CONTENTS

Author:
DAVID BAKER

Design:
BURDA DRUCK INDIA PVT. LTD.

Publisher:
STEVE O'HARA

Published by:
MORTONS MEDIA GROUP LTD, MEDIA CENTRE, MORTON WAY, HORNCASTLE, LINCOLNSHIRE LN9 6JR.

Tel. 01507 529529

Printed by:
WILLIAM GIBBONS AND SONS, WOLVERHAMPTON

MORTONS
MEDIA GROUP LTD

ISBN: 978-1-911639-25-1

THE BIRTH OF
THE JET BOMBER

During the 75+ years since the Second World War, the story of the jet bomber can be divided into three distinct evolutionary phases. Phase 1 was from 1945 to 1960, a period of revolutionary change and the transition from piston to turbojet at a time when strategic deterrence relied on a concept of 'massive retaliation' with nuclear weapons.

Phase 2 was from 1961 to the 1970s when 'flexible response' and burgeoning anti-aircraft defences brought bombers down to low level for high-speed penetration, with both avionics and systems integration maturing. Phase 3 is the period from the 1970s to the present, where stealth, airframe shaping, new materials and advanced avionics have influenced both design and deterrent policy.

Threat assessment has shaped the path followed by planemakers and engine manufacturers but the route was mapped by advancing technologies and shifting geopolitical challenges. Phase 1 set the strategic bomber at the core of US defence policy, even at some expense to land and sea forces.

During this period the US government spent heavily on new technologies and infrastructure

A force of B-17s from the 3rd Bomb Division attacking an industrial plant in Marienburg, Germany, in October 1943. The strategic bomber came of age during the Second World War but its true potential awaited the development of the jet engine. (USAF)

A production line of Consolidated B-24s, classified as heavy bombers during the Second World War. When the war ended in 1945 the USAAF had more than 39,000 combat aircraft – 14,000 of them in this category. (USAF)

The first jet bomber to enter combat, the Arado Ar 234 was the last wartime German combat aircraft to enter British skies. (USAAF)

THE JET AGE

The end of the Second World War heralded a transformation in combat aircraft design, performance and capability. The jet engine allowed both bombers and fighters to reach hitherto undreamt of speeds and spurred technological innovation in other areas of airframe and equipment design.

Some of this innovation resulted from the capture of laboratory test results and wind-tunnel trials data from Germany. Before the D-Day invasion of 6 June 1944, German progress with jet and rocket powered aircraft was well known from extensive reconnaissance photography of airfields and research establishments combined with signals intelligence and reports from agents and partisans inside occupied territories across continental Europe.

The world's first operational jet fighter, the Me 262, was seen in the skies over Europe not long after D-Day and the last enemy aircraft to fly over Britain had been a German jet bomber – the Arado Ar 234 B-1, on 10 April 1945. Initially designed as a pure reconnaissance platform, the bomber variant of the Ar 234 became operational in September 1944 and quickly impressed the Luftwaffe. Its sheer presence was a sobering display of muscular technology already in production and on the flight line.

With its distinctive 'greenhouse' nose, high wing mounting on the upper fuselage and single jet pods in the mid-wing position, the Ar 234 was also developed into a night fighter version with four paired BMW 003A-1 turbojet engines. Sleek and fast, it had the potential to worry the Allies but the war ended before its potential could be realised.

Impressive yet under-developed and bedevilled by under-performing and unreliable engines, along with the Me 262 and the Heinkel He 162 it sent a clear and distinct message that the jet age had arrived.

Yet the Allies had not been idle in developing their own jets. The last two years of the war saw a flurry of requirements for new jet types by both the US and Britain. British jet engine inventor Frank Whittle and his company Power Jets test-flew their creation in the Gloster E.28/39 in 1941 and the technology was soon handed over to the Americans.

Together with American companies' own engine developments, this resulted in several competitive projects – all of which stimulated a surge of interest in applying jet propulsion to fighters, bombers and reconnaissance aircraft.

There were widely differing opinions as to the efficacy of the jet engine at first. Vast manufacturing plants were already churning out thousands of highly developed and highly successful piston engines. These had powered the fighters and bombers that won the

for a global bomber force. Foreign bases proliferated and the jet bomber underpinned a new globalisation of American military might.

Phase 2 saw a transition away from the jet bomber to intercontinental ballistic missiles (on land and at sea) for the nuclear delivery role. Bombers now offered a more flexible application of air power, increasingly challenged by massive air defences. Not a single new bomber made it into service during this time – costs soared, questions were raised regarding the efficacy of massive air power and technology began to reshape the dynamic of combat air power.

Phase 3 was itself shaped by shifting challenges, new technologies which returned the bomber to the deep penetration role and by a re-programmable application of both conventional and nuclear weapons.

Much of what happened within the American aviation industry during these three periods arose from three separate capabilities – general capability in design, development and production; the capability to make key systems, subsystems and technologies; and the unique capabilities of individual companies.

During each of the three chronological phases, the bombers built depended on both the capabilities available and the existing and projected future military needs of the USAF.

The Birth of the Jet Bomber

The Power Jets W.2B/23 jet engine greatly interested the US Army Air Forces and played a significant role in the development of the first US jet-powered fighters. (David Baker)

A direct development from the Power Jets W.1X turbojet, General Electric's J31 was designed in 1942 and produced 1,250lb of thrust. (Sanjay Archarya)

war and there was an understandable reluctance to simply abandon them after so much time and effort spent perfecting their design.

The jet was unproven and its performance, though significant, was limited. Jet aircraft were exceptionally thirsty – severely reducing range compared to piston-engine designs. Early jets were unreliable too and needed high maintenance; in flight they were slow to spool up, making the aircraft sluggish at low speeds. German Me 262 pilots had found this out to their cost when they were mauled by marauding USAAF P-47s while trying to take-off or land.

Despite all these shortcomings, however, there were also undeniable advantages. Even in their rawest most undeveloped form, the weakest jet engines could provide speeds exceeding those of the very best piston engines and the jet had a higher ratio of cruise speed to top speed and became increasingly efficient with altitude, the reverse of the

propeller-driven aircraft which needs dense air to bite on.

Where the piston engine was already at its peak, jet engine development had only just begun.

COMPETITORS

During the early war years, the United States Army Air Corps had watched with growing interest as jet propulsion was developed in Italy, Germany and Britain but had assessed the competition as being largely a technological race rather than one which would have an immediate effect on combat capabilities.

The engine manufacturers themselves seemed disinterested in air-breathing reaction engines and while historians are uncertain as to exactly why this was the case, most agree that the lucrative market for reciprocating engines discouraged investment in questionable technology. And production of piston engines was now growing exponentially, driven by seemingly insatiable demand.

All that changed when British science adviser Henry Tizard visited America in September 1940 and told his US counterparts about progress made with the Whittle engine. In response to this, development of the jet engine in America really began in February 1941 with the establishment of the Durand Committee on Jet Propulsion.

Three companies were invited to build three separate types of gas turbine: Allis-Chalmers was to design a turbofan engine; General Electric, a turboprop engine; and Westinghouse, a turbojet. During a visit to Britain in March, General Henry 'Hap' Arnold, soon to be Commanding General of the US Army Air Forces, acquired access to the Whittle engine, the advanced development of which came as a surprise to the American delegation.

The GE engine development began after the secrets of the Whittle W.1X engine were known in detail. Based on that engine, first run on 18 April 1942, the

America's first jet fighter, the Bell P-59 Airacomet, leaned on the design of the preceding, piston-engine Airacobra, and was powered by two General Electric J31s. (USAF)

General Electric I-A produced a thrust of 1,250lb. When it was seen to run hot, during a visit to GE two months later, Frank Whittle recommended partitions in the blower casing to each chamber and that solved the problem.

The I-A engine powered the Bell P-59 Airacomet, America's first jet fighter, and formed the basis for further developments applied to other prototype test-beds. When in production, the engine was redesignated I-16, reflecting its 1,600lb thrust output.

As intelligence reports came in about emerging jet fighter designs in Germany, and with the certain knowledge about Britain's plans, the newly renamed Army Air Forces urged development of competitive jet fighters – more as development prototypes than definitive designs. But it was foreseen that the development of jet bombers would have to wait until engines with more power and better fuel consumption became available, since a successful bomber requires a decent payload capability as well as good range.

The Me 262, though, demonstrated that efforts to design and build a jet bomber could not wait. It was clear that any enemy armed with jet fighters would make quick work of lumbering piston-engine bomber formations. The drive for a jet bomber therefore began as early as June 1943.

The AAF pushed ahead on two fronts to make such an aircraft viable: firstly, more powerful jet engines were essential, and secondly an appropriately efficient airframe design was needed to attain the highest possible cruising speeds. Industry was incentivised to study both. Only by displaying financial commitment could the AAF get industry interested, accepting that they would be developing a production engine rather than a short-run, experimental prototype.

With work already under way on jet fighter engines, GE was the company to go to, although it had been tasked with looking into turboprop designs, while Boeing was approached to come up with an airframe.

US Army Materiel Command was keen to push design studies for a bomber equipped with four GE TG-180 jet engines and AAF headquarters endorsed this decision in September 1943 when Boeing was given access to information about the Bell XP-59, at the time a highly secret project as was all jet engine research. Boeing openly expressed surprise that jet research had got as far as producing a flying prototype fighter and this mirrored the shock throughout the industry as word slipped out and the AAF revealed all.

Early Boeing studies were presented over the next two months and the chief of the engineering division at Wright Field concluded that "Contrary to the existing belief that jet-propelled aircraft

Alarmed by catastrophic attacks on unescorted bombers over Germany, in early 1944 Bell was encouraged to develop the XP-83 jet-powered escort out of the P-59 but it never went into production. (Bell)

With development of jet engines and rocket propulsion, immediately after the war debate focused on whether to use cruise missiles rather than bombers to attack distant targets, epitomised by the Martin TM-76 Mace with a jet sustainer and rocket booster motor. (US Army)

Typical of a generation of cruise weapons, the ramp-launched Mace had its conceptual origins in the German V-1 flying bomb but was superseded by the ballistic missiles of the late 1950s. (US Army)

The Birth of the Jet Bomber

The ultimate expression of early generation cruise weapons, the Northrop SM-62 Snark missile similarly had a jet sustainer but was boosted by solid-propellant rockets. It was precursor to stand-off weapons launched by bombers. (USAF)

Boeing's KB-50J, a derivative of the B-50 bomber adapted as a cargo-tanker, the last of the piston-engine types pressed into service to support early-generation jet bombers. (USAF)

are limited to short ranges… the Boeing studies indicate that… the range of jet propelled aircraft may exceed that of conventional aircraft".

The big catch here was that, according to Boeing, jet engines would be more efficient if a speed of 600mph could be achieved – but at the time nobody knew how to make a bomber able to fly that fast. Nevertheless, Air Materiel Command (AMC) got excited about the possibilities and approved an informal request for proposals. This resulted in Boeing and North American submitting initial designs in January 1944.

Boeing progressively refined their ideas over a series of models (413, 422, 424, 425 and 426) to end up with a turboprop, rather than a turbojet, concept to make maximum use of the better range over the pure jet. Because the AAF was also interested in speed, Models 424 and 425 featured turbojets. Unaddressed, largely because nobody knew a great deal about it, was the compressibility effect experienced close to the transonic zone. Added to the uncertainty was the sluggish development of the TG-180 engine.

Desperate to get a high-performance bomber, the AAF asked Wright Field to verify the engineering assessment and confirm that such a high-speed jet bomber could be built within two years, which it was not able to do. So little was known about the aerodynamics of high-speed cruise conditions that scientists and engineers were unable to provide the guarantees sought.

In November 1944, the AAF issued a requirement for a bomber with a top speed of 550mph – almost 200mph faster than the B-29 – carrying an 8,000lb bomb load on a 3,500 mile mission and with a

service ceiling of 40,000ft. Questioned by politicians about the strident push for a new jet bomber, the AAF explained that the technical requirement would be set above the requirement for early service introduction and that, by issuing a formal request to industry, higher levels of funding could be released for development.

While Boeing was highly sceptical about a high-speed jet bomber, the AAF was emphatic in its desire to have one and brooked no compromise in the requirement – though it was prepared to accept a delay of up to two years in getting prototypes into the air.

PROPOSALS
As the AAF moved toward a procurement strategy, confidence in the strategic bomber concept was at an all-time high. Across Nazi-occupied Europe, German industry was being pounded into dust, marshalling yards and railroads were being destroyed and cities across Japan were suffering a massive onslaught from the B-29. The atomic bomb had already been tested at Alamogordo, New Mexico.

Bids for the new bomber were requested and four companies had responded by January 1945. Attracted by the prospect of lucrative development contracts, industry quickly switched from an attitude of cynicism over the jet bomber concept to one of enthusiasm. With the Me 262 operational over occupied Europe, the Ar 234 bomber/reconnaissance aircraft rolling off the line and Britain putting the Gloster Meteor into production, American aircraft manufacturers were beginning to relish the challenge of building the nation's first jet bomber.

The procurement strategy would follow a three-phase programme. The first phase would assess the feasibility of meeting the requirement and examine technical hurdles, risks and potential show-stoppers. The second would see designs fully completed, with engineering drawings made and mock-ups of specific proposals constructed.

The third phase involved construction, flight testing and competitive evaluation of prototypes. The emphasis here would be on configuration, flying qualities and actual performance compared to the requirement. There would be less focus on ancillaries and supplementary equipment.

Prototype dimensions and weights would represent those of a definitive, production aircraft but spaces would be left for electrical systems, weapons and general ergonomics of the flight deck.

This was to be a welcome departure from the existing 'concurrency' concept, where development and production ran together, the early airframes off the assembly line having to be retrofitted with any modifications or improvements highlighted as desirable through the development process. This method got aircraft to the front line and in quantity more quickly in theory but it had proven an administrative nightmare on the B-29 and would plague the B-36 too.

The phased development programme shifted the burden of administrative micro-management from the military to the contractor, but there was no other way to run a programme in which so many design and construction variables were unknown. It also made it easier to cancel a competing prototype, since no production had yet commenced.

LEGACY CONTENDERS

The four manufacturers responding with proposals to the November 1944 jet bomber requirement were Boeing, Convair, Martin and North American. All four were given contracts to build flying prototypes for a competitive fly-off. There was only one production contract on offer though – the AAF had expressed a desire for just one in-service jet bomber.

The biggest 'unknown' was the engine itself, followed by uncertainties about compressibility and aerodynamic stability in the high-subsonic regime. The first was a technological challenge, the second and third could only be solved through scientific and engineering investigation.

The overall challenge of mathematically defining flying characteristics close to the transonic zone had already prompted the National Advisory Committee for Aeronautics (NACA, precursor to NASA which it became in October 1958) and the AAF to build the Bell XS-1 rocketplane. Hopes were high that the XS-1 would break through the misnamed 'sound barrier' and explore supersonic flight.

All four jet bomber proposals were ambitious and technically challenging – but to varying degrees. North American's B-45 was the most conservative, adopting a conventional wing design with a proven NACA cross-section and four jet engines.

The Convair B-46 (Model 109) went further into the unknown with an aerodynamically unproven high-aspect ratio wing set on a long, slender fuselage. Thanks to its small cross section, the fuselage had little bomb bay volume yet it weighed more than that of the proposed B-45.

Boeing's B-47, at this stage simply the Model 432, featured a conventional, straight wing with four engines and main landing gear in nacelles. And the Martin B-48 was unusual in having six engines in two nacelles, one on each wing, which had a thickness-chord ratio so low that the landing gear had to go in the fuselage.

The relatively simple B-48 was liked best since it had no glaring flaws and promised an early in-service date. Although the AAF had put performance before availability, it began to see the possibility of an early introduction. Although the unusual features of Martin's design would add a further 18 months to the development cycle, the company projected a top speed of 534mph compared to 486mph for the B-45 and 478mph for the B-46.

Boeing's mighty B-29, left, is dwarfed by the enormous Convair B-36. These two aircraft represent the peaks of wartime and immediate post-war bomber design respectively. (USAF)

With pressurised crew compartments and bristling with defensive armament, the B-29 was an important step forward in the design of bomber aircraft. (USAF)

But the company had an aggressive and demanding marketing approach. Martin VP Harry T. Rowland wrote to the AAF demanding that his company's design be given priority consideration. If he didn't get it, he would take the design to the Navy!

In addition to the four bids from January 1945, there were three other bomber projects where jet propulsion was under consideration – the B-35, B-36 and B-42. The first two of these initially piston-engined types had emerged in the late 1930s and early 1940s during the Air Corps' search for a very long range, strategic bomber. The B-42 had come slightly later as a result of a private company project.

The catalyst for the B-35 and B-36 was the belief that the US might have to fight Nazi Germany from North America – requiring a bomber able to fly to Europe and back without landing. This prospect came closer to reality in 1940 when German forces overran Norway, France and the Low Countries, only being halted short of an invasion of the British Isles by the natural barrier of the English Channel, the RAF and the threat of the Royal Navy.

At this date the only long-range US bomber, the B-17C had a combat radius

Maintenance crews at work on B-36s of the 7th BW at Carswell AFB. Convair built 385 B-36s in total. (Dennis Jenkins)

Legacy Contenders

With 'six turning, four burning', the mixed propulsion B-36J and H variants made numerous reconnaissance and surveillance flights close to and beyond the border with the Soviet Union and Warsaw Pact countries at the height of the Cold War. (Dennis Jenkins)

Early jet fighters lacked the range to escort the B-36 so tests were carried out using modified RF-84Ks to see whether the bomber could carry its own parasite escort fighters. (Dennis Jenkins)

Two B-36Fs were converted into swept-wing all-jet bombers under the YB-60 designation. One is seen here with a standard B-36F for comparison. They proved slower than the B-52 and no more were built. (USAF)

of 900 miles. A flight from New York on the American east coast to Brest on the French coast and back would require a range of 6,700 miles even allowing no margin for error. Under development at the time, the conventional B-15, B-19 and B-29 also fell way short of the required range.

FLYING WING CHALLENGER

The Air Materiel Division had stipulated a range of 10,000 miles for the long-range bomber it wanted – and it would have to carry a 10,000lb bomb load too. Among the bidding manufacturers was Jack Northrop with his flying-wing design. Believed to have tremendous potential, 13 prototypes and 200 production B-35s were ordered by the AAF in November 1942, with the contract formalised on 30 June 1943.

Under this agreement, Martin would build B-35s in its cavernous Baltimore, Maryland, facility in space vacated due to the cancellation of the B-33 – a proposed high-altitude B-26 Marauder variant – on 25 November 1942. Founded only in August 1939, Northrop lacked the capacity or the resources to build the aircraft in quantity itself and needed a major manufacturer's support to do so.

Around the same time, the Materiel Division also approved Convair's B-36 design proposal, a six-engine, pusher type for which a requirement for 100 had been indicated in August 1942. The B-35 was given highest priority while the B-36 suffered from accelerating production requirements for existing bomber programmes such as the B-25, B-26, B-17 and the advanced B-29.

However, the revolutionary flying wing hit persistent problems and technical delays, with an ever-growing catalogue of development issues. By mid-1943 the technical challenges, and engineering problems, were sufficiently great as to relegate the B-35 to experimental status with efforts concentrated on the B-36 instead.

By 1944 events across the Pacific Ocean were taking a different turn and there was increasing confidence that the B-29 would be adequate for the task of bringing the war home to mainland Japan. The urgency had gone away and both types were under threat. During its much delayed first flight on 25 June 1946 the XB-35 was plagued with gearbox and engine troubles from its four pusher engines and contra-rotating propellers.

One way of addressing these problems was to replace the reciprocating engines with jets and in June 1945 an order had been authorised requiring two YB-35 prototypes to be so converted.

Featuring eight 4,000lb thrust J35 engines (formerly the TG-180), the B-49 concept had significant changes, with four small trailing edge fins, four large wing fences and a redesigned leading edge to provide a low-drag intake for the engines. Because it was essentially an adapted YB-35, the overall configuration of the aerofoil remained the same. The initial flight was on 21 October 1947 with a second joining the test programme on 13 January 1948.

There were still supporters of the flying wing concept but the technology needed to make it work was lacking. A fatal crash with the second YB-49 on 5 June 1948 cast doubts on the structural integrity of flying wings and stability concerns were highlighted when bombing trials showed a completely unacceptable degree of inaccuracy.

While the YB-49 did possess acceptable range, it took four minutes for the aircraft to stabilise for a bomb run compared to 45 seconds for a B-29. The performance deficits were just too great and the type was officially cancelled on 15 March 1950. The first YB-49 crashed on the very day that the programme was abandoned.

Parallel to the YB-49 programme, a reconnaissance version, the YRB-49A emerged from the cancelled B-35 and a single example was converted from the third YB-35A. It had six J35s – four mounted internally and two outside the airframe – and the first flight was on 4 May 1950. The test programme came close to experiencing a fatal crash on 10 August when the canopy blew off in a climb at 35,000ft; only the actions of a quick-thinking flight engineer, who clamped an oxygen mask to the pilot's face, prevented a catastrophe. The test programme was brought to a halt 10 days later although a few experimental flights continued to take place before that programme too was scrapped on 6 May 1952.

On paper at least, the YB-49's performance had been reasonably credible – a combat radius of 1,614 miles

and a maximum speed of 463mph at 35,000ft or 492mph at 20,000ft. With piston engines, the XB-35 was about 6% slower than the YB-49 with 7% less range. But while the piston-engine XB-35 could carry 40,000lb of bombs, the capacity of the jet-powered YB-49 was only 16,000lb, the reduction being due to the larger fuel load required.

The two chief advantages often cited for the flying wing concept were a large internal volume for both fuel and bomb load, plus the long-range potential arising from that extra fuel. The YB-49 could provide neither greater carrying capacity nor particularly outstanding range and this, combined with its engine and stability issues, proved to be its downfall.

AN INTERIM STOPGAP
The B-36, developed in parallel to the flying wings, had its own litany of problems. The request for proposals (RFP) for an intercontinental bomber had been issued by the Air Corps on 11 April 1941 with invitations sent to Boeing and Convair, then the Consolidated Aircraft Corporation. Over the course of several months, the requirements shifted and changed before eventually settling on a 10,000 mile range, a combat radius of 4,000 miles and a 10,000lb bombload.

The decision to develop Convair's behemoth was made on 16 October 1941 and two engines were added to supplement the originally proposed four at the suggestion of Wright Field Engineering Division. The long and convoluted path taken by this aircraft in its protracted development has been recounted in all its gruesome detail elsewhere but suffice to say that from its inception the aircraft ran into innumerable problems and technical difficulties. Like the B-29, the B-36 was

to be fully pressurised – a new concept in 1942 made essential by the enormous distances that the aircraft would be expected to cover and the demands this would place on air crew comfort.

It was hoped that the bomber could be rushed into service and used against the Japanese homeland, with General Arnold ordering 100 on 19 June 1942. With China threatened by Japanese forces, it was hoped that the B-36 would bolster China's confidence that the US would soon be able to strike at the heart of the Japanese war machine.

America's primary strategy involved its carrier battle groups island-hopping their way towards the Marianas, where air bases could be established for B-29s – which could then reach Japan. But if this failed, the B-36s would have the range to hit targets in Japan from Hawaii. At this point even the B-29 was still nearly two years away from entering operational service.

Unfortunately for the B-36, it was relying on the massive Pratt & Whitney R-4360-25 Wasp Major 28-cylinder four-row engine and this was encountering significant engineering problems. In addition, the need to retain maximum production of existing bomber types sapped resources from the project – making delays inevitable.

A general letter of intent to procure the 100 aircraft was issued on 23 July 1943 but a definitive contract was not signed until 19 August 1944, with the first aircraft expected in August 1945, the last in October 1946. Slippage occurred as victory neared and on 25 May 1945, aircraft production of all bomber types was cut by 30%, a reduction of 17,000 aircraft over an 18-month period.

With hindsight, this was not the time to press for a sustained development

Nuclear propulsion was considered for future US bombers and a single B-36 airframe was converted into the NB-36H-1 to test the system. The challenges were too great, however, and the idea was dropped. (Convair)

The General Electric J47 turbojet engine provided supplementary power for the B-36 but pressure for its use in other aircraft stressed delivery schedules, a limitation not uncommon in the early days of jet-powered combat aircraft. (David Baker)

Jack Northrop had a strong belief in the flying wing concept and experimented with many configurations before submitting a bomber contender in 1941. Two prototype XB-35s were ordered. (USAF)

programme on a new and unproven type. Yet the price paid in human lives lost in seizing island after island to get those forward B-29 bases in the Marianas continued to give the B-36 a degree of urgency it might otherwise have lacked.

Notwithstanding some quality control issues, strikes at the Fort Worth plant assigned to the B-36, and continued technical problems, the XB-36 made its first flight on 8 August 1946.

But there were detractors, especially General George Kenney, head of Strategic Air Command (SAC) since April 1946, who pointed to a shortfall in range, poor protection for the fuel tanks in the event of an attack and what he perceived as a general inferiority to the Boeing B-50, a development of the B-29. Real problems continued to mount up and delay development, including new requirements from the customer which

called for additional armament and a redesigned landing gear – switching from a single main wheel each side to a four-wheel bogie.

BOMBER MANIA

Another serious threat to the B-36 programme was the US Navy's insistence that it, rather than the newly independent Air Force, should deliver the strategic deterrent. The USAF's bombers needed massive range to reach targets from the continental United States but the Navy argued that such aircraft were unnecessary when it could have much smaller, simpler and cheaper carrier-based bombers on-station around the globe.

Thus began the legendary bomber-versus-carrier debate which almost did away with the B-36 but ended up sinking the super-carrier when Congress selected the Air Force to deliver atomic retribution. But the Navy never abandoned the role of strategic nuclear delivery and adopted carrier-based jet bombers.

Peace brought an end to B-29 production in October 1945 and existing aircraft were declared surplus. Had the B-36 not been so far along in development, with all the investment that this entailed, it is unlikely that the six-engine behemoth would have entered service when it did in 1948. Problems persisted with fuel supply issues, unreliable electrical systems and unsatisfactory armament and gunnery control systems. The aircraft had evolved to have dual dorsal and ventral gun positions with retractable barbettes fore and aft. There were also nose and tail guns in numbers

Powered by four Pratt & Whitney R-4360 engines, initially driving contra-rotating propellers, the XB-35 was considerably delayed and did not make its first flight until 25 June 1946. (USAF)

and configurations that changed regularly as new variants were introduced.

In service from August 1950, the B-36D featured two pairs of J47-GE-19 turbojets under the outer wing sections in addition to the six R-4360-41 pusher engines, effectively serving as a hybrid transition between piston-engine types such as the B-50 and the all-jet B-47 and B-52. A reconnaissance role for the B-36 was inevitable, its incredible range and high-altitude performance seen as ideal for a spy plane in the absence of surface-to-air missiles (these being just around the corner).

Of the 385 B-36 aircraft completed in all variants, 121 were built as RB-36 variants with a further 22 reconfigured into the reconnaissance role, effectively more than one-third of the total production inventory.

The importance of the B-36 cannot be over-emphasised, serving as guardian of the Air Force claim to carry the nuclear deterrent until it was superseded by the B-52 from 1956 and retired from SAC two years after that. Early variants came with a $2.5m price tag while the final production model came in at $4.15m. Averaged out over all variants, the cost ran to $3.6m each, without the cost of engineering changes and modifications factored in.

With a cruising speed of around 230mph it was slow. Even with the addition of jet engines it could only achieve a maximum of 414mph. But although the type's combat radius varied widely between models, all could comfortably top 3,450 miles. It had a flight duration of 30-42 hours with a crew of 15-22 depending upon the mission. With an armament typically consisting of

After serious problems with its contra-rotating prop configuration, the XB-35 was fitted with conventional propellers and tested in flight, with only one example of the YB-35 making it into the air. (USAF)

The XB-35 configuration was adapted into the YB-49 with eight J35 turbojets replacing the four reciprocating engines. It made its first flight on 21 October 1947. (USAF)

16 x 20mm guns, the B-36 was the last heavily armed, self-defensive bomber in the US inventory. It was a transitional aircraft in every sense but also a suitable precursor to the age of the all-jet bomber.

MIXMASTER AND JETMASTER

The first American bomber fitted exclusively with jet engines was not designed as such but rather a modification of the Douglas XB-42 Mixmaster. This was a company-funded experimental bomber concept in which two piston engines inside the fuselage drove contra-rotating pusher props in the tail. The concept originated with design engineer E. F. Burton, who envisaged a twin-engine aircraft with a 2,000lb bomb load. By burying the engines in the fuselage and keeping the laminar wing aerodynamically clean, he reduced drag by a third and thus achieved a high cruising speed.

It was an ingenious concept with a top speed to equal the faster variants of the famously quick British de Havilland Mosquito, but with twice the bomb load. And unlike the unarmed Mosquito B.XVI, it was to carry a defensive armament of four 0.50in machine guns in two remotely-controlled turrets. It was only two-thirds as expensive as the B-29, called for half the maintenance crew, could carry a respectable 8,000lb of bombs internally and only needed three crew, compared to the B-29's 11.

Submitted as an unsolicited proposal in May 1943, it was received with great enthusiasm and two flying prototypes were ordered on 25 June 1943. Initially, the type was cast as an attack aircraft with 16 x 75mm cannon plus two machine guns but it was developed under the designation B-42, making its inaugural flight on 6 May 1944. In early December

1945, however, it was decided that the aircraft would not enter production.

This was despite the type having flown from Long Beach, California, to Bolling AFB, Washington DC, in 5hr 17min, setting a speed record of 433.6mph over the 2,300-mile distance. The AAF wanted to wait for the more powerful jet bombers then in development. Instead, the XB-42 prototypes would be employed as experimental aircraft and would incorporate two auxiliary Westinghouse 19XB-2A turbojets, one under each wing. In this configuration, the hybrid made its first flight on 27 May 1947 – in the process becoming the first US jet bomber.

Aviation history is replete with missed opportunities and overlooked concepts, ideas which never really caught on. Seminal designs which deserve a prominent place in the annals of aeronautical achievement are rare – yet

Originally developed by General Electric as the TG-180, the Allison J35 was the first axial-flow jet engine built in the United States and was a technology outgrowth from the T31 axial-flow turboprop engine. (via David Baker)

the XB-43 Jetmaster was arguably just such a design, though it never gained the popularity nor the acknowledgement it deserved.

When reviewing the initial concept of the XB-42 in October 1943, the AMC proposed replacing the inline piston engines with two turbojets and on 31 March 1944, following preliminary designs from Douglas, the company received a contract for two jet powered XB-43 aircraft. With essentially the same fuselage and wing configuration as the XB-42, the Jetmaster would have two 3,750lb thrust GE TG-180 engines, later re-designated J35-GE-3 in production form.

The design adaptation was simple; the turbojets were installed in the same bays previously occupied by the piston engines in the XB-42 and flush air intakes were located on the upper fuselage sides immediately aft of the cockpit. The only significant change to the tail area was the removal of the dorsal fin and enlargement of the upper fin and rudder to maintain positive control. The AMC agreed that the static XB-42 airframe could be used to form the first XB-43 (44-61508) but despite relatively modest changes, the first flight of this aircraft would not take place until 17 May 1946. The second aircraft (44-61509), designated YB-43, followed it into the air on 15 May 1947.

Had events not overtaken the XB-43, a series production version could have had a credible career. Its excellent qualities and performance characteristics gave it a top speed of 515mph at sea level, a range of 1,100 miles and a cruising speed of 420mph.

However, it was passed over for a preferred four-jet bomber and would instead serve only as an engine and aerodynamic flight test aircraft. That

The YRB-49 saw four J35s removed from the wings and placed in two external pods, one of which can just be seen protruding beneath the starboard leading edge, making space for more fuel. (USAF)

The decision to pick the B-36 over Northrop's flying wings was fiercely contested, particularly by General George Kenney, head of Strategic Air Command from April 1946. He feared that the giant bomber had little effective protection. (USAF)

work ended only when the XB-43 had an accident in February 1951. The YB-43 was sent to the AMC's Power Plant Laboratory at Muroc where it was employed as a test bed for the TG-190 (J47) engine. Spares from the XB-43 were used to keep it flying, contributing more than 300 flying hours to a comprehensive test programme. In December 1953 it was discharged from further duty and went to what is now the National Air & Space Museum in Washington DC.

A CLOSER MATCH

It was thus against a backdrop of developments in the B-35, B-36 and B-42 programmes that the pure jet bomber projects of Boeing, Convair, Martin and North American lined up in January 1945.

Convair's design, Model 109, was the first submitted, on 6 November 1944, and took the form of a conventional fuselage with the high aspect-ratio Davis wing which evolved from that employed on the B-24 Liberator and XP4Y Corregidor. Named after David R. Davis, the wing was designed for high lift and low drag, the mathematics of which were ill-defined, with the physics as to why it worked little understood. When Davis approached Reuben Fleet, President of Consolidated in 1937 for funding to develop the wing, he was unlucky and only gained moderate support before Fleet's chief engineer, Isaac M. Laddon, had a change of heart and got tests conducted at a wind tunnel operated by the California Institute of Technology.

After fine-tuning of the CalTech tunnel, the results were astounding; the Davis wing displayed the promised ability to generate lift at low angles of attack and had a very low drag coefficient. The

uncertainty as to precisely why it worked so well would not come until much later but it did provide a satisfactory solution for both flying boats and land aircraft in that it greatly improved low-speed lift-over-drag (L/D). Subsequent tests showed that the shape of the Davis aerofoil maintained laminar flow farther back from the leading edge, although subsequent developments with alternative wings designs greatly improved on this.

By the time Model 109 was approved by the AAF on 17 January 1945, with a letter contract for three prototypes designated XB-46, the Davis wing was better understood. As applied to the B-24, it had a high aspect ratio of 11.55:1 and presented a zero-lift drag coefficient of 0.0406 compared to 0.032 for the much more conventional wing on the Boeing B-17. Due largely to the high aspect-ratio wing of the B-24, the maximum L/D of the two aircraft was about the same.

The problem with applying the Davis wing to the XB-46 was that as the speed of the air across the wing increased, the advantage of the aerofoil design diminished markedly – high speed drag more than offsetting the reduction in low speed drag. The higher the air speed, the less advantageous it became. It is therefore somewhat surprising that Convair chose this wing form, albeit with a much thinner Davis aerofoil to reduce the wave drag encountered with a thicker cross-section.

The mock-up was completed within three weeks and several recommendations made, after which a supplementary agreement was signed on 3 March but due to budget restrictions it was converted to a

Legacy Contenders

fixed-fee contract. The three XB-46s were given serials 45-59582 to 45-59584 and each would be powered by four 4,000lb thrust J35-A-3 engines in pairs within a single nacelle under each wing. There was provision for three crewmembers including a pilot and co-pilot seated in tandem in a pressurised enclosure beneath a single canopy with a bombardier in the nose section. This tandem arrangement was novel and attracted the attention of other manufacturers, with support from the AAF which enthusiastically embraced the layout.

As had been the case with the B-24, Convair chose the Emerson Electric Company to provide the remotely controlled tail turret with APG-27 sighting system and equipped with two 0.5in machine guns. The maximum bomb load of 22,000lb was carried in a single bay directly beneath the shoulder-wing. The XB-46 had a maximum take-off weight of 94,400lb and boasted a maximum speed of 545mph with 2,870-mile range. Top speed was 489mph, cruising speed 438mph and combat radius 693 miles.

The AAF became interested in an attack variant of the XB-46 proposed by Convair towards the end of 1945, which would have had a battery of machine guns in its nose. Budget limitations prevented a dedicated prototype but Convair offered to build two of the three fully-funded XB-46 prototypes as XA-44 attackers under the same contract. The AAF agreed to this but interest in the XB-46/XA-44 rapidly waned when the limitations of its slender fuselage, with little space for weapons or equipment, became clear.

When the XB-46 was defeated by the XB-45 (see below), Convair was allowed to continue with the XA-44 – which then underwent a dramatic redesign, a change of role to light bomber, and acquired a new designation – XB-53. Almost unrecognisable as any sort of XB-46 relation, the XB-53 had a forward-swept wing shape with a sweep of 30-degrees and a dihedral of 8-degrees.

This was heavily influenced by German wartime research on the advantages of forward swept-wing configurations, notably the Junkers Ju 287, a flying mock-up of which had flown on 16 August 1944. It had been thought that by placing the wingtips forward of the main lifting component of the wing, early and slow-speed stall could be avoided. However, the reverse can be the case where the tip bending mode is sufficient to increase the angle of attack and cause the tips to stall first.

The design of the XB-53 allowed for a conventional vertical tail assembly, with pitch and roll control achieved through surfaces on the wing trailing edge; elevators on the outer sections, ailerons inboard and variable incidence tips.

Power was to have been provided by three J35 engines in the fuselage with

The XB-42 was redesigned into the XB-43 Jetmaster along the same basic lines but equipped from the outset with two General Electric J35 engines. Note the strange configuration of the main gear well and door arrangement. (USAF)

two lateral air intakes. A wide array of armament was proposed, including 40 HVARs (High Velocity Aerial Rockets) and up to 12,000lb of bombs and assorted ordnance. The XB-53 had a very short life however, and was cancelled by the AAF in December 1946.

The sole XB-46 emerged on 2 April 1947 for an initial 1hr 30min test flight from San Diego, California, to Muroc Army Airfield. Stepping from the prototype, test pilots E. D. Shannon and Bill Martin had high praise for the aircraft and its handling.

It did have some fine design qualities, although the prototype was only finished to a standard necessary for basic airworthiness and handling. There was no installation of mock armament and no

ancillary equipment. Fowler flaps were carried along almost the entire trailing edge span of the wing with roll control effected by spoilers, the ailerons being only 6ft long. The main landing gear retracted up into the engine nacelles and the nose leg into the forward fuselage below the tandem cockpit. Unusually for the time, a pneumatic system and not hydraulics powered the actuators for landing gear, bomb bay doors, crew doors and brakes.

Despite Shannon and Martin's positive reviews, the programme was formally cancelled in August 1947. The USAF accepted the prototype on 7 November and took delivery five days later. One of the reasons for selection of the B-45 over the B-46 was its lighter dry weight, which

The XB-43 had a two-place crew station on top of the fuselage with a bombardier-navigator in the glazed nose section. (USAF)

What would turn out to be the first all-jet US bomber began life as an experimental aircraft with two reciprocating engines driving contra-rotating propellers. Designated XB-42 only two were built but it led directly to the XB-43. (USAF)

Experimental flights with the first Douglas XB-42 Mixmaster, redesignated XB-42A, were made carrying two Westinghouse 19XB-2A turbojet engines, one under each wing. It flew at Edwards ADFB on 27 May 1947. (USAF)

Legacy Contenders

America's first all-jet bomber, the XB-43 ended up as a test bed for different jet engines but had already earned its place in history. (USAF)

Only one of three Convair XB-46s ordered was completed as the type lost out to North American's B-45 Tornado. Note the large trailing edge flaps inboard of the ailerons and the tandem crew arrangement favoured by the Air Force. (Convair)

was interpreted as indicating a better performance overall. But that slender fuselage was the main reason cited for cancellation.

Nevertheless, as is typical with funded but cancelled prototypes, the XB-46 soldiered on as an experimental test vehicle for a wide range of investigations, stability and control tests being conducted at West Palm Beach AFB, Florida between August 1948 and August 1949. Having logged 44 flying hours, spares ran out and maintenance became difficult, calling a halt to these tests. The aircraft was flown to Eglin AFB, Florida, in July 1950 for four months of low temperature pneumatic systems tests in the base climate simulation hangar. From November 1950 the XB-46 was of no further use. The nose section was removed and flown to the Air Force Museum at Wright-

Patterson AFB, Ohio, on 13 January 1952, preceding the rest of the aircraft being scrapped on 28 February.

A PAIR OF MARTINS

The Martin jet bomber proposal, Model 223, was shaped by a somewhat different requirement to that of its competitors – a top speed of 550mph, 3,000-mile range, 45,000ft maximum altitude and 40,000ft tactical altitude. The proposal was submitted on 9 December 1944 and the company received a letter contract. On 29 January 1945 the AAF modified the requirement and now wanted the aircraft to carry a specified range of weapons including the 10,000lb M-121 earthquake bomb, a US development of the British Tallboy used against large fortified structures during the Second World War.

A definitive contract followed on 26 March 1945, with the type designated

XB-48, but no prototypes were ordered. Martin proposed a single prototype for basic aerodynamic and handling verification during the summer, to be followed by three complete XB-48 aircraft with all ancillary and armament equipment installed.

There then followed months of financial negotiations between Martin and the Air Technical Services Command over the work to be done and how much would be paid for it. With the war over, budgets for new military hardware had been slashed, but eventually Air Technical Services Command came up with a fixed-fee agreement in December 1945.

Not signed off till 13 December 1946, the definitive contract agreed on two prototypes, spares to keep a flight test programme current and a bomb bay mock-up. It also required that all wind tunnel testing be completed by 1 January 1947. The first prototype had to be fully tested and delivered to the AAF for evaluation by 30 September 1947 and the second by 30 June 1948. However, as with all these early post-war proposals, each was heavily dependent on the engine and here the XB-48 was compromised by the decision to use the TG-180 (J35) as its powerplant. The first aircraft would use the J35-B-1, the second the J35-D-1, both with the same power output of 3,820lb. But that was in the future and technical development of the design introduced some novel features later adopted by other manufacturers as well as setting a trend toward unique and innovative design ideas.

The basic layout of the medium bomber incorporated a high wing mounted midway on a circular cross-section fuselage supporting a two-seat tandem cockpit with a conventional tail. As with the XB-46, the bombardier sat in a glazed nose. Six TG-180 engines were arranged in groups of three attached to the underside of each wing in a lift section, with intakes between the pods and adjustable exhaust pipes.

This layout made it difficult to incorporate a conventional tricycle landing gear, so Martin placed the main legs fore and aft of the central bomb bay with extendible outriggers in the outer engine nacelles – an arrangement that would later become a feature of the B-47. Some tests with this layout had been conducted on a converted Marauder designated XB-26H and painted red for that purpose.

The XB-48's bomb bay incorporated retractable doors so as to accommodate either an atomic bomb or an earthquake bomb. Like the XB-46, it also carried a single defensive position consisting of two 0.5in guns in the remotely controlled tail turret with an AN/APG-27 radar.

Bearing the tail serial 45-59585, the first XB-48 took to the air on 22 June 1947 and flew from the company plant at Baltimore, Maryland, to the Patuxent Naval Air

Originally designated XA-44, as an attack aircraft, this Convair forward-swept aircraft design (shown here as a model) was redesignated XB-53 when the company developed it into a candidate bomber. (Convair)

Station, a distance of about 80 miles. But this first flight revealed issues with the aileron on the starboard wing and the rudder steering, which proved inadequate. The aircraft was unable to stop after touchdown and ran off the runway, albeit without any noticeable damage.

These issues paled compared to problems that arose with the TG-180 engines, however. Some 14 different engines were required to complete the first 44hrs flying time as unit after unit failed. The second aircraft (45-59586)

did not fly until 16 October 1948, three months after the expected date, by which time the fate of the programme had been sealed. Not only was it deficient in several technical respects – excessive turbulence when the bomb bay doors were open shattered the hydraulic system – the XB-48 was 50mph slower than calculated before the test series began and maxed out 14,000lb overweight. The writing was on the wall when the XB-47 went into the pre-production planning stages in December 1947.

It came down to these two types and the XB-47 performed significantly better than its competitor on almost every count, including the potential for growth compared to the Martin contender. The straight wing of the XB-48 could not provide the performance displayed by the swept-wing XB-47 and the general layout made it much easier to change engine types as new types became available.

Even on paper, the performance of the XB-48 was woefully inadequate. Carrying the required 22,000lb bomb

The Martin XB-48 displays a clean configuration with wings reminiscent of the B-26 Marauder upon which it was based. The type was considered a back-up to Boeing's B-47. (USAF)

Challenged to come up with an all-weather air support medium bomber, Martin produced the swept-wing XB-51 (originally XA-45) powered by three J47s. (Martin)

With a clean aero-profile and variable-incidence wings, the XB-51 had a single engine in the fuselage and two on pods cantilevered from the lower forward fuselage section. (USAF)

load it had a combat radius of 498 miles and an average cruise speed of 414mph with a service ceiling of 39,400ft. And at 7,900ft, the takeoff run under full load was excessive. It is perhaps disingenuous to blame all of the type's problems on its troublesome engines. Other manufacturers had the same powerplant and were able to get much better performance.

The military requirements which had informed the XB-45, -46, --47 and -48 prototypes for a medium bomber were paired with a new requirement for a light, all-weather close support bomber through a separate competition announced in February 1946. Already busy with the B-48, Martin submitted a design bid and received a contract for the XB-51 on 23 May 1946, including two flying prototypes which were to be preceded by wind tunnel tests and the usual mock-ups.

Martin had originally submitted a proposal on April 1, 1946, which was given the designation XA-45. This was for an aircraft accommodating a crew of six, power provided by two TG-110 turboprop

engines and two I-50 turbojets. The initial design submission showed a potential top speed of 505mph with a cruise speed of 325mph and a combat radius of 800 miles. Unhappy with this, the Air Force examined the possibility of seeking a second or third contender but opted not to, saving time otherwise lost in reopening the bidding process. AMC decided to tweak the work from Martin and the resulting redesign transformed the aircraft such that the XB-51 contract was for a very different aircraft, a variation on the initial role.

After working through several iterations and design changes, virtually rewriting the specification, Martin eliminated four crewmember positions. It was then asked to provide an aircraft with a 713mph top speed, 533mph cruise speed and 378-mile combat radius. It couldn't match those demanding requirements and in further discussions with the Air Force the requirement was reduced to a 600mph top speed and a cruise speed of 500mph. Because of the freshly redefined tactical support

role, the stipulated combat radius was lowered to 230 miles, coincident with the SHORAN short-range navigation system which was to be an integral part of the aircraft's equipment in its tactical support role to ground operations. The XB-51's armament would consist of 8 x 20mm cannon plus a 4,000lb bomb load.

Reworking the initial design, Martin fixed on a high-wing three-engine configuration using J47s, two in nacelles on pylons either side of the lower section of the forward fuselage and one in the rear fuselage with an inlet on top immediately forward of the vertical T-tail, the exhaust outlet being at the rear of the fuselage.

These engines had a water/alcohol thrust augmentation system for better take-off performance and an innovative system for temperature control to prevent overheating, plus fuel tanks with a continuous purge system. Martin also allowed for the provision of four RATO motors attached to the rear fuselage for an additional 1,000lb of thrust during take-off. Provision was made for two fuel tanks to be installed in the bomb bay in addition to the three integral fuel tanks for range extension.

Variable-incidence wings were an important aspect of the XB-51 and featured a 35-degree sweepback with 6-degree anhedral, unusual in that they had spoilers rather than ailerons together with leading edge slats and full-span flaps, flight surfaces augmented by hydraulic power units and artificial feel control units. The second aircraft had a bullet at the juncture of the vertical and horizontal tail surfaces to inhibit flutter and to cure vibration experienced during flight tests with the first prototype.

Employed primarily to change the glide path angle, an airbrake was fitted to the underside of the fuselage and a braking parachute was attached on the right side of the upper fuselage. The landing gear was similar to that selected for the B-47, and not unlike that of the XB-48, with twin-wheel sets on the centreline of the fuselage, fore and aft of the bomb bay, and wingtip outriggers for lateral stability on the ground.

The crew positions closely followed the trend for the majority of new light and medium bombers with the pilot on the aircraft centreline and the navigator behind and to the right under a fixed bubble canopy. The navigator's position was close to the access bay for the advanced avionics equipment with a small window as the only view out. Electronics included AN/APN-3, SHORAN, the AN/ARN-6 radio compass, AN/APT-16 radio countermeasures equipment, a VHF radio and radar and marker beacons. Neither prototype had any radar equipment installed. The bomb bay had a rotating door to which the ordnance was attached and exposed to the airflow when in the fully rotated, open position. The bomb release expelled the ordnance well clear of the aircraft using a pneumatically operated actuator. Bomb aiming was aided by the A-1-B sight operating with the SHORAN system. Due to its ground-attack role, the XB-51 also had armoured sections including the forward windshield to protect the pilot.

The first prototype (46-0685) took to the air for the first time on 28 October 1949, flying from Middle River to Patuxent Naval Air Station piloted by Pat Tibbs – who gave a positive report on its handling. Only on conclusion of this flight did the company receive a formal contract for the two aircraft and all the supplementary equipment, formally signed on 1 November. As accepted, the XB-51 became the first jet close-support bomber in the US inventory and thus began Phase I Air Worthiness tests which were completed at the end of March 1950. Afterwards, a highly positive report was issued on the overall design, its functionality and the overall handling. The Phase II trials which were held to verify contractor compliance were conducted between 4 April and 4 November 1951. Martin test pilots had flown the aircraft for 211hrs on 233 flights and the USAF pilots added a further 221hrs.

The second prototype (46-0686) meanwhile, took to the skies on 17 April 1950 with full armament installed and the capacity for a bomb load of up to 10,400lb (4,700kg) on internal and external stores positions. Company pilots flew the aircraft for 125hrs on 168 flights with the Air Force adding 26hrs in 25 flights. Tragedy struck when the second aircraft crashed and burned, killing the pilot, during aerobatics over Edwards AFB on 9 May 1952. By this time the Air Force had decided to cancel the XB-51 programme in favour of buying the English Electric Canberra bomber, which was engaged in fly-off trials with the Martin bomber in early 1951. The winner was announced on 23 March 1951 and an order for 250 Canberra aircraft followed, to be licence-built by Martin with the designation B-57. Formal closure of the XB-51 programme was announced that November.

The XB-51 had proven faster than the Canberra but its endurance was poor – the latter could loiter for 2.5hrs over a target 898 miles from base, whereas the XB-51 could only manage 1hr over a target 404 miles from base. It was also thought that the XB-51's wingtip outrigger wheels would be unsuitable for rough field operations.

The importance of the XB-51 programme is generally under-appreciated, even by some aero-historians. It provided an extensive set of test data on a design which contributed greatly to a wide range of research activity on aerostructures, aerodynamics and innovative design trends. The variable-incidence wing proved particularly useful in trials and tests. This type of wing was researched in detail by several German manufacturers, notably Blohm & Voss with the BV 144 transport. It was also applied by the British on the Supermarine Type 322 which appeared in 1943 as a candidate torpedo bomber. After the war, the Republic XF-91 also had a variable incidence wing.

Much too was learned from the extensive work on bomb-release dynamics, work which would find application in several other projects that matured to production levels. Also important was research with the T-tail configuration and on the landing and takeoff characteristics driven by the four-leg landing configuration. Some of the work fed across and improved the B-57. Sadly, the first aircraft was lost on 25 March 1956 when it crashed on take-off from El Paso International Airport at the start of a planned flight to Eglin AFB, Florida.

Martin produced only two XB-51 prototypes. There were only seats for a pilot and a navigator but the spacious bomb bay could take almost any bomb in the tactical inventory. (USAF)

NORTH AMERICAN B-45 TORNADO

First Flight: 17 March 1947

Of the four contenders for the 1944 jet bomber requirement outlined earlier in this book, only North American and Boeing would get to build production aircraft accepted by the US Air Force. The decision to select North American for its XB-45 was dated 8 September 1944, authorising development and testing of three prototypes based on NA-130. The design was the essence of simplicity for operation and manufacture – a mid-wing monoplane with its four jet engines in pairs in underwing pods, it featured a horizontal tail with dihedral and conventional fin and rudder, a semi-glazed nose section enclosing a bombing radar, and a teardrop cockpit canopy.

The wing was based on NACA 66-215 aerofoil section at the root, tapering to a NACA-212 at the tip. Much of the aircraft was reminiscent of the B-25 Mitchell bomber, particularly the fuselage and the arrangement of formers and stringers supporting the sheet panels.

The Air Force changed a lot between the contracted order and the first flight in spring 1947. What had started out as a medium bomber would be recategorised as a light bomber, reflecting the existence of vast superheavy bombers such as the B-36, which effectively turned what had been heavy bombers into medium bombers.

The Air Force decided on full series production of the B-45 straight off the drawing board on 2 August 1946, authorising 96 B-45A aircraft based on NAA Model 147 as well as a static test version. Not a little of that decision had been settled when Colonel J. S. Holtoner, Office of the Chief of the Air Staff, endorsed the aircraft for its basic simplicity, asserting that it "presented no questionable features" and that he anticipated "few development problems".

The first aircraft was trucked in sections from the Inglewood facility to Muroc Field where it was assembled and put through various ground tests and taxi trials. The first flight took place on 17 March 1947 and lasted 1hr 4min.

The three XB-45 prototypes (45-59479/80/81) would each be instrumented according to a pre-set allocation of test requirements for specific aircraft. Aboard the first XB-45, 28,800 instrument readings would be gathered every 60 seconds through a range of equipment, including five photo-recorders covering 120 dials fitted in a small space and with a mirror to reflect 35 large instruments. The camera incorporated an electro-magnetic actuator and was attached to an adjustable rail so that it could be accurately aligned.

Data would be recorded on film strip showing control forces recorded

The clean lines of the North American XB-45 (45-59479), the first of three prototypes. Powered by four J35 engines, it would become the first US jet bomber to enter service. (USAF)

on micro-ammeters, vertical forces up to 12g monitored by accelerometers, yaw, roll, pitch and attitude recorded from gyroscopes and angular displacement of small control surfaces measured by dials. Tiny adjustments would be picked up by selsyn indicators, essentially electro-mechanical devices used for precise angular differences between two points. The selsyn indicators were linked together by braided steel cables to the aircraft control systems. To get highly accurate data, two selsyns were attached to each transmitter, one geared to rotate at four times the speed of the other. This ensured a direct correlation between measurement frequencies.

The output of strain gauges was recorded on three oscillographs provided by Consolidated Engineering, attached to three bridge-balances each with 12 separate channels and 36 cables connecting them to selected points on the strain gauge terminal board. Measuring devices were placed in locations which would never see any measurements taken on a production aircraft – one example being the attachment of pitot tube intakes within the engine air inlet. To get greater accuracy and direct readout of pressure gauges, North American chose to connect tubes to the air-speed indicators rather than to direct-read pressure gauges.

Jet exhaust was measured by pressure tubes leading to a stainless steel rake

As Chief of the Air Staff, Colonel J. Stanley Holtoner played a significant role in pushing for the introduction of the B-45, claiming it had 'few development problems'. (USAF)

mounted in the tailpipe of the engine. The tubes were connected to sensitive manifold pressure gauges. Power for all the test equipment was obtained from two 24V and four 12V batteries in the tail section.

There was much about the B-45 which was novel and new to air crew and ground personnel alike. It was acknowledged early in the design process that atmospheric friction would raise the temperature of the

aircraft's skin and conduct heat into the pressurised cabin. A refrigeration system was incorporated to lower the inside temperature by up to 30°F (16°C) below the outside temperature. Maintenance crews liked the displacement of the engines in paired pods, extending beyond the leading edge of the wing for ease of access. When major and many other minor items were addressed, the Air Force had its own test pilots conduct an extensive sequence of tests, logging 181hrs between August 1948 and June 1949.

The first batch of production B-45A-1 aircraft arrived in service with the 47th BW during April 1948, two months after initial delivery. Some defects and faults with the early deliveries brought unexpected problems to the induction programme and the Wing wrestled with training issues. The next batch, designated B-45A-5, had the more powerful 5,200lb J47-3 engine, replacing the 4,000lb J35-A-11 with the X-45. Apart from a larger tail, increasing the span to almost 43ft, the latest aircraft had a completely revised fuel system, a more refined tail cone with turret installed, a vertical row of powered flaps to provide a windbreak ahead of the crew door to protect the navigator exiting in an emergency, and a new cockpit canopy. The last of the initial 96-strong production lot had been delivered by June 1949 but the introduction of the B-45 to service was compromised by inadequate provision of ground handling equipment and

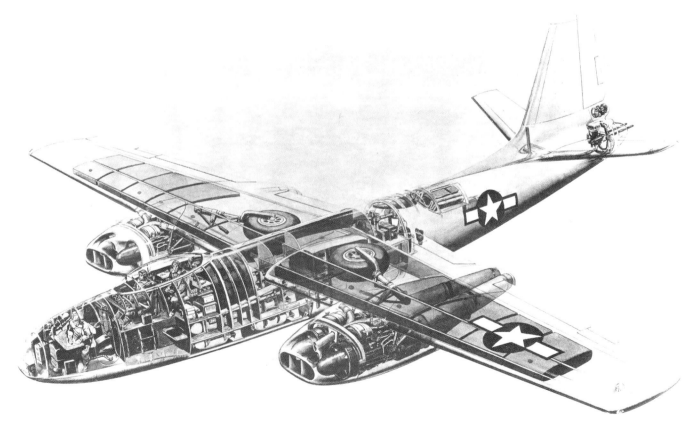

This period cutaway displays the layout of the B-45 including its paired engines under each wing, the main landing gear wells, the fuel tanks and the crew positions. The radar-sighted tail-gun shown was replaced by a tail gunner in the actual aircraft. (North American Aviation)

North American B-45 Tornado

B-45As of the 47th Light Bomb Wing at Langley AFB prior to a transatlantic flight to RAF Sculthorpe, England. The new jet bomber force made several operational deployments overseas. (USAF)

specialist maintenance tools, with some aircraft offline for several weeks.

There is no known record of precisely when the Air Force formally introduced the B-45 into service, various dates being recorded with several highly contradictory. The press of the time did not record it either. The Air Force discouraged publicity of new aircraft types at this time, especially as tensions with the Russians built up and there were concerns over leaks to a potential adversary. These security fears reached a new level with the Berlin blockade, beginning in July 1948, which brought an end to any hope that the post-war world would enjoy an age of mutual peaceful coexistence. This had a significant effect on the evolution of both the B-45 and the B-47 and would have a determining influence on the need for a fitting B-36 replacement.

INTO SERVICE
Initial assignments for the B-45 began with the Far East Air Force (FEAF), with deactivation of the 47th BG at Barksdale so that its aircraft could replace the B-26Cs with the FEAF's 3rd Light Bomb Group at Yokota AB, Japan. But the limited range of the B-45 prevented it reaching Hawaii from the continental US. The B-45A-1s had a ferry range of 2,440 miles with a take-off weight of 86,341lb and an internal fuel capacity of 5,800 US gallons. Almost half this fuel was carried in two fixed bomb-bay tanks. Consideration of how to get the aircraft to Japan was rendered superfluous when it was decided that, without fire-control or bombing equipment, the B-45A-1 aircraft was nowhere near operational standard and plans to move them to Yokota were cancelled.

There were other reasons not to deploy overseas. Some structural defects had been discovered and the J47 engines were showing operating deficiencies. Each engine had to be inspected after only 7.5hrs and if shown to be serviceable, could be flown for an additional 7.5hrs before a complete overhaul. By mid-1949, Tactical Air Command (TAC) estimated that it would require an additional 900 engines just to keep the aircraft operational in US bases. Demand for J47s was extremely high with the J47-powered F-86 Sabre in service from 1949. AMC decreed that only aircraft with jet engines providing 100hrs between overhauls would be allowed abroad. There is some justification to the idea that engineering

problems with jet engines of all types were directly responsible for the shaping and reshaping of US combat aircraft deployment during this period.

TAC bomber units had no experience of these relatively high-speed aircraft. The B-45 used a Gyrosyn gyro-compass which integrated the directional gyro synchronised with the horizontal component of the Earth's magnetic field by way of a flux gate that detected the direction of magnetic lines of force and transmitted that to a precession instrument. Troublesome in high-speed flight, the E-4 autopilot caused problems when the bomb doors were open. Hooks and shackles in the bomb bay came loose through poor design and detached during manoeuvres. In addition, the

A B-45A in overall aluminium finish with anti-glare panels on the upper forward fuselage in front of the cockpit and on the paired engine nacelles. (USAF)

Positioned for a public relations shot, the second of ten B-57Cs delivered from 1949 with strengthened airframe and canopy but here without the tip tanks with which it was supplied. (USAF)

The RB-45C followed as a tactical photo-reconnaissance aircraft. Wingtip tanks greatly improved range and the type had a prolific array of optional camera positions. (USAF)

North American B-45 Tornado

The first B-45C off the production line (48-001) in May 1949.

An impeccable shot of the last B-45C produced, showing the standard nose and reinforced cockpit framing. (USAF)

A Boeing YKB-29 tanker at Yokota, Japan of the type used to top-up the B-45 – the first jet to carry out mid-air refuelling. (USAF)

emergency brake slaved to the primary hydraulic system proved unreliable.

Avionics too were proving troublesome and issues with the AN/APQ-24 bombing-navigation system were compounded by a lack of experience in operating and maintaining this unique piece of equipment. The pressurisation pump was consistently breaking down and troublesome when apparently operating correctly and the altitude at which the receiver and transmitter equipment could operate was also limited. One problem arose from the absence of pressurisation in the modulator and a faulty positioning of the radar antenna confused target coverage above 40,000ft (12,192m).

Even the poorly designed arrangement of the cockpit controls and readouts caused problems. In operating the APQ-24, the observer was required to manipulate the mileage control dials located to his right and about 1ft behind his back, while simultaneously observing the radar scope directly in front of him. The situation was made worse by the shortage of ground technicians proficient in the field of avionics. There were frequent shortages of spare parts, ground handling equipment and all the stands and hoists required to service the aircraft too.

Development of the B-45C began on 22 September 1947, three months after the production decision for the B-45A. It would have air-refuelling for the first time, wingtip tanks as standard and a forward oblique camera would be installed on the nose tip for the TB-45C reconnaissance version. These would have water-injection for extra take-off thrust, with two 214 US gallon drop-tanks suspended beneath the

engine nacelles. But most of the changes were on the interior, where stations for 10 different types of camera were installed. The B-45C first flew on 3 May 1949, followed by the RB-45C in April 1950. Overall, 10 B-45Cs and 33 RB-45Cs were accepted by the Air Force, with deliveries beginning in May 1949 and completed in October 1951; the last B-45C had been accepted on 13 April 1950. Two aircraft, one of which was a B-45C, were used as director aircraft for guided weapons development and appropriately designated DB-45.

THE B-45 BUILD

Heavily influenced by its requirement to serve as a tactical bomber, the B-45 borrowed much from North American's experience with the B-25 Marauder. The crew included pilot, co-pilot/radio-operator, bombardier/navigator and a tail gunner. In the operational version, the two pilots had tandem ejection seats while the other crew could bale out through nose and tail hatches. The forward pilot had all the primary controls while the back-seater served as navigator.

Structurally, the aircraft consisted of three prime sections: the forward assembly from the nose back to the forward bulkhead, which contained the station for the bombardier/navigator situated above the radar scanner; the main centre section from the front bulkhead back to the rear fin post; and the aft assembly which contained the tail gunner's position and vertical and horizontal stabiliser. There was limited access between the pressurised compartments, and only when the bomb

bay was empty and its doors closed. The main centre section was assembled from seven primary frames with lighter sub-frames which were all riveted to load-bearing longerons and stringers covered by aluminium alloy skins.

The wing was built around a single main spar with secondary spars fore and aft, shaping provided by nose ribs, interspar ribs with fuel tank cutouts and stressed skins. In locations where the engine nacelle mounts were situated, and at the attachment points for the main landing gear legs, special strengthening was built in to the wing assembly. The wing was attached to the fuselage with upper and lower bolts aligned both horizontally and vertically to shift loads from one assembly to the adjacent fixture.

Either side of the engine nacelles, flap sections were located on the trailing edge with ailerons attached to the outboard wing panels. These flying surfaces were supported by a single spar incorporating nose ribs and aft ribs to form a taper, skinned with aluminium alloy. The tailplane sections, both horizontal and vertical were of conventional two-spar construction similar to the wings, incorporating trailing edge elevators and a fin and rudder of similar construction to the ailerons.

All the control surfaces were fitted with hydraulic boosters and the ailerons and elevators were controlled by a wheel incorporating a communications button, nose steering switch and elevator trim control. The wing flaps too were hydraulically driven, with four separate sections on each side. The pilot could

North American B-45 Tornado

Built as the last of ten B-45As (47-096) and redesignated JRB-45A, this Tornado was used to test Westinghouse turbojet engines on a pylon under the fuselage. (USAF)

select flap position at pre-selectable values to a maximum 40-degrees with power provided by the engine-driven pumps. Hydraulics also controlled the landing gear, the main gear retracting inwards with the nose leg retracting aft. In the approach phase, the main gear doors remained open to operate as pseudo drag brakes. The nose wheel steering unit was also hydraulically controlled with appropriate anti-shimmy units. Brakes were of standard design, with toe pedals on the rudder pedals or, for emergency use only, levers at both pilot positions.

Only the B-45A-1 was powered by the Allison J35, both the A-9 and A-11 variants being used on these aircraft. The B-45A-5 and the B-45/RB-45C were powered by either the GE J47-7, or J47-9, utilising a pressurised oil system similar to that provided by the J35. The RB-45C had an additional fuel tank in the aft fuselage and a 1,200 US gallon droppable tank in the aft bomb bay with an optional fuel tank of the same quantity in the forward bomb bay; two 1,125 US gallon drop tanks could also be carried. As with the B-45, the RB-45C could jettison the bomb bay fuel tanks. The in-flight refuelling capability incorporated the AN/APN-68 system for guiding the aircraft to the tanker. The receptacle and slipway were fitted to the top of the fuselage and forward of the fin, the system capable of filling all fixed and wingtip tanks at the rate of 300 US gallons per minute.

Central to the avionics was the E-4 autopilot, also used with automatic approach equipment as the airborne element of the instrument landing system. A drawback prevented it from being engaged in any path other than level flight but when engaged a sidestick controller could be used to change attitude. The auto-approach system also allowed the aircraft to follow the radio beam from the localiser, which would engage directional control of the flight path, riding the beam to just above the runway when the pilot would switch it off and land manually.

The primary avionics equipment included the AN/APQ-24 bombing/navigation radar, the AN/ARC-3 communications system and the AN/ARN-6 gyro compass. Other equipment included the RC-103/AN/ARN-5A instrument approach set, the AN/ARC-2A for inter-communications and the RC-193-(A) marker beacon together with the AN/CRT-3 emergency radio for the emergency dinghy.

The bomb capacity of the B-45 remained largely unchanged across the three variants, optional extremes being 27 x 500lb bombs or a single 22,000lb Grand Slam bomb with various intermediate options. Defensive armament comprised two M24 0.50in machine guns, each with 500 rounds of ammunition, controlled by a gunner within a pressurised compartment forward of the turret and equipped with an MD1 hemispherical optical sighting station and gun camera. The gunner could switch to an optical system if selected. The absence of a tail gun in the RB-45C made the aircraft highly vulnerable to attack and this was to prove fatal in a couple of instances during the Korean War.

The specialised reconnaissance equipment varied according to operational requirements and cameras were housed in the fore and aft compartments, provision for one and up to three respectively in each. With an optional 12in or 24in lens, a K22A camera would be installed in the forward oblique position for day reconnaissance, or an A-6M film camera with optional 25mm, 50mm or 250mm lenses. The main group of cameras would be installed in the aft compartment, the T-11, K-22A, K-17C, K-38, K-37 or S-7A. In addition, an oblique mounting was available for a K-22A or an S-7A film camera. A split-vertical mount was provided for either a pair of K-38s with 24in lenses or a pair of K-37s with 12in lenses for night reconnaissance work.

GOING NUCLEAR

In early 1946 it was decided that all new Air Force bombers would need to be capable of carrying atomic as well as conventional bombs – but the B-45 had not been designed with nuclear bombs in mind. North American had not been made aware of the dimensions of the early atom bombs and as such they would not fit within the B-45's bomb bay due to a large spar which extended across its width.

The problem could be remedied but only with expensive and time-consuming modifications. Approval was given to begin making these modifications in December 1950. The programme, known as 'Backbreaker', started out with nine aircraft and went from there with the last one being completed in April 1952 – just a month prior to the deployment of nuclear-capable B-45s to the UK.

The seventh RB-45C became the JRB-45C (48-017), carrying the engine test pylon for a single jet. This view was taken on 22 July 1952. (USAF)

Between May and June 1952, 40 B-45s were sent to RAF Sculthorpe in Norfolk, England.

One anticipated use for the B-45 was in retardation strikes – where nuclear weapons would be employed to slow enemy troop advancements and their lines of supply by interdiction. It quickly became clear that the B-45 was incapable of carrying out such a role or any other ground support mission due to the limitations of the airframe. It was the search for a tactical nuclear-armed ground support aircraft that led the Air Staff to look to the B-57 and the Douglas B-66 Destroyer but delays and similar difficulties plagued those prospects too.

While the intended mission for the B-45 had been to provide a jet-powered tactical bomber, its initial adaptation was to the tactical nuclear role and in that capacity it partnered the Convair B-36 which provided the strategic nuclear strike deterrent for SAC. By January 1958 fewer than 50 remained in the inventory and their phaseout became a priority as the B-66 entered service. By July the aircraft had departed Sculthorpe for deployment to other bases around Europe and North Africa where they found an inglorious second life as airframes for training firefighters. A few were retired to Moron AB, Spain, where they were parted out and sold for scrap.

The third and arguably the most valued role for this aircraft was for reconnaissance and intelligence gathering operations and it was in this capacity that the RB-45C had the most interesting life. In service from 1950 with the 91st SRW at Lockbourne AFB, Ohio, and its three operating squadrons, the 322nd, 323rd and 324th, all 33 RB-45C delivered to the USAF were operated by these units. Never officially logged as having participated in the Korean War, three RB-45Cs were sent to Yokota AB in September 1950 to replace outdated RB-29s of the 91st RS. On 4 December 1950 an RB-45C (48-015) crewed by Capt Charles E. McDonough, Col James Lovell (a Pentagon intelligence officer), Capt J. E. Young and Lt J. J. Picucci, was shot down by a MiG-15. Capt McDonough and one other were held by Russian intelligence for some time. One was hanged and the other man died under interrogation.

Other flights were made over China and some to Vladivostok and additional spy flights were undertaken with the assistance and cooperation of the CIA as well as the Pentagon. FEAF's Bomber Command took control of these aircraft on 31 January 1951 but on 9 April another RB-45C narrowly escaped after being set upon by four MiG-15s and on 9 November another incident saw a lone RB-45C escape from nine jet fighters. Discouraged from approaching heavily defended targets, in January 1952 crews were assigned to night reconnaissance duties only.

A cat-and-mouse game ensued with various methods of deception applied to flights which were, at best, classified intelligence-gathering operations, accounting for the absence of this type from official registers of aircraft operating in theatre during the Korean War.

Between 1952 and 1954, the Royal Air Force operated four aircraft which had been leased to Britain from the 91st SRW, forming a Special Duties Flight with crews assigned to 35 and 115 Squadrons as part of Operation Jiu-Jitsu. Their purpose was to overfly Soviet-controlled airspace and obtain intelligence information which SAC wanted but was disallowed by the Truman Administration for political reasons. Because the USAF was prohibited from flying into Warsaw Pact airspace, the request to the British originated in late 1950 from General Nathan Twining, the Air Force Chief of Staff, and General LeMay, commanding SAC.

The phasing out of the B/RB-45C took place quickly. By June 1959 only one remained on the inventory. Grossly underrepresented in the history of the US Air Force, the B-45 was a pivotal tool – filling a vital role as a tactical nuclear bomber (a natural choice given its hefty bomb-carrying capacity) and proving itself a vital asset for intelligence gathering over Eastern Europe and South-East Asia.

BOEING B-47 STRATOJET

The B-47 would end up being arguably the most aesthetically pleasing of the four designs submitted for the AAF's jet bomber competition by January 1945. Boeing had gone through a wide range of alternative design concepts beforehand, starting with Model 413 of January 1944. This had straight wings and four TG-180 turbojet engines in widely spaced underslung nacelles, essentially a jet version of the B-29.

This was followed by Model 422, which replaced the turbojets with turbofans, and Model 424 with four turbojets bolted directly to the wing in paired nacelles. Model 426, with turboprops, appeared in March 1944 and Model 432, drawn up in December 1944, had four jet engines in the bulged upper part of the fuselage, the side-intakes feeding directly to the engines

with jet pipes exhausting either side of the vertical tail.

While the projected performance of Model 432 was inadequate, on 31 January 1945 the USAAF gave Boeing a contract for engineering development, wind tunnel assessment and structural tests. On that day Model 432 became the XB-47 – although this design had little in common with what would eventually emerged as the built aircraft.

As well as being Boeing's chief aerodynamicist, George Schairer was a member of the Air Force Scientific Advisory Board. As such, he was among the American experts sent to Germany just as the war was ending to evaluate captured German documents and data. Even before he set off he was aware of NACA research on swept wings which indicated their favourable properties at high subsonic speeds.

In occupied Germany, Schairer was part of the group assigned to work at the aeronautical research institute in Brunswick – poring over advanced German studies under the guiding hand of leading aerospace engineer Theodore von Karmen. Coming across some of the test data on swept wings, von Karmen and Adolf Busemann, one of the institute's leading aerodynamicists, engaged in a conversation which verified NACA's conclusions.

Boeing may never have built what became the B-47 had this serendipitous meeting never taken place, since the company was on the point of withdrawing from the competition. On returning to the US in August 1945, Schairer set to work and quickly produced dramatically improved designs for the firm's jet bomber entry. The first of these, submitted on 6

The epitome of US global power projection in the 1950s, Boeing's sleek B-47 emerged from a plethora of preceding design options, very few of which were powered by jet engines, to become the standard-bearer for the newly independent Air Force. (USAF)

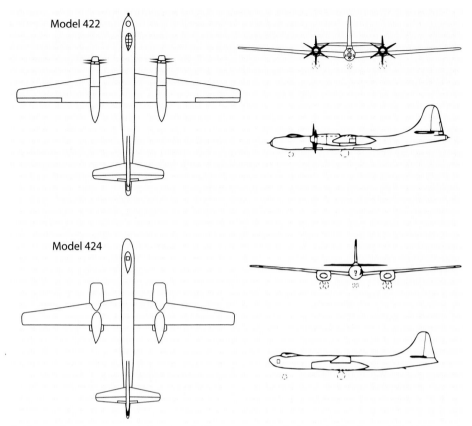

Model 422

Model 424

Boeing produced numerous designs for a B-29 successor prior to the end of the Second World War, such as the turboprop Models 422 and 426, and the turbojet Models 424 and 425. (Boeing)

September 1945, was Model 446 with swept wings and four turbojets buried in the fuselage. The engines were in the top of a bulbous section immediately behind the cockpit, with the hot exhaust gases flowing across the top of the fuselage and past the tail – it was a start.

Then, later that month, came Model 448 with two additional jets, one either side of the rear fuselage and swept tail surfaces, followed by the refined Model 448-2-2 offering better visibility. The net result was a more efficient aerodynamic profile and a top speed calculated to be in excess of the Air Force requirement. The Air Force had not liked engines buried in the fuselage, if only for the fire risk, so further refinement was required.

This was achieved with Model 450-1-1, which Boeing produced in October 1945. This time chief engineer Edward C. Wells and project engineer George C. Martin had worked together to get the optimum configuration for both wings and engines. They leaned somewhat on the work of graduate student Victor Ganzer from the University of Washington, who determined the optimum sweep angle of an efficient wing was 37.5-degrees.

With the engines mounted on pods well forward of the leading edge, wing efficiency was brought to the maximum achievable and the unique Boeing aerofoil had a 12% thickness ratio with an aspect ratio of 9.6:1. Moreover, the placement of the wing pods allowed better internal wing design for meeting both flexure in bending

and torsion while the location of the outer engines at the wingtips reduced flutter.

The Air Force had invested in Boeing even when its Model 432 submission seemed doomed to failure and it was money well spent; Model 450 was a winner. There remained uncertainty about the properties of swept wings however, and it would be nearly two years before the swept wing North American XP-86 proved the concept, a few weeks before the XB-47 itself.

The AAF issued a note of negotiation on the original contract on 6 December 1945, authorising two XB-47s which would not have any operational equipment but would demonstrate the viability of the solutions proposed for many technically challenging issues. The thin, swept wing was accepted despite being unproven by flight testing, in the expectation that issues might be encountered with high-speed flutter, stall characteristics and instability.

Aerodynamically cleaner than a thick wing, it would not have the same stress and fatigue margins where strength and durability were essential, particularly since it was designed to carry six jet engines on pylons. Another issue was the lack of space for either undercarriage or fuel in the wings. Boeing's solution for this was to adopting a tricycle landing gear and with outriggers at the wingtips for stabilising the unloaded aircraft on the ground.

TRIAL BY FLIGHT
A conference at Wright Field on 1 November 1945 concluded that Model

450 was a step beyond the B-45, B-46 and B-48 and estimates of top speed went as high as 635mph at 35,000ft. The problem of high subsonic compressibility would put a limit on the speed achievable with the straight-winged competitors, while the B-47's higher subsonic capability would open possibilities for fitting more powerful engines and reaching higher cruise speeds. Following this, on 6 November the USAAF Engineering Division at Wright Field praised the boldness of design and acknowledged it as superior in performance to any of the other contenders. It was this that prompted the AAF to approve two XB-47 prototypes precisely one month later.

There would be differences from the 450-1-1. The outer engines were brought inboard and placed on pylons like the inner engines and the wing was given greater area, with the outriggers brought in to the twin-engine inner pylon nacelles. All three crewmembers would have ejection seats, a tail turret was added, all fuel would be carried in self-sealing fuselage tanks, the vertical fin would be swept and a more refined tandem landing gear was added. The latter saved 1,500lb and resolved an issue with drag during retraction on take-off, which was calculated to act as a speed brake. This configuration would carry forward to the B-52.

The XB-47 mock-up was inspected in April 1946 and several changes were requested in the nose and in the seating arrangement. But all was not well at Boeing, with detailed technical and engineering changes to the definitive XB-47 prototypes in addition to labour troubles at the company where a lack of overtime pay contributed to a six-month slippage in the schedule.

It took until 10 July 1947 to get a definitive contract signed for the two prototypes but the completion of the first aircraft progressed well during the middle of that year and when the first aircraft (Model 450-3-3 configuration) with serial 46-065 was rolled from the Seattle factory on 12 September 1947 it signalled a new age in air power – coming as it did in the same month that the Air Force became independent of the Army.

After poor weather forced a delay of several days, the first aircraft was flown from Seattle across to Moses Lake AFB, Washington, on 17 December to begin flight tests – exactly 44 years to the day after the Wright Brothers first took to the air. Powered by six 3,750lb thrust J35-GE-7/9 engines, the overall performance of the first aircraft was disappointing despite the pilots giving it high marks. One Boeing pilot remarking that, "The plane is still doing much better than anyone had a right to expect. We're still exploring one thing at a time, not every door we kick in has had good things inside."

The second aircraft (46-066) made its first flight on 21 July 1948, with

Boeing B-47 Stratojet

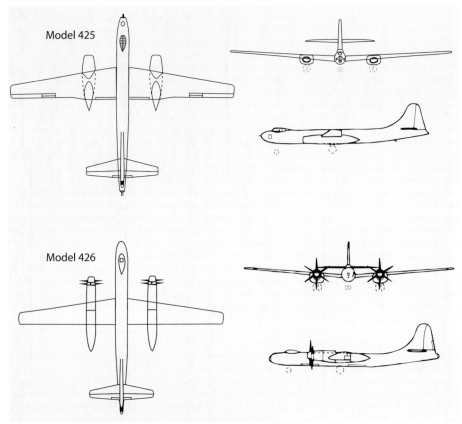

Model 425

Model 426

Boeing's turbojet Model 425 and turboprop Model 426. (Boeing)

six 5,200lb thrust J47-GE-3 engines installed, these also being retrofitted to the first prototype. By this date the Phase I tests had been completed on the first prototype, logging about 45hrs, and between 8 July and 15 August 1948 it completed a further 38hrs with Air Force pilots completing Phase II trials. The Air Force accepted the first XB-47 on 29 November 1948, conditional on the fitting of specific items of equipment deliberately left off to accommodate the weighty volume of test equipment and recorders. Boeing logged an additional 100hrs on the second prototype and the Air Force added 237 more.

The Air Force began to plan for B-47 production during December 1947, with some issues identified during flight testing being earmarked for resolution on the assembly line. The first production run would see 13 B-47As built. These were considered pre-production aircraft (Model 450-10-9) preceding the B-47B (Model 450-11-10) which was considered the fully developed service model. The initial plan was for 54 aircraft – the 13 B-47As plus 41 B-47B.

However, a letter contract dated 22 November 1948 specified an initial order for only 10 B-57As for $28million, with the remaining three being assigned to a future procurement plus the B-47Bs.

The final configuration for the B-47 was based on Boeing Model 450 with swept wings and tail assembly and a slender fuselage with two crew seated in tandem and additional crewmembers in the fuselage. (Boeing)

This contract was then subject to several changes, amendments and cancellations.

The first prototype was flown to Andrews AFB on 8 February 1949, setting an official transcontinental speed record in the process, so that it could be shown to members of the House Armed Services Committee. The three additional B-47As were cancelled on February 28 but the order for B-47Bs was raised from 41 to 55. Simultaneously, design and assembly of a ground test rig for a jet-assisted take-off system was ordered. This was deemed necessary if the aircraft was to satisfy its field performance requirement. During this period, the impact of budget cuts under the Truman administration hit the Pentagon and as a consequence stimulated a pruning of contenders for both medium and strategic bombers, including the B-50 and the prospective B-54 on 18 April 1949.

The Air Force eventually finalised an order for 87 B-47Bs on 14 November 1949, all to a revised specification issued in September 1948. These included a single-point refuelling capability for speed, a tactical RATO capability for short take-off runs, an increased gross weight of 202,000lb after aerial refuelling, installation of the K-2 bombing and navigation system, and a remotely operated tail turret. Taken together, these changes required redesign of the fuselage, wings and landing gear. The 10 B-47As were scheduled for delivery between April and November 1950, with the B-47Bs between December 1950 and December 1951. The first flight of a B-47A took place on 25 June 1950 but it would be another year before all 10 aircraft had been delivered to the Air Force.

However, continued testing indicated serious deficiencies in these aircraft – they were underpowered and had critical braking issues after aborted take-offs. They were also hazardous to fly following a refused landing due to their low rate of acceleration. The solution was clearly bigger and more powerful engines but these would be a long time coming.

TRIAL AND TEST

For all the problems encountered, the B-47 represented arguably the biggest step forward in combat aircraft design since the shift from fixed-undercarriage, open cockpit, biplane configurations to closed-cockpit, monoplane fighters of the mid-1930s. In testimony before the Senate Government Operations Committee, George Schairer summed it up: "In the case of our B-47… we had no idea what would turn out when we built the airplane. At least we had no idea it would turn out as well as it did. There was no way to predict that it was going to come out that well. We thought we were terribly optimistic in our predictions. We guessed our drag would be about two-thirds of what anybody in his right mind

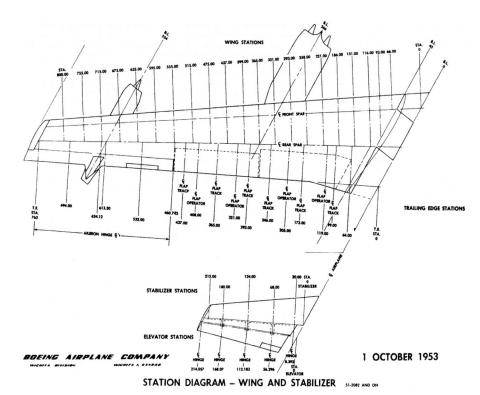

The 36.5-degree swept wing was a radical departure but timely considering the wealth of information emerging from German research data and studies in the US. The engines were suspended from pylons beneath the wing. (Boeing)

The first XB-47 (46-065) is rolled out at Boeing Field with some low-level celebration and much anticipation. (Boeing)

would have estimated, and it turned out to be another 25 percent lower than our optimistic estimate."

The B-47A entered service with the Air Force in May 1951, the 10 aircraft arriving with the 306th BW (Medium), MacDill AFB, Florida. Initial training had been assigned to this unit, with its air crew being responsible for training other units – but when the programme almost doubled the Air Training Command took that job on from December 1951.

None of the B-47As were armed and they were devoid of the systems being

assigned to the next variant. They did incorporate ejection seats, but these troublesome units had already been deleted from the initial production lots of the B-47B series. With so much development work under way, these aircraft proved invaluable for testing and several remained with the Air Proving Ground Command.

The B-47B was the first operational production variant and was subject to a considerable number of upgrades and improvements. The first 87 (Model 450-11-10) were followed by a second

Boeing B-47 Stratojet

The first XB-47 prototype made its first flight on 17 December 1947, on the 44th anniversary of the Wright Brothers' first flight. (Boeing)

The first B-47A off the line, essentially a production version (rather than a variant) of the two XB-47 prototypes. (USAF)

Government owned but Boeing-operated Plant II, Wichita, Kansas, 26 January 1951. The three aircraft closest the camera are B-47As, of which only ten were built. (Boeing)

lot of 202 (Model 450-67-27) and these, plus the last 110 (Model 450-157-27), were powered by the 5,800lb thrust J47-GE-23. Each was equipped with two 0.50 calibre tail guns which could be fired manually by the co-pilot, who was also known as the 'weaponeer', or by the radar system. The B-47B also had the B-4 fire-control system, K-4A bombing-navigation equipment and the AN/APS-54 warning radar together with the latest electronic equipment, including AN/APT-5A electronic countermeasures. For reconnaissance work, it also carried two K-38 cameras, one K-17 and one K-72.

Initial design for this model began in September 1948 and it was at first set up to meet a USAAF requirement for a reconnaissance aircraft, dropped before the need for a medium bomber was prioritised. By the time the production go-ahead had been authorised, the Air Force wanted a bomber capable of carrying a full suite of nuclear weapons in addition to a full photo-reconnaissance role. Because of increases in production of the type and due to a sense of urgency instilled by the Korean War, Air Force planners anticipated a production rate of 149 aircraft a month.

Douglas Aircraft was awarded a contract in December 1950 to build 10 at its Tulsa, Oklahoma, plant followed shortly thereafter by a deal whereby Lockheed would built eight at Marietta, Georgia. Actual production get started until 1953 however. Yet in August 1950 the Air Force identified 2,000 changes necessary before full scale B-47 assembly commenced.

The first example was accepted by the Air Force in March 1951 and 87 aircraft from the initial production lot had been delivered by early 1952, but these had J47-GE-11 engines. The next two lots of 312 aircraft would get the 23-series. It was quickly apparent that because of enduring problems with getting the type fully operational as required by SAC, there would have to be a specially configured suitability test.

Under Project WIBAC (Wichita Boeing Aircraft Company), as aircraft were delivered to SAC they would cycle through a system where personnel from SAC and the Air Proving Ground Command compiled comprehensive logs of parts, components, subsystems and systems – recording any failures and malfunctions. Specialist data was also gathered on testing, maintenance procedures and base operations.

All elements of the B-47 programme – not just its equipment – were assessed for full operational efficacy. This resulted from a stringent, some would say overbearing, emphasis placed on readiness, operability and effectiveness by SAC's commander, General Curtis LeMay. This track and trace policy transformed the manner in which the Air Force operated, irrespective of the importance of the job, and through the

The last B-47A (49-1909) shows its impressive take-off performance courtesy of the RATO bottles as boost-assist – aiding the aircraft's less-than-impressive J47-GE-11 engines. (Boeing)

A B-47B (51-2171) representing the first fully evolved variant and the first to enter full service with the Air Force. (Boeing)

B-47 programme too subcontractors and suppliers from the ancillary industry were made to sharpen practices, improve quality and weed out defective or substandard equipment before it was delivered for integration into the production line.

Aircraft sometimes get the blame for the ineffectiveness of the companies supplying their parts and so it was with the B-47. Many within industry at the time believed that the aircraft required higher standards than those applied by existing manufacturers of relays, fuel selector valves, booster pumps and similar subsystems and components.

As an example, the K-2 bombing-navigation system had 41 major parts incorporating 370 vacuum tubes and almost 20,000 separate components. Because the B-47 was a very compact aircraft, these components were distributed around the airframe and a lot of the parts were outside the pressurised area. This prevented any in-flight attention and made ground servicing and change-outs extremely time consuming – eight hours to pre-flight the system compared with one hour for similar equipment in a B-36. Only after several tiers of modification had the K-2 become reasonably reliable by mid-1952. The added improvements had effectively made it a completely new piece of kit, and it was redesignated K-4.

Similar problems were encountered with the A-2 tail defence system which had been specifically designed for this aircraft. It was initially believed that the Emerson A-1 fire control system which had been selected for the B-45 could equally serve for the B-47 and in June 1948, without reference to Boeing, Emerson was tasked with designing a tail turret cab for the B-47 similar to that for the B-45, with comfort improvements appropriate for the much longer flight times.

Complexity was added to over-engineered designs and the concept became unworkable, a remote-controlled tail gun system operated by the co-pilot being selected instead. This became the A-2 fire control system which was also tasked with providing search and track by radar. Under Project Hornet, a test mock-up was trialled in a B-29 and while appearing, theoretically, to be superior to the General Electric APG-32 for the B-36 there were insurmountable problems

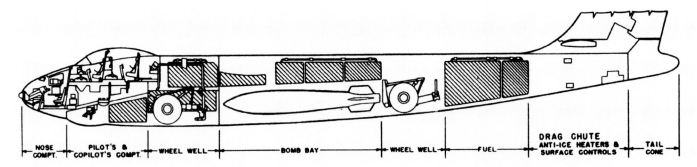

NOSE COMPT. | PILOT'S & COPILOT'S COMPT. | WHEEL WELL | BOMB BAY | WHEEL WELL | FUEL | DRAG CHUTE ANTI-ICE HEATERS & SURFACE CONTROLS | TAIL CONE

The B-47's bomb bay was designed to allow carriage of oversize bomb loads, including the Tallboy shown here. (USAF)

Using externally mounted RATO packs, a B-47B executes a dramatic takeoff on 15 April 1954. (USAF)

A B-47B (51-2212) streams its brake parachute after touchdown at MacDill AFB, Florida. (USAF)

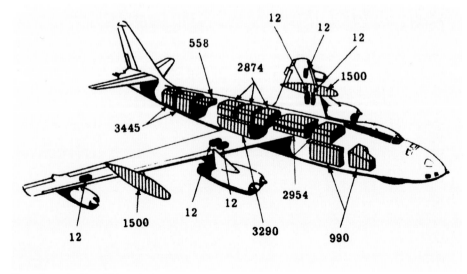

Reconfigured with additional fuel for greater range, the interior tank arrangement of the B-47B differed from that of the B-47A. (via David Baker)

unique to the B-47 and it was cancelled in late 1952. The twin-gun turret was selected with the N-6 optical sight. The B-4 fire control system would later be installed.

Further difficulties were encountered with fuel boil-off, which shortened range, and purging, which required the use of dry ice. New JP-4 fuel solved the former problem while AMC was obliged to develop a new portable gas purging supply unit to end dependence on the availability of dry ice.

Because the aircraft did not have the range specified by the Air Force during the initial competition, aerial refuelling was essential. But the skills involved in fuelling a fast-jet from a slow tanker were not easily acquired. When the first aircraft arrived with Air Training Command the problems arrived with them. There were too few KC-97 tankers and too few trained crew able to do the work. Increasing numbers of trainees were therefore imported to learn the processes involved in one of the trickiest operations conducted between two aircraft. On bases at home and abroad, increased numbers of mechanics, supervisors and trained personnel disrupted planned housing provision, maintenance facilities, equipment and fuel supply chains. All of which had a major impact on readiness levels as the new Air Force adjusted quickly to very different ways of doing business.

'B' FOR BUSINESS
The first B-47B destined for SAC (50-008) was flown from Wichita to MacDill AFB by Col. Michael N. W. McCoy, commander of the 306th BW on 23 October 1951. It was still not combat ready but a celebration held on 19 November named this aircraft 'The Real McCoy'. It was only a start. Six aircraft scheduled for delivery to MacDill that month were rejected for deficiencies, although a total of 12 were accepted by the end of the year. Production plans shuffled around as anticipated and production quotas changed frequently.

Starting in January 1952, SAC began a refinement programme involving 310 B-47Bs through the Grand Central Depot at Tucson, Arizona. But the need to push them through was greater than the capacity of that facility so Boeing agreed to modify 90 aircraft itself and gradually incipient problems, including that of fuel leakage began to slow production once more. Douglas became involved as well and the last modified B-47Bs were delivered back to SAC in October 1953. The refinement modifications were incorporated into the production line for subsequent variants, including the 'Baby Grand' update adding the A-5 fire control system and 'Field Goal', modifications undertaken by Douglas.

The last production B-47B was delivered in June 1953 but the variant saw a wide range of applications. That same year B-47B 51-2186 was modified as the YDB-47B to carry the Bell GAM-63 Rascal missile which could be guided to its target by a controller aboard the aircraft. There would be 74 DB-47Bs, each stripped of armament and converted to carry radio gear for controlling QB-47s and other remotely controlled aircraft. There would also be 66 TB-47B trainers – 48 converted by Douglas, the rest by the Air Force – with a fourth seat added for an instructor. One WB-47B (51-2115) was converted to weather reconnaissance work.

Early in 1953, two B-47Bs were converted into a KB-47G tanker and KB-47F receiving aircraft for evaluation trials with the British probe and drogue aerial refuelling system. The system was first demonstrated in flight during September 1953. However, the need to retain much needed B-47s as bombers rather than wasting them as tankers put an end to this idea. SAC remained concerned about the inability of the prop-driven KC-97 to reach the optimum altitude for the B-47, wasting time and fuel in having to refuel at lower altitudes. In order to avoid the B-47 stalling during the transfer, which it was prone to do at low speed, SAC developed a procedure whereby the two aircraft went into a shallow dive during fuel transfer to maintain a safe speed.

There was no B-47C production variant, despite hopes that this could be the definitive medium jet bomber with a radius of 2,300 miles without refuelling. Boeing's 88th production B-47B (50-082) was assigned to conduct experimental flights in late 1951. Replacing the six J47s with four 8,500lb thrust Allison J35-A-5 engines promised less weight and greater power but proved insufficient for the task. The redesigned aircraft was redesignated

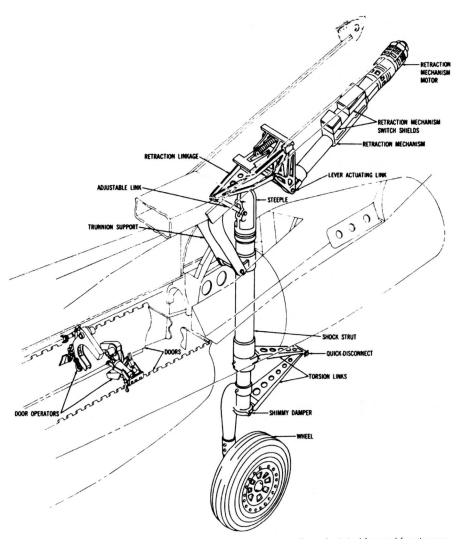

The aircraft's outrigger gear retracted up into the inner engine nacelle and rotated forward for stowage. (Boeing)

The B-47's unique landing gear with main legs fore and aft of the bomb bay required outriggers seen here located between the inner engine pairs on each wing. (USAF)

Boeing B-47 Stratojet

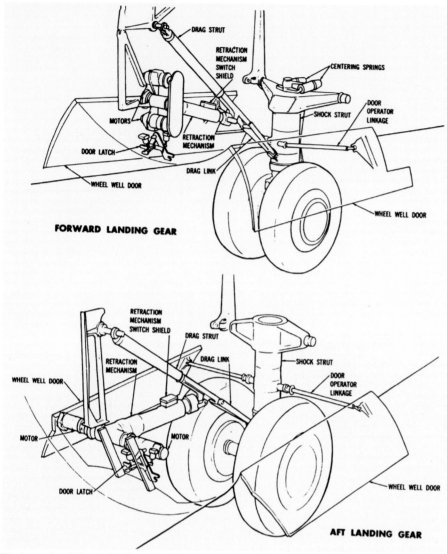

FORWARD LANDING GEAR

AFT LANDING GEAR

The forward and aft main landing gear which had already been proposed by other manufacturers for their own designs found its way onto the B-47, due to the extremely thin and high-set wing position. (Boeing)

YB-56 and earmarked for a rework on the fuselage structure to incorporate titanium and magnesium materials, which would be lighter but just as strong. The idea was that this would serve as the prototype for an RB-56A reconnaissance version but that was abandoned. Instead, the aircraft received another designation, YB-47C, and was to be powered by the 17,000lb thrust J57. Already planned for the B-52 as a priority, the J57 took longer to develop and the J57-powered B-47C concept was dropped. This also marked the end of a further version, the YB-47Z, which was to have side-by-side seating and a fourth crewmember.

Back in February 1951, the Air Force was keen to explore the possibilities of greater efficiency through turboprop engines compared to turbojets and paid for two Boeing test aircraft (51-2103 and 51-2046) with the designation XB-47D. These retained their outboard J47-GE-23 engines but the inboard pair on each wing were replaced by a single Curtiss-Wright YT49-W-1 turboprop, which was derived from the J65 Sapphire and drove 15ft diameter four-bladed propellers.

The complexities of integrating this mixed jet/turboprop propulsion caused considerable delays and the YT-49 engine failed to pass its 50hr qualification run. The first flight of the first aircraft took place on 26 August 1955 followed by the second on 15 February 1956. Each logged many flying hours but the concept was impractical and was ultimately never developed.

During the initial planning stage for the B-47B, the Air Force had been keen to develop a dedicated reconnaissance version and asked Boeing to come up with several optional configurations for entry into service during 1953 as the RB-47B. Plans were laid for a production series of 278 aircraft.

However, the B-47B's technical problems, outlined previously, preoccupied both Boeing and the Air Force. Meanwhile, the RB-47B was redesignated YRB-47B and work to convert B-47Bs into YRB-47Bs, involving a reconnaissance pod to be built by Aeronca, was split between Douglas at its Tulsa facility and Lockheed-Marietta.

The recce-pod incorporated four K-38 cameras with a 36in focal length lens,

three K-17 cameras with a single 6in lens and a forward oblique camera position with three K-22s with 6in lenses. A K-36 with a 24in lens or a K-37 with 12in lens could be carried in the pod for high altitude night operations. Some historians credit the Air Force with having completed conversion of 24 standard bombers into YRB-47Bs while others claim up to 132 but the official records are contradictory. SAC shows various figures between 85 and 88 conversions, while Aeronca records disclose 95 pods as being delivered.

It is most probable that 91 aircraft were converted into the YRB-47B configuration, although many were retrofitted back as bombers. The first flight of this variant (51-2194) was on 25 April 1953 and the last had been delivered to the 26th SRW and the 91st SRW by September. In the meantime, the first RB-47E had taken to the air on 3 July and would soon render the RB-47B redundant.

There is a tragic footnote to the story of the RB-47Bs. Late in 1954, Lockheed began conversion of two YRB-47Bs (51-2054 and 51-2141) into a unique configuration incorporating a camera with a 100in (254cm) lens in the forward left side of the bomb bay, facing left and gyro-stabilised 15 to 20-degrees below the horizon. Pointing through the fuselage just forward of the wing root, the target would be framed using a 0.50cal machine gun sight.

The two aircraft received the designation RB-47B-I and they were to be used for a particular reconnaissance mission – a photographic pass along the Kamchatka Peninsula. 51-2054 took off from Eielson SFB, Alaska, on 18 April 1955 but never returned. It was assumed that the aircraft had suffered a technical problem and crashed. Russian forces offered assistance and directed rescue teams to specific areas where they believed it might have crashed. Only 37 years later did Russian premier Boris Yeltsin admit that a Soviet fighter had shot it down, with the loss of all on board.

E FOR 'EXCELLENCE'

Boeing Model 45-157-35, the B-47E, represented the refined evolution promised by the basic design and its first flight was on 30 January 1953. The Air Force had gone through a time of great uncertainty and this continued into the beginning of President Eisenhower's first term in office. An armistice would be signed by mid-year, bringing the Korean War to an end and casting doubt on vast budgets earmarked for defence spending.

By September, the Air Force would shrink to an interim 120 Wings and the anticipated procurement of 2,190 B-47s was cut by 140. An additional 200 were saved by an agreement on extended delivery with phased payments as Boeing was about to get into full-scale production of the B-52. But on no occasion was the B-47 threatened with cancellation. The B-47 replaced the piston-engine B-29/B-50 and the B-52 would replace the mixed-propulsion B-36. More than that, these two aircraft represented an entirely new force – one which would carry the strategic nuclear deterrent to a new level. Most of the B-47's flaws had now been identified and those that had not yet been resolved were addressed with the B-47E.

Equipped with J47-GE-25 engines, an integral 18-unit RATO system and the promise of a jettisonable rack of 33 rockets each delivering 1,000lb of thrust, a revised nose section, reinforced and stronger landing gear for heavier take-off and landing weights and three ejection seats, the B-47E was a significant improvement on the B-47B. It also had twin 20mm cannon in its tail turret and later would acquire the MA-7A bombing radar, the AN/APS-54 warning radar, the AN/APG-32 gun-laying radar and a new suite of advanced electronic devices.

The first unit to get the B-47E was SAC's 303rd Medium Bomb Wing at Davis-Monthan AFB, Arizona, with the 22nd Wing at March AFB, California next, replacing its B-47Bs which were sent on to Air Training Command. Most welcomed by crews was the A-5 fire control system which replaced the virtually useless B-4. It could automatically engage pursuing fighters, tracking them with radar and directing fire from the tail turret.

Production issues had been sorted out and deliveries progressed as planned. By December 1953 SAC had eight fully equipped Wings, one partially equipped and five more receiving their aircraft during 1954. The anticipated phase-out of the B-29s and B-50s was well under way, the last being removed from the inventory of the 97th Wing by July 1955, the year SAC's B-47 inventory exceeded 1,000 aircraft.

The flow of new aircraft continued and by December 1956 SAC had 27 combat-ready Wings, an increase of 15 within the preceding six months. The aircraft was widely respected but the very different piloting style – and skill – required to fly all-jet aircraft was relatively new to SAC. Only the B-45 had been in service by this date, with the B-57 imminent, but the massive influx of B-47s, with the B-52 hot on its heels, challenged flying training programmes.

Instructors had a tough job transitioning piston-engine pilots to the new jets but best practice and a better aircraft helped give the B-47 the lowest major accident rate per 100,000 flying hours. Still, 55% of accidents were down to human error, 43% being air crew and 12% ground crew. Few ever expressed a 'liking' for the B-47 though. It was difficult to handle, unforgiving in many instances, and the workload per crewmember was far greater than experienced with the B-29 from which so many crew transferred.

Up to 12 B-29 crewmembers worked about 130 instruments but the three

The last Block 60 B-47E from Boeing-Wichita, on test with an external horse-collar RATO pack. (Boeing)

The B-47E entered service from April 1953 and most were given anti-flash white undersides to protect the aircraft from thermal radiation after a nuclear detonation. (Boeing)

The Mk 28 thermonuclear bomb was carried by the B-47B and E variants. (USAF)

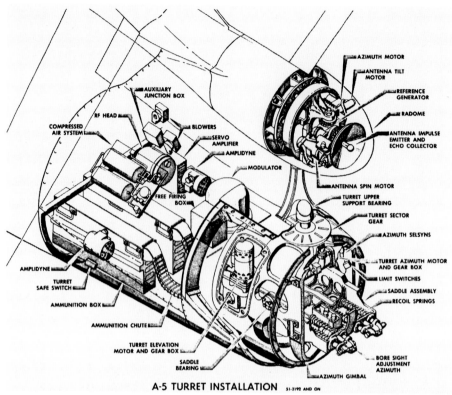

A-5 TURRET INSTALLATION 51-2192 AND ON

As part of the 'Baby Grand' update programme, beginning in 1953, B-47Bs began receiving the A-5 fire control system for their defensive tail turrets. (Boeing)

Two B-47B Stratojets, armourers attending to the tail gun servicing access panels of the one in the foreground. (USAF)

crew aboard a B-47 had 300 gauges, dials and control levers to command. It was also difficult to set the aircraft down on its bicycle undercarriage; getting it wrong on touchdown usually resulted in a catastrophe. Some instructors have remarked that the unforgiving nature of the B-47 raised the alertness level and commanded attention in a way that more forgiving aircraft did not.

During February 1955, the B-47E-IV programme commenced to beef up landing gear for heavier take-off weights, raising it to 230,000lb from the previously permissible 202,000lb. The increase was attributable to fuel load for increased range. Initially the B-47E had a combat radius of 2,014 miles, but the E-IV types extended that to 2,359 miles – almost twice that of early B-47s.

The work was so successful that in March 1955 it was decided to upgrade all B-47Es to this standard, which changed the aft landing gear and added an emergency boost to the elevator to assist with safe take-off and flight. With these improvements and upgrades the bomb load capacity was increased to 25,000lb. It also allowed introduction of the MA-7A bomb and navigation system, including the AN/APS-64 radar with a range of 242 miles. This set could also be used as an IFF transponder interrogator to allow an E-IV to locate another B-47 or a tanker and as a high-resolution, ground-targeting radar. It did retain the conventional bombsight but this was rarely used.

Even as the undercarriage upgrades were being rolled out, consideration was being given to switching from high altitude bombing to low altitude bombing. Tests showed that this was feasible and delivering nuclear weapons from low altitude at high speed would make the aircraft less vulnerable to enemy radar and fighter interception. Moreover, it would split the defences between high and low threats, compromising the enemy's focus.

The Air Staff approved low-level drop tests but these came to an abrupt halt when a B-47 was lost during a test run over Bermuda. Boeing and the ARDC did further structural analysis to show that the aircraft could carry out low-level attack and Air Proving Ground reinstated trials in June 1955, this time with a 6,000lb dummy bomb. On a separate flight, a B-47 successfully released an 8,850lb dummy from a 1.5g pull-up, culminating in an Immelmann turn.

The tests proved conclusively that such operations could be carried out and that it should be instated as a functional role for weapons delivery. In May 1956 Boeing received authorisation to modify 150 aircraft for low-level nuclear weapons delivery. This brought new training requirements and under what was known as 'Hairclipper', the orientation programme began in December 1955.

The Air Force publicly demonstrated SAC's Low Altitude Bombing System (LABS) technique in May 1957 before a mixed civilian/service attendance at an aerial firepower demonstration. By this date the technique was already five years old, it having been developed first for the Republic F-84. It came at a price for the B-47, with the added stress on its airframe necessitating increased maintenance and renewed ground crew training.

FIND AND FIX

There were accidents too and on 5 March 1958, SAC Commander in Chief General Thomas S. Power called a halt to Hairclipper. It was replaced with Pop-Up, a technique which put less stress on the B-47's flexible wings. The B-47 came in at low level, pulled up sharply to high altitude, released the weapon and entered a high-speed dive to get away, achieving the same separation as with the LABS technique. Fatigue cracks were discovered in B-47 wings in April 1958, which led to severe flying restrictions, but the Pop-Up programme resumed in September and training activity had been completed by the end of the year. Even so, there were further accidents and reports of structural fatigue which made a significant increase in the inspection and repair regime necessary.

Solving the fatigue crack problem was initially achieved through the interim Milk Bottle programme, named after the pin fittings of the same shape.

Structural parts of the aircraft were disassembled and suspect bolt holes were reamed oversize so that a boroscope and dye penetrant could be used to see whether cracks were present, following which the holes would be reamed a second time. This operation was carried out on the milk-bottle fittings and Boeing completed fixes on 457 aircraft which were returned to service, each having taken 1,700 hours of work. This allowed aircraft to continue flying the Pop-Up technique but the more permanent fix was a work of art in itself.

This called for repairs to the splice that joined the outer and inner wing panels, the place where the lower wing skin met the fuselage. It also required reworking the milk-bottle pin fittings and the associated forging on the forward fuselage close to the navigator's hatch. It was difficult and costly work but it significantly improved safety.

By the end of July 1955, 1,230 aircraft had received Milk Bottle treatment, with 895 returned to SAC, the entire fleet having been modified by that October. The programme formally ended in June 1959 with only a few aircraft remaining to be treated, all of which were processed during the normal inspection periods.

The cracks may have been cured but there was uncertainty about why they had appeared at all – since the Pop-Up technique only imposed loads on the aircraft that it should have been able to deal with. Several programmes were therefore launched to investigate metal fatigue and why the B-47 was susceptible to it.

An effort to acquire engineering data through extensive loads analysis across all aircraft helped build a coherent understanding and industry worked with the service chiefs to organise a learning-tree, incorporating both scientific and mathematical analyses. Manoeuvre-loads data was a new tool in the kit and did much to help better understand these events across the inventory. It helped to better understand such loads and stresses on the B-52 too as it was also brought down to low-altitude. In flight

tests, the WADC instrumented a Douglas B-66 to research the issue and this information was fed across industry for projects already in development or those still on the drawing board.

All this research also fed in to Boeing's work on life-extension. Static airframe tests in August 1958 showed that the upper fuselage longerons were prone to fatigue and fracture when service aircraft approached 2,000 flying hours. Boeing and the Air Force consulted the NACA, together with Douglas, but they initially failed to find any problems. Then Douglas brought testing to a halt when a fracture appeared in one of its test aircraft's wing stations. The tests at Boeing did not encounter those effects but Douglas continued until January 1959 when it discovered a 20in crack after a 10,000hr test run. Additional inspections were made and 11 other B-47s were discovered with defective longerons, resulting in AMC modifying all support beams on the B-47.

The Air Force had never seen engineering results on aircraft with 10,000hrs but in mid-1959 SAC put a 3,300hr life expectancy on the B-47. Next the test equipment itself came under suspicion, with the oscillograph recorders used for tracking stresses and strains on low-flying aircraft found to be far from satisfactory.

Further problems were encountered when the mission sought by SAC outran

Two distinctly different anti-flash schemes seen on this line of B-47Es. (USAF)

Boeing B-47 Stratojet

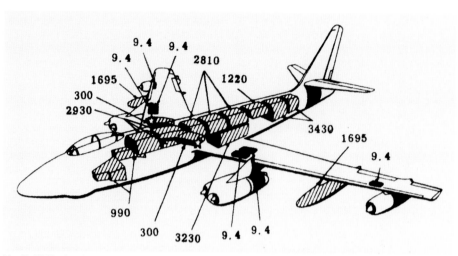

The B-47E had underwing tanks between the inner and outer engine positions which gave the variant even greater range and a better performance for long duration reconnaissance missions. (Boeing)

the technical development of systems essential to carrying it out. General Powers wanted to fly low at night or in poor weather conditions but the necessary absolute altimeters, terrain-avoidance devices and Doppler radar were only then entering the research and development phase and certainly did not exist for service aircraft such as the B-47.

SAC was also under extreme budgetary pressure, its mission now not only embracing full scale introduction of the intercontinental B-52 but also the expensive development of ICBMs and associated ground infrastructure. The costs of Milk Bottle, Pop-Up and other modifications could not support the high number of aircraft assigned to low-level bombing operations. SAC responded by halving the B-47 Inventory assigned to that role – to 500.

This occurred simultaneously with the Air Force concluding that the B-47 lacked

missile penetration aids and that it was only marginally suited to high-altitude weapons delivery. The Air Force gave the B-47 until 1963 to maintain currency in role and with awareness of significant improvements in air-defence technology – Russia sealing its airspace against hostiles with advanced surface-to-air missiles and new high-altitude interceptors – it was the low-level role or nothing. SAC soon set its sights on just 350 B-47s being modified for low-level flying and by mid-1959 plans to equip the B-47 with a defence from infrared missiles were abandoned.

The last B-47E (53-6244) of 931 was delivered on 18 February 1957 to the 100th BW at Pease AFB, New Hampshire – the famous 'Bloody Hundredth' of the Second World War, the 27th and last Wing to be equipped with this aircraft. The switchover to the B-52 was already under way; the 93rd had converted to that aircraft in 1955.

The B-47E was expected to remain in service until at least 1963 in the low-level role but the appointment of Robert McNamara as Secretary of Defense in 1961 changed all that. Under his new and transformative approach to defence, many projects were cancelled or curtailed with the B-47 scheduled for accelerated retirement. This was delayed during the Berlin Crisis of 1961-62, when the Soviets built a wall around the Russian occupied sector. Under operation Fast Fly, initiated in 1965, the B-47 was pulled from the SAC inventory and by 1966 it had gone, redundant aircraft being flown to David-Monthan AFB, the last on 31 October 1969.

A range of derivative B-47E variants had been produced, including an electronic warfare aircraft. One hundred B-47E-Is had been modified to carry removable external electronic countermeasures pods, one on each side of the bomb bay, containing four AN/ALT-6B jammers, known as Tee Town pods after Topeka, Kansas, which was the location of Forbes AFB.

The E-I was followed by the E-II with minor changes and the E-III had an ECM suite including a radar jammer in a bulge under the fuselage as well as a chaff dispenser and improved electrical alternators. This line of development led to the dedicated EB-47E platform, which was sometimes known as the E-47E.

There were 40 EB-47Es, each with a crew of five, and they filled a wide variety of roles and tasks. Some carried a specialist electronic rack in their bomb bay, in which case a crew of three sufficed. Some 35 aircraft were converted to the EB-47L configuration, equipped with communications gear for serving as airborne relay stations

Seen here represented by a much later variant, in the 1960s the Tupolev Tu-95 caused Western defence planners great concern, this Soviet bomber considered the equivalent of the B-47. (RAF/MOD)

A JB-47E (53-2280) landing on 12 August 1957. This was one of several used for specialised tests with weapons-related avionics and advanced control systems, including fly-by-wire trials. (Boeing)

A B-47E supporting the Operation Teapot nuclear tests, a series of 14 detonations which took place at the Nevada Test Site in 1955. (USAF)

Teapot tests aimed to evaluate nuclear weapons of very low yield and to measure their effect on ground structures as well as aircraft. (DoD)

between aircraft and ground command systems. These also carried a three-man crew but served only until replaced by types such as the EC-135 in the mid-1960s.

As the EB-47E neared retirement with the rest of the B-47 fleet, the Navy took over two aircraft (52-0410 and 52-0412) and had Douglas modify them in a programme started in mid-1968 for its Fleet Electronic Warfare Support Group (FEWSG). They received additional equipment for passive and active electronic tasks and their external wing tanks were replaced by ECM pods and additional chaff dispensers.

These aircraft were designated SMS-2 and SMS-3 and were incorporated within the Navy's Surface Missile System, where it was planned they would be used into the late 1970s to operate both as research and as technology demonstrators for electronic countermeasures throughout the Navy. The last flight of an operational B-47 took place on 20 December 1977 when 52-0410 was flown to Pease AFB.

Three EB-47Es were adapted for a highly specialised role involving the collection of radio and telemetry signals from Soviet missile tests and satellite launches under the Tell Two programme. This was precursor to the RC-135S Rivet Ball and Cobra Ball programmes and featured a special capsule in the bomb bay loaded with appropriate equipment and two electronic warfare officers known as 'Crows'.

Each of the aircraft was distinguishable by the proliferation of unusual antenna and protrusions from the underside of the fuselage and all three were operated from NATO bases in Turkey. They were retired in 1967, their job taken over by other aircraft and ELINT satellites.

As with the B-47B, the E-series had the ETB-47E training version with some converted to carry a fourth, instructor, crew member. Stripped and remotely piloted QB-47E drones were used for missile target tests but due to the cost of their adaptation ($1.9m each for the 14 aircraft) they were not destroyed, the missiles programmed to make a near pass instead. One aircraft was modified as a flying test bed for the MA-2 radar bombing and navigation system under the designation YB-47J.

Some 34 were converted for weather reconnaissance, designated WB-47E, carrying air-sampling equipment and data-recorders in place of nuclear weapons. Nose-mounted cameras were installed for recording cloud formations. The conversions began in 1956 and followed the initial trial modification of a B-47B into a WB-47B by General Precision Laboratories.

The first WB-47E was delivered on 20 March 1963 and began to replace existing WC-130 and WC-135 aircraft in 1965. The last flight of a WB-47E took place in October 1969, the month the bomber and reconnaissance versions disappeared from the inventory.

Boeing B-47 Stratojet

Aircraft of different types were employed to measure and record the atmospheric effects of nuclear weapons and the MET (Military Effects Tower) test on 15 April was far below anticipated yield due to the scientists incorporating U-233 in the core without premature announcement. (DoD)

The gathering of intelligence information by clandestine overflight of Soviet airspace was driven by concerns over missile development, such as those which evolved from these R2 and R5 sounding rockets. (USAF)

A VITAL RECONNAISSANCE ROLE

As with so many aircraft of this period, the only B-47s to get anywhere close to combat or engagement were the 240 Boeing-Wichita RB-47Es completed as strategic reconnaissance aircraft, the first 52 based on Model 450-126-29, the rest on Model 450-158-36. These aircraft differed from the B-47E bomber in several important respects. The nose section was lengthened by 34in and contained an air-conditioned compartment housing up to 11 cameras and other equipment such as an optical viewfinder, photo-cell shutters actuated by flash lights for night photography and intervalometers for large-area photography at fixed intervals.

The RB-47E lacked the fittings to carry and release bombs but did retain the 20mm tail cannon and A-5 fire control system. The bombardier was replaced by a photographer/navigator and an additional 18,400 US gallons of fuel to increase its range. It could also be refuelled in flight, which was on occasion the only way it could complete its mission. Optional camera loads could include an O-15 radar camera and a forward oblique camera, both for low-altitude work, a K-17 trimetrogon (tri-axis) camera for panoramic shots and K-36 telescopic cameras.

The first flight of the first production aircraft (51-5258) took place on 3 July 1953 and the Air Force took delivery of the last one in August 1955, in all receiving 255 aircraft. Just two years later, on 14 October 1957, the Air Force started phasing it out.

An order for 15 dual-role weather and reconnaissance aircraft with side-looking radar, designated RB-47K, was placed on 5 November 1954. These aircraft also had air-sampling sensors which sniffed out radioactive fallout from above-ground nuclear tests and served for several years in that capacity. Initial deliveries were to the 55th SRW and the type became operational in mid-1956.

The RB-47E was also used as the basis for an electronic reconnaissance and countermeasures platform designated RB-47H. These would feature a separate pressurised compartment in the area formerly occupied by the bomb bay which housed their electronic equipment as well as three operators – bringing the aircraft's total crew complement to six. The new compartment was to be permanently installed, rather than being a 'pod' as seen on the EB-47E.

Original plans envisaged 30 aircraft but in 1955 that was increased to 35, including three ERB-47Hs for some specialised tasks. The aircraft had a blunt, rounded nose and showed blisters and several pods for equipment and antennas. Three crewmembers were in the RB-47H but only two in the ERB-47H. Defensive tail cannon were retained and the ERB aircraft had a distinctive antenna under the rounded nose.

The first RB-47H arrived with the 55th SRW on 9 August 1955 and almost all had been delivered by the end of the following year. But along with its existing work, the 55th had to induct both aircraft and crew – which required specialised training and integration using specialised staffers working the advanced electronics.

Problems included noise within the pressurised compartment, leaking fuel and trouble with engines on the early aircraft. Most debilitating was the absence of an automatic electronic direction finder. Two different systems became available in December 1956 and Douglas fitted them to two different RB-47Hs, which were then delivered to the 55th. Yet more direction finders were received in March 1957 and all RB-47Hs were eventually fitted with one by Douglas – though not necessarily the same model.

Technology was advancing at a rapid pace during this period and the development of more sophisticated equipment soon necessitated a

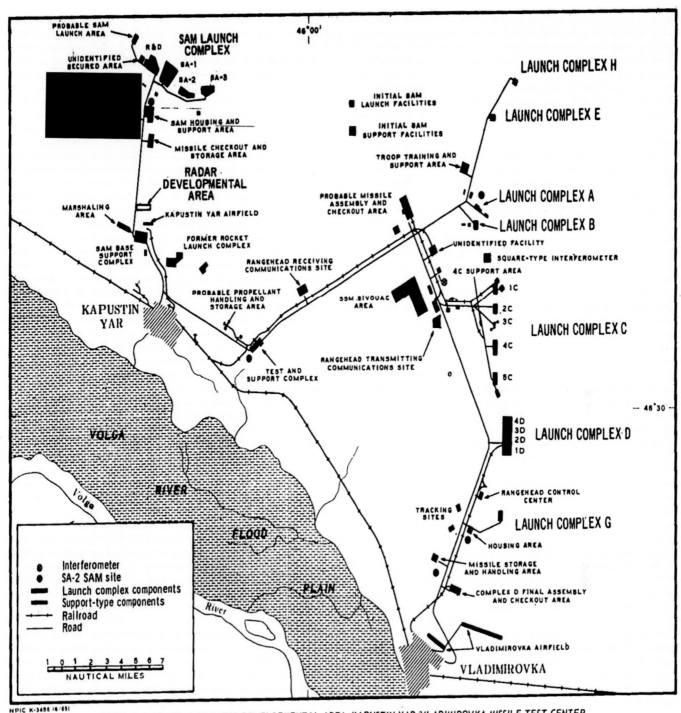

PROBABLE SAM LAUNCH AREA

SAM LAUNCH COMPLEX

R&D

UNIDENTIFIED SECURED AREA

SA-1

SA-2 SA-3

SAM HOUSING AND SUPPORT AREA

MISSILE CHECKOUT AND STORAGE AREA

RADAR DEVELOPMENTAL AREA

MARSHALING AREA

KAPUSTIN YAR AIRFIELD

SAM BASE SUPPORT COMPLEX

FORMER ROCKET LAUNCH COMPLEX

KAPUSTIN YAR

RANGEHEAD RECEIVING COMMUNICATIONS SITE

PROBABLE PROPELLANT HANDLING AND STORAGE AREA

TEST AND SUPPORT COMPLEX

VOLGA

RIVER

FLOOD

PLAIN

River

Volga

46°00'

INITIAL SAM LAUNCH FACILITIES

INITIAL SAM SUPPORT FACILITIES

TROOP TRAINING AND SUPPORT AREA

PROBABLE MISSILE ASSEMBLY AND CHECKOUT AREA

SSM BIVOUAC AREA

RANGEHEAD TRANSMITTING COMMUNICATIONS SITE

LAUNCH COMPLEX H

LAUNCH COMPLEX E

LAUNCH COMPLEX A

LAUNCH COMPLEX B

UNIDENTIFIED FACILITY

SQUARE-TYPE INTERFEROMETER

4C SUPPORT AREA

1C

2C

3C

4C

5C

LAUNCH COMPLEX C

46°30'

4D
3D
2D
1D

LAUNCH COMPLEX D

RANGEHEAD CONTROL CENTER

TRACKING SITES

LAUNCH COMPLEX G

HOUSING AREA

MISSILE STORAGE AND HANDLING AREA

COMPLEX D FINAL ASSEMBLY AND CHECKOUT AREA

VLADIMIROVKA AIRFIELD

VLADIMIROVKA

Interferometer
SA-2 SAM site
Launch complex components
Support-type components
Railroad
Road

1 0 1 2 3 4 5 6 7
NAUTICAL MILES

NPIC K-3456 (6/65)

FIGURE 1. LOCATION OF RADAR DEVELOPMENTAL AREA, KAPUSTIN YAR/VLADIMIROVKA MISSILE TEST CENTER.

Activity at Russia's Kapustin Yar rocket and missile development site became the area of principle concern during the 1950s and beyond, with EB-47Es from Incirlik AB, Turkey, orbiting the border with Russia to monitor telemetry from test shots. (CIA)

redesign of the RB-47H's pressurised compartment. A mock-up of this was inspected in September 1959 and the first aircraft fitted with the real thing, which now included six different radar systems in addition to other electronic systems, flew in August 1960. Boeing had made the prototype but Douglas again did the retrofitting in series. The 55th began receiving these in November 1961.

Another RB-47E modification was the ERB-47H, which was fitted with electronic 'ferret' equipment for detecting, locating, recording and analysing electromagnetic radiation. Three were modified as such by

Boeing before the end of 1957.

A lot of the ERB-47H's capability was exported to the satellite community where ferrets became common piggy-back payloads launched by the Air Force on other specialised and highly classified military payloads. It was during this period that the Air Force began integrating air-derived and space-based assets to form a holistic picture and to direct aircraft to targets acquired by satellite. The operational role of the RB-47E/ERB-47H types was limited by the decision to retire the entire fleet and the last RB-47H was flown to Davis-Monthan

AFB for storage on 29 December 1967. But this aircraft (53-4296) had one other task to perform – to test avionics equipment for the FB-111 and for that it was given the Aardvark's nose for tests well into the 1970s.

BUILDING THE STRATOJET

The basic Model 450 went through several iterative design changes as reviewed earlier but the basic layout incorporated two twin-engine nacelles which were set below and forward of the wing at the approximate 40% semi-span point but the single nacelles were moved

Boeing B-47 Stratojet

Characterised by its longer nose containing an air-conditioned section for cameras, the RB-47E emerged in 1953. Later examples carried the Universal Camera Control system developed by the Air Force. (USAF)

Frequently called upon for longer reconnaissance missions, RB-47Hs would be topped up by KC-135s. (USAF)

back inboard from an original location at the wing tips. Careful examination of the wing's aeroelastic properties relocated those 10ft inboard of the tips. The B-47 was a pioneering influence in the engineering of the wing structure which would greatly influence the design of the wing for the B-52.

With a span of 116ft, it had to be built with great strength. It was capable of flexing 17ft before breaking and was also flexible chord wise. The nominal upward deflection was 45in with a downward deflection of 16in but on the ramp the tips would droop by up to 5ft. At speeds above 489mph the ailerons acted as tabs and above 525mph they were totally ineffective, rigidly locking the control wheel. It incorporated two huge spars at 17% and 58% of the chord, the rear heavier than the other, connected by conventional ribs and stringers. Wing loadings on the rear spar would reach 154lb per square foot.

The wing had skin panels of varying thickness on both top and bottom of the primary torsion box. These panels were each separately machined for particular locations, 0.625in thick at the wing root and tapering to 0.187in at the tip. The stressed skin was fabricated from the new 75 ST aluminium which called for a double heat treatment in manufacture and variations had to be no more than 0.005in.

Despite being spectacularly heavy, compared to other designs, the Boeing-145 laminar section delivered a cruising lift coefficient of 0.35-0.45. The wing sweep was fixed at 36.5-degrees at the quarter-chord line rather than the optimum 37.5-degrees theoretically calculated as the best for performance but not its properties. Having a total surface area of 1,426sq ft, it possessed an exceptionally high wing loading, more than 113lb per square foot at maximum loaded take-off weight of 162,000lb, while production aircraft would eventually have a loading of 140lb per square foot when the gross takeoff weight reached 200,000lb. Selected for high-speed operation, the wing had a 12% thickness ratio and a 9.4 aspect ratio.

Designed for high-speed, high-altitude performance, the wing was incredibly efficient and the aircraft could out-manoeuvre most fighters of the day above 20,000ft but it brought difficulties at slow speeds and during landing. Large Fowler flaps were fitted to the trailing edge, affording a 25% increase in lift while adding only 5% to the wing area. These were operated by a hydraulic motor in the carry-through box driving torque-tubes operating screw jacks on each flap section.

The angle was determined by the curved steel tracks on the rear face of the torsion box. The inboard section operated like a conventional flap while the smaller outboard section worked as a flaperon for additional roll control at low speeds. There were no leading edge lift devices and all the primary controls

Reconnaissance EB-47Es carried a crew of five, raised to six for the 35 RB-47Hs, one of which (53-4299) is seen here at the USAF Museum. (USAF)

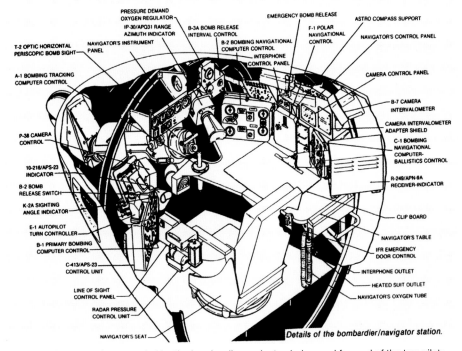

Details of the bombardier/navigator station.

The forward crew station occupied by the bombardier-navigator, below and forward of the two pilots seated in tandem. (Boeing)

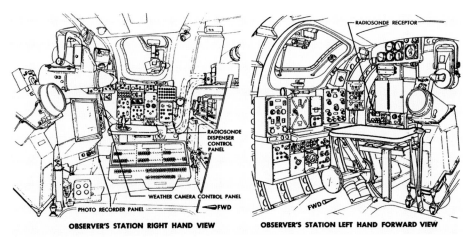

OBSERVER'S STATION RIGHT HAND VIEW OBSERVER'S STATION LEFT HAND FORWARD VIEW

The interior compartment of the EB-47L, a converted B-47E, was fitted with communications equipment for airborne relay and operations as early command-post aircraft. (Boeing)

were hydraulically boosted at 3,000lb per square inch, incorporating artificial feel through torsion-springs on the split-section ailerons with additional springs on the elevator and rudder. Twin rows of vortex generators were located close to the wing leading edge and forward of the tab-controlled inboard ailerons.

The semi-monocoque fuselage was oval in cross-section and covered with the same 75 ST aluminium as used on the wing skins. The electrically-heated windscreen was bulletproof with a wiper on the front face beyond which was a 'yaw string', the simplest of all pilot aids placed there to help the pilot coordinate the rudder during a turn.

Up to the mid-production of the B-47E, the canopy slid rearward by 14in but the later models had a clamshell canopy which opened up by the same amount for ventilation. Protection for crews dropping nuclear weapons was provided by flash curtains with a small hole for the sextant periscope used for celestial navigation. Only from the 400th B-47B did the aircraft get ejection seats but the previous 264 aircraft were retrofitted with them. The co-pilot's seat could rotate to allow him to operate the tail gun via panels behind. If required, the ejection seats – made either by Republic or Webber – for the two pilots fired upward while that for the navigator fired downward with a minimum safe ejection altitude of 500ft.

The forward crew compartment was pressurised, taking bleed air from the final engine compressor stage and partly cooled by a refrigerator unit but, as mentioned earlier, aircraft configured for ECM work had an air conditioned compartment in the bomb bay, with web seats for two to four electronic warfare operators. Conditions for these 'crows' were cramped and claustrophobic, with some reconnaissance or ECM missions lasting more than 10 hours.

The arrangement of the forward compartment changed gradually, and significantly, over time, especially as special requirement for access evolved and additional, or replacement, systems were installed. The early decision to build the aircraft cockpit around the requirements of a three-man crew left little flexibility for design engineers and the position of the navigator, accessed via a narrow aisle to the left of the two pilots, added to the discomfort.

The wing dominated the internal layout and the three main fuel tanks, forward, aft and centre, were positioned atop the bomb bay and between the two landing gear bays. With forward and aft auxiliary tanks. From 12in aft of the cockpit canopy to the leading edge of the vertical fin, the upper part of the fuselage was occupied with these self-sealing fuel bags along a distance of more than 73ft. Capacity would vary between 14,600 US gallons and 17,000 US gallons depending on aircraft variant.

Flight testing of two XB-47Ds, converted B-47Bs with the outboard J47s supplemented by single Curtiss-Wright YT-49 turboprops inboard, took place in August 1955. The programme was never developed. (Boeing)

The XB-47D was equipped with four-blade 15ft (4.5m) diameter propellers to measure the impact a turboprop/turbojet mix on a swept wing would have, interest stimulated by the Tupolev Tu-95. (Boeing)

Two standard B-47Es were converted to YDB-47E configuration for testing the GAM-63 Rascal stand-off missile and then employed as drone controllers when Rascal was cancelled. (USAF)

Under normal operating conditions, the forward fuel tank fed engines one and six, the centre tank engines two and five and the aft tank engines three and four. Internal capacity could be supplemented by the addition of 1,500 US gallon jettisonable tanks between the two engine pylon positions.

The weapons bay was located beneath the wing carry-through structure, a location that ensured minimal influence on stability under different bomb loads. Nevertheless, the bay for the prototype and the B-47A occupied all the space between the two landing wheel trucks. This was a requirement driven by the general recommendation to allow a weapon of up to 20ft in length to be carried so that the unspecified dimensions of an atomic bomb could be accepted. In this period there was no direct information on the dimensions of atomic devices but by the time the production B-47B and B-47E variants entered service, a 20MT thermonuclear bomb was no bigger than

a conventional 2,000lb device,

As said, the arrangement of the high-mounted wing brought an additional advantage by allowing the engines to 'hang' in a position highly accessible for attention and servicing, disengaging them from access to other structural elements such as the wing and the fuselage. With the decision to design a spectacularly thin wing for the period, it nevertheless provided problems for the location of the landing gear.

The entire weight of the aircraft on the ground was supported by tandem wheel-trucks, each carrying a single shock strut retracting forward on an electrical, motor-driven ball bearing system. Lateral balance was provided by small, single-wheel outriggers mounted between the inner, paired engines and retracting into the nacelle enclosure. Boeing did examine the possibility of adopting the castoring assemblies for the main landing gear trucks applied to later B-52s to counter crosswinds but this was never pursued.

The aircraft was given progressively more powerful engines, beginning with the J35-7, previously known as the TG-180, for the XB-47, the J-47-11 for the B-47A, the J47-23 for the B-47B and the J47-25 or -25A for the B-47B and B-47E. Nominal continuous rated thrust increased from 3,420lb for the J-35 to 5,320lb for the J-47-25. But throughout its service life, the aircraft was underpowered and was never cited for its sparkling leap into the air. Accordingly, augmented thrust in the form of a RATO system was designed in from the outset and was essential kit, especially for an overweight reconnaissance mission with additional fuel load or a maximum bomb capacity.

Located in the aft fuselage, the integrally-mounted RATO system had nine exhaust ports on each side delivering a total thrust of 18,000lb for 14 seconds, adding 43% thrust to the 41,820lb delivered by the J-47-25 on maximum rated takeoff thrust. The spent rockets were dead weight and the orifices caused flow breakaway on the fuselage and drag so later models had this system removed and replaced with a jettisonable horse collar arrangement which could carry between 19 and 33 rockets depending on requirements. The space vacated by removal of the internally-mounted RATO rockets was filled with ECM gear and chaff dispensers.

The vertical and horizontal tail surfaces had a 35-degree sweepback and were of stressed skin construction with a thinner cross-section than the wing so that the critical Mach number was always above the diving speed of the aircraft. The fin spar was situated at 47% chord with the ribs at 9in to the spar. The fixed horizontal tail was mounted low but above the jet wake and wing turbulence, with the single spar at 50% chord and

One of three RB-47Hs (53-4288) converted to EB-47H standard with electronic 'ferret' equipment for detecting and measuring electromagnetic radiation. (USAF)

The two US Navy EB-47Es seen here at Naval Air Station Point Mugu, California, were part of the Surface Missile System (SMS) programme, spending almost 10 years advancing the fleet's electronic countermeasures. (USN)

Airshow fodder – a B-47B's sleek lines and unmistakeable profile photographed at one of numerous public events in the US and overseas during the 1950s and 60s. (USAF)

ribs spaced at 8in. Rudder and elevators were attached to the aft sections of the fin and horizontal stabiliser. The tip of the fin was a removable, fibreglass cover for the AN/ARN-14 VOR and AN/APN-69 rendezvous radar antennas. The fin itself was the aft termination point for the AN/ARC-65 communications radio wire antenna.

COMBAT OPERATIONS

Spy flights over the Soviet Union had been going on since 1946 and within 10 years of that date more than 200 overflights had been approved at the highest level. Those that became public knowledge were the scant few examples that attracted publicity; the vast majority were covered up by opposing sides and for good reason.

Of all US overflights and penetrating spy missions, more than 30 were shot down, including two B-47s on such operations.

Neither side wanted to have this 'phantom' war open up a public hysteria. But only after the collapse of the Soviet Union did Boris Yeltsin and US President Bill Clinton meet to agree a pledge that neither side would probe further into

Precursor to the WB-47E, the only WB-47B (51-2155) was operated by the 55th Weather Reconnaissance Squadron, Military Air Transport Service, logging 126.5hrs before retirement in 1963. (USAF)

the whereabouts of those airmen who never returned, closing the book for all time on incidents kept secret. Some US airmen shot down had been killed by their captors, many had been sent to remote regions and assimilated into communities, their conscious awareness of a different past erased by mental torture. Today, their families continue to lobby politicians in the hope their fate may be made known.

Those events and many adventures have been told several times in numerous places and need not be repeated here. Suffice to say that the RB-47s played a vital role in transitioning the Air Force from Second World War fighter or bomber types adapted for reconnaissance to dedicated reconnaissance aircraft such as the Lockheed U-2 and the SR-71. As noted earlier, the very existence of the B-47 as a reconnaissance platform stimulated technology and encouraged industry and government laboratories to develop previously unimagined equipment. More than 80% of overflights carried out by the US involved the B-47.

From its inception, the high-speed, high-altitude role of the B-47 as a medium bomber filled the need for overseas deployment stimulated by tensions between Western powers and the USSR in 1948, when a Soviet coup tightened the communist grip on Czechoslovakia and began to close access routes to Berlin. In response, the first of two squadrons of B-29s of the 306th BW had arrived in the UK on 18 July and the US presence was back – this time to stay.

Being the same type of aircraft as those which had dropped atomic bombs on Japan, the inference was that the Americans were not messing around and would threaten the USSR with similar treatment if pressed hard enough. Soviet intelligence was well aware that none of

these aircraft were capable of carrying atomic bombs but the message was good enough.

The B-47 was ready for overseas deployment from 1953. Some specially modified B-45s had been in the UK in 1952 but on 4, 5 and 6 June the 306th landed at RAF Fairford on their way to RAF Mildenhall, accompanied by KC-97s with support personnel and equipment. They were there to replace the B-29s on 90-day rotation since 1948. This was a seminal moment and had been engaged with some trepidation by the Americans, until reassured from British Foreign Secretary Ernest Bevin that the British public would welcome them back and that they would support the move – which, for the majority, was the case. So began the first routine deployment overseas of a jet bomber Wing and the 305th BW took over after 90 days. The B-47 would continue to support that role until 1958.

The operational phasing out of the B-47 began on 14 October 1957 when an RB-47E (51-5272) was sent by the 91st SRW, Lockbourne AFB, Ohio, to Davis-Monthan AFB, Arizona. Rotational training with the B-47 was discontinued in the UK, the last being the 100th BW, completed at RAF Brize Norton. The last B-36 was retired on 12 February 1959 and SAC became an all-jet bomber force. As airborne alerts became standard practice at SAC, the need for low-level training to accommodate the new role for the B-47 prompted the establishment in November of that year of seven special air routes across the US, each 20 miles wide and up to 500 miles long for practicing these flight patterns. In further dispersal options, on 9 June 1960 SAC tested the ability of the B-47 to operate out of civilian airfields in times of crisis, greatly expanding the survivability of the bomber in wartime.

The Cuban Missile Crisis of October 1962 became the first opportunity for this civilian dispersal programme to be deployed, as B-47s were dispersed across the US, the arrival of a six-jet SAC bomber raising a few eyebrows across the mid-West. Fearing surprise attack from submarine-launched missiles, SAC was at full alert, fully armed and with a high level of readiness. As a sea-search got under way for Soviet ships bringing missiles to Cuba, the RB-47s and KC-97s patrolled vast areas of the Atlantic Ocean. On 27 October an RB-47 of the 55th SRW crashed on take-off at Kindley AFB, Bermuda, killing all four crewmembers. After the tension dissipated and the Russians withdrew, accepting a secret protocol for the Americans to withdraw Jupiter missiles from Europe, on 7 December President Kennedy visited SAC headquarters to thank the Command for their outstanding response to the crisis.

With the drawdown of medium bomber forces and the gradual reduction in B-47s, during 1963 foreign bases were realigned and operations ceased at locations across the world. Fewer overseas support bases were required and the diminishing KC-97 inventory, replaced by the KC-135, removed the last vestiges of Second World War-era aircraft from the cargo-tanker role. By the end of 1964 only four overseas bases supported the B-47: Moron and Torrejon in Spain (they would go the following year) and Brize Norton and Upper Heyford in England; one remained at Elmendorf AFB, Alaska. In a prescient sign of the times, on 21 April 1964 the number of Atlas, Titan and Minuteman ICBMs on alert equalled the manned strategic bomber force. By the end of February 1966, the last B-47 had gone.

BOEING B-52

First Flight: 15 April 1952

The origin of what would become the longest serving bomber of all time can be traced back to the heavy losses suffered by US B-17 bombers during raids on Regensburg and Schweinfurt in late 1943. It told the AAF that no manner of fighter escort nor self-defence armament would be sufficient to protect those aircraft. The only viable options for survival – particularly against the newly emerged threat of the jet fighter – were speed and altitude.

Neither the B-35 nor the B-36 were fast enough and both had shortcomings that limited their potential. In August 1944 the AAF issued a demanding set of requirements for a long range heavy bomber greatly exceeding the capabilities of any existing aircraft. It brought little interest and no response from industry. In June 1945, with the war in Europe over and victory over Imperial

Japan inevitable, the AAF directed AMC to put together a formal specification calling for a new post-war bomber to 'be capable of carrying out the strategic mission without dependence upon advanced and intermediate bases controlled by other countries'.

Mindful of the difficulty encountered when trying to reach Japan with strategic bombers, this reflected growing concern that international tensions, particularly with the Soviet Union, would call for particular measures to counter future threats.

The first statement of characteristics was issued on 23 November 1945 and called for an operating radius of 5,000 miles – roughly equivalent to a 12,000 mile range – a speed of 300mph at 34,000ft, a crew of five, an unspecified number of 20mm defensive cannon, a six-man relief crew and carrying a 10,000lb bomb load. A design directive

was issued on 13 February 1946 and this time three companies – Boeing, Martin and Convair – offered initial design concepts and cost quotes. The concepts proposed by Martin and Convair were not developed, each manufacturer already heavily involved in existing aircraft and lacking either production capacity or experience.

Boeing had been working on several early design studies, notably Models 444A and 461, but the AAF had indicated that it wanted a gas turbine engine, with which the Model 462 was proposed in April 1946. It was a conventional design and looked a lot like a B-29 but with six Westinghouse 827 GTA-1 (T35) turboprop engines.

With a gross weight of 360,000lb, the aircraft had a classic Second World War look with four fuselage gun turrets and a tail turret. It could carry a 50,000lb bomb load but its radius of 3,570 miles

A B-52H arrives at Andersen AFB, Guam, supporting a Bomber Task Force deployment from Barksdale AFB, Louisiana, on 26 January 2020. (USAF)

fell short of the required operating radius due to the heavy engines and armament. Nevertheless, Boeing was announced the winner on 5 June 1946 but financial restrictions limited the formal contract on 28 June to only Phase I development, covering a full mock-up of an XB-52, design engineering and test rigs for engines, guns and structures.

And in October 1946 Major General Earle E. Partridge, Assistant Chief of Air Staff for Operations, criticised the concept for its 'monstrous size' and raised such concern that two months later Boeing modified the design into Model 464-17. This had four much improved T-35-5 turboprop engines, a maximum bomb load of 90,000lb and a mission radius of 3,752 miles. Slimmed further still, Model 464-18 had only two turboprop engines but drop-tanks ensured its range was not much less than for the 464-17.

While accepting that Model 464 had merit, the AAF began to focus on speed and in December asked Boeing for a proposal with a design range of 12,000 miles, powered by four engines and capable of carrying an atomic weapon. Boeing had already proposed a Model 464-16 which would carry only a 10,000lb bomb load and the Air Force felt that it could not fund the two, selecting the Model 464-17 instead.

This too failed to last.

The Air Force began to question its own general specification of November 1945 and looked again at requirements. And then there was uncertainty about the T-35 turboprop engines and, in a further deliberation, about the speed required. The air chiefs looked at the design and believed it to be too big and potentially too expensive so that at most 100 could be bought and operated. They deemed the XB-52 would be little improvement over the B-36 and that it would be obsolete before it entered service.

General LeMay urged caution and did not endorse scrapping the project but the Air Force decided to shelve the 464-17, which spurred Boeing to propose three more versions with suffix numbers 23, 25 and 27, finally settling on Model 464-29 in March 1947 which got the approval of the AAF. With a cruising speed of 455mph, a range of 9,000 miles and a maximum weight of 400,000lb, it was favoured by the Air Staff.

Independence for the Air Force during the second half of 1947 prompted a rethink on several strategic decisions and a reassessment of the long-range, heavy-bomber requirement. In September the Aircraft & Weapons Board (AWB) set up the Heavy Bombardment Committee which would determine the optimum way to deliver "mass atomic attacks against any potential aggressor nation from bases within the continental United States".

Everything was on the table – from nuclear war delivered by pilotless

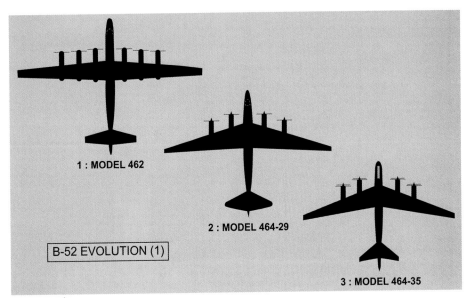

1 : MODEL 462

2 : MODEL 464-29

B-52 EVOLUTION (1)

3 : MODEL 464-35

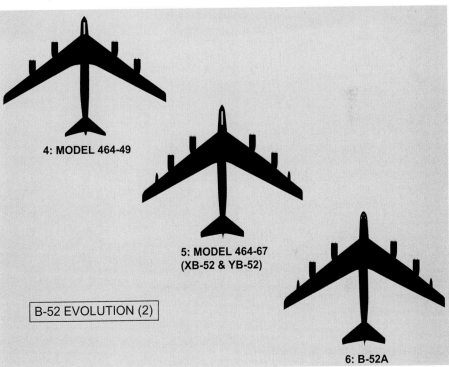

4: MODEL 464-49

5: MODEL 464-67
(XB-52 & YB-52)

B-52 EVOLUTION (2)

6: B-52A

The Wright T-35 turboprop-powered Model 462 was submitted to the requirement for a B-29 replacement in early 1946. This was followed by designs from the 464 series – 464-29 of March 1947 and the more refined 464-35 later that year. Model 464-49 of late 1948 began the configuration change which resulted in Model 464-67 – approved in March 1950 as the XB-52. (via David Baker)

Boeing XB-52 with a Convair B-36B (49-2088) behind. (USAF)

The XB-52 (49-230) with its distinctive forward fuselage and crew compartment, in front of which is the experimental Northrop X-4. (USAF)

The only other tandem seat variant in the series, the YB-52 (49-231) displays the sleek profile of the massive bomber. (USAF)

The YB-52 with an unusual placement of the 'stars and bars' between the inner and outer engine pairs. (USAF)

cruise missiles to one-way manned bombers. Air-to-air refuelling came into the picture as a way of getting around the range problem and the committee established an 8,000 mile minimum range requirement with a cruising speed of 550mph. At a stroke, this eliminated the Boeing Model 464-29. But these minimum requirements were modified by the AMC on 8 December when it reduced the cruise speed to 500mph, that being the price for achieving the desired range.

Boeing's efforts stood on the cusp of cancellation in favour of a completely new competition with a fresh set of proposals from an industry-wide contest. The Air Staff were in favour of that but the AMC stood by Boeing as the best qualified to do the job. Nevertheless, fearing an accusation of favouritism, and on the basis that if Boeing really was the best it would still win out, the XB-52 contract was cancelled on 11 December.

Boeing protested vigorously and its objections were partially upheld. Air Force Secretary Stuart Symington decided that the contract would stand pending further analysis of competing technologies such as the B-35, which had already made its first flight.

AMC endorsed continued development of a suitable B-52 programme and eventually the flying wing was disregarded, being considered too problematic to continue. In March 1948 Boeing was informed that its present contract would be modified to meet the December 1947 requirements. The following month Model 464-35 was accepted for a Phase II contract.

This iteration had the desired speed and range but weighed less, at a maximum 300,000lb and a further revision was made before the final turboprop version on 15 December. But that was eclipsed by the emerging consensus that turbojets had reached a development level where they were now preferable to the turboprop, promising faster speeds and greater range. There was, in addition, the inevitable cost effectiveness of increasing the number of combat aircraft using turbojets, increasing production and lowering the price per engine.

Boeing executives met with the AMC at Wright Field on 21 October 1948 to confer on the 464-35 and learned that it was now seeking a more advanced bomber based on the Pratt & Whitney J57 turbojet engine. Seven days later Boeing delivered a 33-page report on a turbojet bomber, Model 464-40 and revealed a hand-carved model. Model 464-49 had swept wings and eight J57s slung in pairs on four underwing pylons in an overall configuration much like the B-47. It was a design layout which did not evolve from that medium bomber but rather as the result of a year or more in which Boeing had independently researched a turbojet-powered heavy bomber.

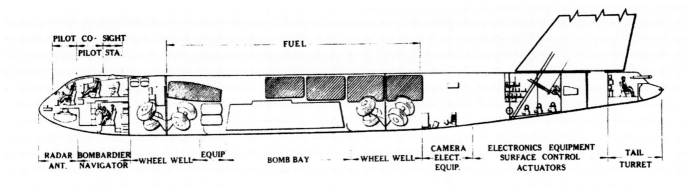

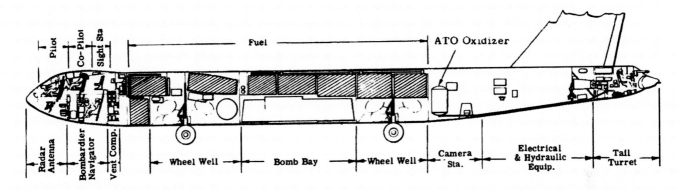

Several changes were made to the XB-52 between the preliminary and the critical design reviews, notably the additional fuel tank added to the XB-52 as built and flown. (Boeing)

The Board of Senior Officers liked it and endorsed its projected performance, indicating a top speed of 572mph and a range of 8,000 miles, delivering a 10,000lb bomb load from 45,000ft.

Boeing received word on 26 January 1949 that this was the favoured configuration but this was only a few weeks after it became apparent that President Truman would deliver an austere defence budget for the financial year beginning 1 July. The US economy had slipped dangerously toward 'bust' (albeit temporarily) after the 'boom' of the war years. Boeing's white knight appeared the following month in the form of the AMC, which pointed to Model 464-49's outstanding characteristics.

A Model 464-49 mock-up was examined by the Air Force inspection board at the Boeing facility over the course of four days, 26-29 April 1949, and it was noted that the necessary J57 engines – replacing interim J40-6 units for the XB-52 – would not be available before 1954. The only caveat was insufficient range, driven largely by the smaller airframe size favoured by the Air Force. Responding to this in November 1949, Boeing produced Model 464-67, a heavier aircraft with more fuel capacity. With a maximum weight of 390,000lb, it would have a combat radius of 4,356 miles with the potential to achieve 4,816 miles by 1957.

This version greatly impressed the Air Force and at a conference on 26 January LeMay threw his weight behind it. Despite unsolicited proposals from

Fairchild, Convair and a concept from the RAND Corporation, formed in 1948 from Douglas Aircraft as a research and analysis think-tank for the Air Force, on 24 March 1950 Model 464-67 was approved by the Air Board and would lead directly to a production decision.

In a classic example of concurrency again being preferred over the construction of multiple prototypes to iron out discrepancies before production, on 9 January 1951 Gen. Vandenberg approved the Board's decision. A

production contract was issued to Boeing on 14 February which covered long-lead items on 13 B-52A aircraft planned for delivery from April 1953. An amendment added 17 detachable reconnaissance pods and in July 1951 four more B-52As were added. A further letter contract in September ordered 43 RB-52s but all that changed due to the repercussions of the Korean War which modified requirements.

Meanwhile, development of the two prototypes continued as a debate arose over the tandem seating of the

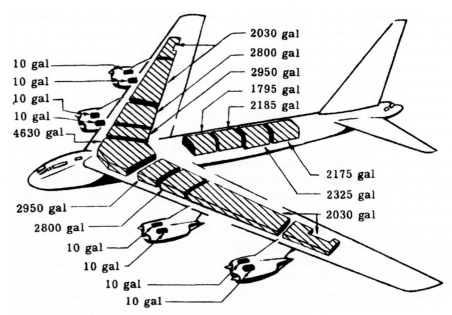

The fuel tank distribution of the unmodified XB-52 showing quantities in US gallons, the four tanks in the upper central fuselage would be replaced by five on the XB-52 as built. (Boeing)

The first of three production B-52As (52-001) which made its first flight on 5 August 1954. This configuration would remain largely unchanged throughout the next several decades, apart from the reduced height of the tail, introduced with the B-52G. (USAF)

The robust and skew-angle B-52 articulated landing gear allows for side winds, as seen here with an aircraft deploying its brake 'chute. (USAF)

A clear shot of the track of the two pairs of side-by-side landing gear legs fore and aft of the bomb bay. (USAF)

prototypes. LeMay wanted side-by-side seating to enhance coordination and to elevate the second crewmember from flight engineer to full co-pilot. He got his way. All but the two prototypes would have the now familiar nose section and crew configuration.

Boeing was originally expected to build two XB-52 prototypes but the company proposed the second as a YB-52 production prototype to reduce costs prior to production of the B-52A.

Rolled out under covers to hide its configuration, the XB-52 (49-0230)

emerged after dusk on 29 November 1951 and after some systems and taxi tests it was returned to the factory for the addition of its pneumatic system and to have a modified rear spar incorporated, already built in to the YB-52 (49-231) which would be rolled out on 15 March 1952. It was this second aircraft that made the first flight of the type, exactly one month later, from Boeing's Seattle facility to Larson AFB, Washington, lasting 2hr 51min. The XB-52 made its initial flight on 2 October 1952.

The test programme revealed some issues but in general, certainly for an aircraft of this size and complexity, there were few major problems. In fact, the B-52 is generally regarded as having set a record for the most extensive testing of any type thus far. In addition to the two prototypes, the contractor Phase III tests required six B-52s for both airframe and engine manufacturer testing.

The development of the B-52 had been long and protracted but the corporate effort had been unprecedented. Where the B-29 cost Boeing 153,000 engineering man-hours, the B-52 took three million and the competition was there throughout. Only in August 1952 did the rival YB-60 – the all-jet derivative of the B-36 – disappear and not until the end of that year did a proposed B-47Z get rejected on the grounds that it was too small for some of the multiple nuclear payloads envisaged versus range. It would be mid-1953 before the B-52 programme was finally released from challenges and competitors.

PRODUCTION LINE VARIANTS

Only three B-52As (Model 464-201-0) would be built because the remaining 10 on the initial order were completed to B-52B (Model 464-201-3) configuration. They differed from the prototypes in several respects: the forward compartment was extended by 21in to accommodate additional equipment in the new side-by-side arrangement for pilot and co-pilot. A four-gun 0.50cal tail turret was also added together with ECM equipment, a chaff dispensing system and water-injection J57-P-1 engines. The normal 35,600 US gallon fuel load was supplemented by an auxiliary fuel tank under each wing holding 1,000 US gallons to increase range and by an aerial refuelling receptacle.

Rolled out on 18 March 1954, the first flight of the B-52A (52-001) took place on 5 August 1954 at Edwards AFB, with the third aircraft delivered the following month.

During the first half of 1953 several important decisions were made, including a commitment to build 282 aircraft to equip seven SAC Wings. Deliveries would be made between October 1956 and December 1958. A second production facility was opened in Wichita, Kansas, where most B-52s would eventually be made. Air Force Chief of Staff General

Nathan Twining gave an address to the several thousand Boeing personnel at the Seattle plant, formally inducting the aircraft into SAC on 18 March 1954. He claimed that, "The long rifle was the great weapon of its day… Today this B-52 is the long rifle of the air age."

The last B-52A (52-003) was significantly modified and redesignated NB-52A for NASA in 1959, being adapted to carry the rocket-powered North American X-15 hypersonic research aircraft for flights continuing into 1968.

The B-52B was cleared to a higher gross take-off weight following trials conducted with the B-52A at Edwards, although detailed design had begun as early as February 1951. It had a maximum weight of 420,000lb, more powerful J57-P-19W, -29W or -29WA engines and the addition of a reconnaissance capability for an RB-52B variant.

Through a series of contractual changes and revisions, a total of 50 B-52Bs were produced. The first flew in December 1954 but SAC would not receive its first example (52-8711) before 29 June 1955. A press release of the time pointed out that the B-52 had a wingspan greater than the total distance traversed by Orville Wright during the world's first powered flight.

The aircraft was certainly impressive and quickly became the poster-plane for SAC, despite some ongoing problems and operating challenges: fuel leaks, fuel system icing up, troublesome water injection pumps for the engines, faulty alternators and inadequate bombing and fire control systems. Out of 170 engineering change proposals submitted by AMC, 110 had been eliminated by March 1955 and SAC took delivery of the last B-52B in August 1956.

Originally planned for service as the RX-16, the RB-52B was to be a dual-mission aircraft, its reconnaissance function supported by an Aeronca-built pressurised capsule which could be cable-winched into the bomb bay and locked in position. This capsule, which weighed only 300lb, converted the bomber into a reconnaissance aircraft in less than four hours. Two crewmembers sat inside it to operate a suite of six cameras or ECM gear. The first B-52B with the capsule installed was flown at Seattle on 25 January 1955 and of the total production order of 50 B-52Bs, 27 became RB-52Bs.

Ordered originally along with the first production contract (see earlier), the capsules had downward ejection seats

but these early ones were essentially flight test articles and operational units had an AN/APR-14 radio receiver, and two AN/APR-9 radar receivers, each station having two AN/APA-11A pulse analysers for processing data. The AN/ARR-88 triple panoramic receivers and all the electronic signals were stored on an AN/APQ-1A wire recorder. The camera equipment included four K-38s at the pod multi-camera station and either a T-11 or K-36 at the vertical camera position. The capsule also had three T-11 cartographic cameras for mapping.

A significant milestone occurred on 21 May 1956 (local time) when an ARDC B-52B became the first aircraft to drop a thermonuclear device. It took place at Bikini Atoll in the Pacific Ocean from an altitude of 50,000ft at 1.51am during Operation Redwing. It was intended as a demonstration of US nuclear capability to the USSR and involved a TX-15-X1 carried by a B-52 from Eniwetok Island. Ground zero was directly over Namu Island and was to have provided a wide range of data from instrumentation set out across the area. The bomb was 34.5in wide and 11.3ft long with a total weight of 6,867lb delivering a yield of 3.8MT. The crew mistook the target point

A ground technician closes out pre-flight access panels. The general alignment of the two forward landing gear legs is well displayed together with lights on the starboard bogie. (USAF)

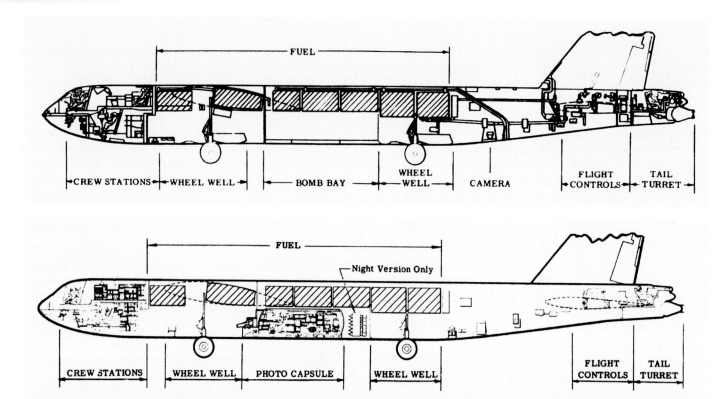

CREW STATIONS — WHEEL WELL — BOMB BAY — WHEEL WELL — CAMERA — FLIGHT CONTROLS — TAIL TURRET

FUEL

Night Version Only

CREW STATIONS — WHEEL WELL — PHOTO CAPSULE — WHEEL WELL — FLIGHT CONTROLS — TAIL TURRET

The general layout of the B-52B (top) and the reconnaissance version of the B-52C, the latter showing the photo-capsule and associated equipment location. (Boeing)

Developed to give the B-52 a stand-off capability, originally designated GAM-77, the AGM-28 Hound Dog missile served with the Air Force between 1960 and 1977. (USAF)

as an observation facility on an adjacent island four miles away, preventing recorders from getting any data.

Nevertheless, this new eight-engine bomber certainly succeeded in sending a message to the Soviet Union about US air power, as well as to US taxpayers that their defence dollars were being wisely invested for national security. In another public relations coup, on 18 January 1957, three B-52Bs of the 93rd BW arrived back at Castle AFB, California, after flying non-stop around the world, covering a distance of 24,325 miles in 45hr 19min. As LeMay expressed it while congratulating the crews and presenting each with the Distinguished Flying Cross, it was a "demonstration of SAC's capabilities to strike any target … on Earth".

One RB-52B (52-008) was supplied to NASA on 8 June 1959 and became the NB-52B. It carried X-15 hypersonic research aircraft on 140 flights from 23 January 1960, the other 59 flights with the X-15 being supported by the NB-52A.

It also carried X-24, HiMAT, lifting-body vehicles, the X-43 and early launches of the Pegasus satellite-launcher rocket. Retired from NASA on 17 December 2004, it is still on display near the north gate of Edwards AFB today.

With a range of technical improvements and a rated maximum take-off weight of 450,000lb, the B-52C (Model 464-201-6) began to take shape in December 1953 but its first flight would not occur until 9 March 1956. Its unrefuelled range was extended by the addition of two 3,000 US gallon auxiliary fuel tanks, bringing fuel capacity to 41,700 US gallons.

A total of 35 B-52Cs were built, the first going to the 42nd BW at Loring AFB, Maine on 16 June 1956 – but this was not combat ready until the end of the year. The 'C' was the first variant to carry the improved A-3 fire control system which had initially been installed on the B-52A and B-52B but which proved so troublesome that it was replaced by the A-5. This turned out to be equally troublesome though, pushing corrective upgrades to the A-3. Its woes persisted and it was eventually replaced by the MD-9 in this and subsequent aircraft.

The B-52C was the first to get the anti-flash white undersurfaces from straight off the production line, a precise operation since an extra 0.005in of paint would add 450lb to the weight of the aircraft. Internally, it was equipped with the ASQ-48(V) bombing navigation system which had the ASB-15 radar under the nose and the APN-108 navigation radar looking directly ahead.

Carried under each wing inboard of the inner engine nacelles, the Mach 2.1 Hound Dog was powered by a single 7,500lb thrust J52 turbojet engine and had a range of up to 780 miles. (USAF)

Equipped with the N5G inertial navigation system, the GAM-28 would take position information from the B-52 with an astrotracker, stable platform and Verdan digital computer to maintain a pre-planned trajectory to the target. (USAF)

A new tail turret carried four 0.5-calibre M3 guns set in a square format within a fixed structure, with a horizontal pivot allowing elevation or depression. This was carried within a main barbette on a vertical axis allowing movement left or right. The gunner's pressurised compartment was located above the four ammunition boxes, which held 600 rounds for each gun.

THE GAP MYTH
Intelligence reports on a new generation of Soviet jet bombers, the Tupolev Tu-16 and the Myasishchyev M-4, together with early reconnaissance imagery from the U-2 spyplane, was interpreted as indicating mass production of Russian aircraft capable of striking North America. National Intelligence Estimate reports persisted in warning the political and military leadership of America about a

surge in Soviet combat aircraft numbers and thus was born the 'Bomber Gap Myth' – which would endure for many years before a more nuanced approach to intelligence gathering finally showed it to be false. The West had been duped by maskirovka, Soviet deception techniques to deliberately lay false trails along which the uninformed could be led.

The result of this was near panic, the Pentagon calling for mass production of both the B-47 and the B-52. SAC authorised a massive programme to convert eight B-36 Wings to B-52s by 30 June 1958, the end of the financial year. The KC-97 was inadequate for the role of aerial tanker now that the SAC force was going all-jet and the Air Force therefore accelerated production of the KC-135, putting together a plan for 20 jet tankers and B-52s to be produced each month.

This stretched production and expanded the delivery plans Boeing had meticulously put in place. Development of new variants was expedited and added another dimension to the rapidly expanding nuclear deterrent, now with ICBMs and SLBMs quickly forming a triad of land, sea and air-based strike systems.

Of the 50 B-52Cs, 35 could be fitted for reconnaissance work, deploying their high-thrust engines to good effect and extending their reach through the added range from the extra fuel this variant could carry. Assembly of all B-52Cs was completed in 1956 and its successor, the B-52D (Model 464-301-7), embodied all the changes and refinements standardised in the B-52C. It was built exclusively as a bomber though, without the option of a reconnaissance capsule.

The B-52D marked the beginning of large-scale production and the 170 built (101 from Seattle; 69 from Wichita) were ordered across four contracts issued between August 1954 and January 1956. All had been accepted by November 1957. The first B-52D (55-049) made its initial flight on 4 June 1956 followed by the first from Seattle (55-068) on 28 September, about the time the type entered service with SAC, initially going to the 42nd BW at Loring AFB in direct replacement for their B-52Cs. Ironically, this represented the low point in combat-ready crews, with only 42 available for almost 100 B-52s in the inventory. By mid-1958 however, SAC declared 402 combat-ready crews for 380 aircraft.

Persistent and irritating (because they were easily solved), problems affected the B-52D as they had earlier variants. Failure of the water injection pumps was found to be caused by their continued operation when the water tanks were empty – so a simple water sensor for a low-level cut off was fitted.

Other problems were not so easily solved. Bases built to support the B-36 and B-47 were severely compromised by the B-52 wings, each with 45 bombers and up to 20 tankers at a single location. Expansion of the bomber force was outstripping infrastructure at SAC bases.

Facilities designed for the B-47 and KC-97 struggled to cope with the demands of the much larger and more complex B-52s and KC-135s – their impact affecting everything from runways, ramps and hangars to the quantities of fuel, oils and lubricants that needed to be accommodated.

Thanks to the emergence of the Soviet ballistic missile threat, dispersal became necessary too and while money was poured into new infrastructure, B-52 wings were broken into three equal units of 15 aircraft apiece, two of which were co-located with other units. In this, each B-52 squadron became a strategic wing, usually accompanied by an air refuelling squadron of 10-15 aircraft.

Boeing B-52

A Strategic Air Command B-52G (57-6491) of the 456th BW. Its Hound Dog missiles are each equipped with a W28 nuclear warhead and the aircraft has the anti-flash white undersurface finish. (USAF)and 1977. (USAF)

The first B-52D (55-049) off the Boeing-Wichita production line in June 1956. A total of 170 B-52Ds were made, production being split between Wichita and Seattle. (Boeing)

Almost a sub-variant of the type, the B-52E (Model 464-259), was produced by Wichita and Seattle. Externally this type, of which 100 were built, was largely indistinguishable from its predecessor. Inside, however, it introduced a better standard of electronics, getting the improved AN/ASQ-38(V) bombing navigation system which replaced the AN/ASQ-48 fitted to the B-52D, and that resulted in a redesigned pressurised compartment.

The AN/ASQ-38(V) was the product of a major development effort by IBM-led specialised teams and incorporated nine of their computers and related displays, including the ASB-4 or 4Aradar, APN-89 Doppler, the Kollsman astro-compass, Kearfott true-heading indicator and the radar strike camera from GE, eventually bringing a greater degree of operability

and reliability as well as accuracy – but not for some time.

Making its first flight on 3 October 1957, the B-52E began trickling into SAC two months later with the last delivered in June 1958.

The second B-52E (56-632) was committed to a series of test programmes for improved landing gear, engines and major subsystems intended for the definitive production variants yet to emerge. As the NB-52E, it sported various appendages at different times, including small swept winglets attached to the side of the nose, a long probe extending forward and a wide range of new and innovative control surfaces, the mechanical and hydraulic linkages replaced by experimental electric and electronic systems. Backed up by a large range of specialised electronic

measuring systems, it was applied to a programme designed to develop an electronic flutter and buffet suppression system to reduce crew stress and fatigue levels.

This aircraft also participated in the LAMS (Load Alleviation and Mode Stabilization) project incorporating sensors to activate control surfaces and reduce fatigue stress on the structure. With canards attached to eliminate 30% of the vertical and 50% of the horizontal vibrations caused by air gusts, the aircraft flew 11.5mph faster than the speed at which it would normally disintegrate due to flutter. This single aircraft made arguably the greatest contribution to the overall programme, and to future aircraft design, of any B-52.

Unlike the B-52D, which went to other operational wings when SAC's bomber fleet was reduced by Defense Secretary McNamara, the B-52E was stored with operational units and non-active squadrons.

Although maintained in a serviceable state, they were flown only periodically and no additional flight or ground crews were assigned to them. Some were permanently retired as early as 1967 as they reached the end of their flying hours but, surprisingly, in mid-1973 there were still 48 of the original 100 in the inventory but no longer part of any operational unit. Of the B-52E, it can only said that it provided a workable development platform for new avionics and contributed towards later variants. Before that, there was a further development which refined some of the more aged elements and systems.

The B-52F (Model 464-260) came about due to the fitment of a new engine – the J57-P-43W. This incorporated a single 40KVA alternator in the left-hand unit of each pair, replacing the air-driven accessory units and alternators located in the fuselage of the B-52E. This did require a large bulge in that left-hand engine for the air-cooled alternators, the ram air intake being located near the front of each pod. By removing troublesome armoured accessory-driven packages from the front truck bays it also removed hot ducting from the wing and that allowed Boeing to install integral wing tanks, something it had wanted to achieve for a long time.

Design of the B-52F began in November 1954 with some modification to the wing structure to allow two additional water tanks, providing the injection system with increased capacity – this being the defining feature of the variant. Built in Seattle, the first of 89 B-52Fs made its initial flight on 6 May 1958. The last of 44 Seattle-made examples was completed in November 1958; the other 45 being assembled in Wichita, where all future engineering would be located. B-52Fs were the first examples of the type to enter the war in Southeast Asia, where Arc Light bombing missions were carried out from 18 June 1965. The first operational B-52 losses were recorded on that day when two aircraft collided on their way to the target.

Just as with the B-52Es, the B-52Fs were retired at the end of their service life and no attempt was made to keep them operational. The 93rd BW kept all of its aircraft but the phaseout began in 1971 when retirees were sent to Davis-Monthan where they were placed in storage. Only very slowly did the B-52F disappear from the inventory.

THE DEFINITIVE STRATOFORTRESS

The single biggest change to the B-52 appeared with the B-52G (Model 464-253), of which 193 were built. The first was delivered on 1 November 1958 and the variant entered service with the 5th BW at Travis AFB, California on 13 February 1959 – the day after the last B-36 retired – and the last was delivered on 7 February 1961.

The B-52G resulted from a Boeing proposal offering a significant improvement in performance, promising up to 30% increase in range, a 25% decrease in maintenance costs, a decrease of 15,000lb in empty weight and a 70% increase in ECM capabilities. The B-52G's contribution provided a comprehensive step-change in the type's evolution and created an aircraft which was totally transformed, giving it a life lasting several decades and leading directly to the B-52H.

Even though the basic design of the B-52 had great development potential, the urgency of the production programme focused all resources on churning out operationally satisfactory aircraft rather than on a 'super B-52'. But concern about the viability of the Convair B-58 (see later) prompted some awareness of the need to make improvements to the B-52 as a hedge against serious delays to the supersonic bomber. Which is why, from a package put together in January 1955, development of the B-52G was not begun until June 1956, when the reality of the B-52's unique capabilities eclipsed plans to halt its development.

There had been a proposal to develop the G-series aircraft with powerful 17,000lb Pratt & Whitney J75 engines but this had been judged a step too far. Nevertheless, the B-52G had a fully 'wet' wing with integral fuel tanks, the much improved engine from the B-52F and still further improvement to the water injection system. The nose radome was enlarged, the size of the vertical fin was reduced, the tail cone was modified and the ailerons removed. Gross weight was increased to 488,000lb.

The B-52G kept the AN/ASQ-38 bombing navigation equipment but had the new AN/ASG-15 fire control system, improved ECM, a powered stability augmentation system and emergency ejection seats for the full crew, including the gunner whose position was moved from the discomfort of the pressurised tail turret to a rear-facing seat next to the electronic countermeasures operator in the forward pressurised compartment. The position of the other crewmembers was unchanged, with the bombardier and the navigator seated behind and below the pilots.

A B-52D (65-091) instrumented to participate in nuclear effects monitoring during atmospheric tests in the Pacific Ocean, one of several employed to take over similar activities conducted by the B-47. (USAF)

A B-52F (57-0162) dropping 750lb bombs during an Arc Light mission over Vietnam. (USAF)

Most aircraft were equipped to carry two Hound Dog stand-off missiles, one on a single pylon under each wing inboard of the inner engine nacelles. The first SAC launch of a Hound Dog missile took place by the 4135th SW on 29 February 1960. Also developed for the B-52G, the Quail decoy was designed to mimic a full-size bomber and was first dropped on test by the same unit on 8 June 1960.

Most produced of all variants, the B-52G became a victim of the 1991 Strategic Arms Reductions Treaty (START) which entered into force in 1994 and limited the number of strategic nuclear delivery systems including manned strategic bombers. Under this agreement, which for the first time reduced the offensive nuclear forces of both the United States and Russia, 375 B-52s were flown to Davis-Monthan AFB, parted out and chopped into pieces by a gigantic guillotine which severed wings, tail and fuselage, the latter into three sections. Left in the open for Russian surveillance satellites to count them, the metal was sold for scrap. Under the treaty, the US could retain 75 heavy bombers (B-52 and B-1B) with non-nuclear capabilities. Almost all B-52Gs were destroyed but

the last operational example (58-0224) was dismantled in December 2013.

Defined and in preliminary design in January 1959, one month before SAC got the B-52G, the B-52H would have a significant improvement in power with the use of the 17,000lb Pratt & Whitney TF33-P-3 engine, the first turbofan fitted to the B-52. Without water injection, it had new engine-driven generators, a new ECM suite and the enhanced SN/ASG-21 fire control system which operated a Gatling gun in the remotely operated tail mounting.

From the outset the B-52H was equipped to carry four Skybolt missile which were never deployed. Procurement proceeded under four separate contracts, the first on 2 February 1960, but the last was delayed due to uncertainty regarding the numbers actually required. It had already been decided that this would be the last B-52 variant.

The first B-52H took to the air (as the YB-52H) on 10 July 1960, requiring 500ft less runway thanks to the additional power. Although the first production B-52H made its first flight on 6 March 1961 and was accepted by the Air Force that month, it remained with Boeing for tests on the aircraft's entire flight

envelope – finding that the new turbofans worked better than predicted.

The first B-52H to enter service (60-001) arrived with the 379th BW, Wurtsmith AFB, Michigan, on 9 May and by the end of the year a further 19 had arrived. Not all initially had all-weather low-flying capability but those that did not had been brought up to standard by September 1962. There were persistent concerns about the TF33 engines and several corrective fixes were required. A major programme called Hot Fan saw most of the problems resolved, though this was temporarily held up by the Cuban Missile Crisis of October 1962. By the end of 1964 all work had been completed.

Production of the B-52H ended on 26 October 1962 when the last of 102 (61-040) arrived at the 4137th SBW at Minot AFB, North Dakota. As with the preceding variant, all B-52Hs had been built in Wichita. But the Air Force was not so convinced that it was the last production aircraft and on 17 October 1962 got Boeing to retain all the tooling until July 1963. The contractors and subcontractors were obliged to do the same. This was a difficult time for SAC and for the entire bomber inventory. The B-70 programme had been terminated and the prospect of a supersonic bomber appeared to evaporate as the cost of operating the B-58 soared out of sight.

No one could have foreseen, in 1963, that the B-52H would still be in front line service 60 years later – but it was already showing its capabilities. On 10-11 January 1962 a B-52H of the 4136th SW at Minot AFB completed a record-breaking, unrefuelled flight of 12,532.28 miles from Kadena AFB, Okinawa, to Torrejon SAFB, Spain, flying literally halfway around the world. It flew at altitudes of 40,000-50,000ft and with a top speed of 662mph.

While outright performance is essential it is not the sole measure by which an aircraft's value can be assessed – efficiency and cost-effectiveness, particularly with a long-lived type are also essential criteria. One crucial factor is the fuel efficiency and operability of the engines, seemingly always a factor in assessing the value of retaining the B-52. And for some time there has been growing concern about the dated TF-33, the design of which, now more than 60 years old, has failed to keep up with new technologies and operating capabilities.

On 19 May 2020 the Air Force released a request for proposals on the B-52 Commercial Engine Replacement Program to General Electric for the CF-34-10 and Passport options, Pratt & Whitney for their PW800 and Rolls-Royce North America offering the F130.

On 24 September 2021, the 17,000lb thrust F130 was declared the winner. The engine will be built at Rolls-Royce's Indianapolis, Indiana, facility and according to the company, "Once installed, the F130 can stay on wing for the entire planned B-52 lifetime. In addition, the F130 will provide vastly greater fuel efficiency, increased range, and reduced tanker aircraft requirements. As importantly, the engine is ready for integration." The $2.6bn deal includes 650 engines – the 608 direct replacements (eight each for the 76 B-52Hs in service) plus 42 spares.

According to the Air Force, today the B-52 is a multi-mission aircraft for long-range precision strike, combat air support, air interdiction, defence suppression and maritime surveillance. All the more remarkable given that it was designed to meet a requirement issued 75 years ago for a very long range bomber capable of dropping nuclear bombs on an enemy halfway round the world.

A B-52D (55-0085) on display at Warner Robbins Museum of Aviation, Georgia, before it was broken up and scrapped. (USAF)

With a lift capacity of 3,000lb, a MJ-1B 'Jammer' lift truck was the mainstay of base operations from the 1950s, seeing service all over the world, especially during the Vietnam War. (USAF)

Boeing B-52

Busy days at Andersen AFB, Guam, on Arc Light operations during the Vietnam War. (USAF)

A stick of bombs laid down during Arc Light operations in Vietnam. (USAF)

Bomb Damage Assessment (BDA) on Bach Mai, just outside Hanoi, 22 December 1972, following a heavy raid by B-52s. (USAF)

The Combat Network Communication Technology (CONECT) programme has recently seen the replacement of existing cockpit displays and communications equipment with Link 16 and integrated machine-to-machine tasking and retargeting capabilities. The first reconfigured aircraft was delivered back in 2014 with CNS/ATM (Communications, Navigation, Surveillance/Air Traffic Management) digital equipment replacing the analogue systems, allowing greatly improved airspace operations and better integration with civil air traffic control.

And the Internal Weapons Bay Upgrade programme, also now completed, has seen the fitment of the new Conventional Rotary Launcher. This doubles the advanced weapons payloads and also reduces drag to increase range. It was deployed to Afghanistan in 2017 for the first time and supported transition

from the conventional ALCM to the AGM-158B JASSM-ER, a non-nuclear long-range cruise missile.

Future upgrades include provision for the GBU-84 laser JDAM and take account of the 38 B-52H attributable to nuclear weapons delivery missions and the 31 modified so as to be useable only for conventional weapons delivery. A new radar is in the offing too, again a commercial product already in use elsewhere added to further upgrades to the voice/data encryption systems and providing the pilots with colour multi-functional displays to improve situational awareness and for enhanced targeting precision.

The Tactical Data Link is also due for an upgrade to lower the latency value, to add jam-resistant communications in concert with CONECT and to improve GPS and cryptographic upgrades. Thus is the US Air Force rebuilding the B-52 to complement the B-21 well into the 2050s, after the B-1B and the B-2 have been retired.

BUILDING AND EQUIPPING THE B-52
Much of the technology and design innovation that had produced the B-47 was on hand for the B-52 but the aircraft had a very different origin. The exceptionally thin wing of the B-47 required a strong and weighty structure, leaving little room for fuel or landing gear – but this was deemed a necessary price to pay for the advantages of the swept wing.

Extensive wind tunnel studies, however, indicated that the critical point for drag rise was not the wing root but further out and this led the design of the B-52 wing. With a thicker wing root overall weight was reduced and internal

A crew briefing at Andersen AFB during the intense phase of Linebacker raids on North Vietnam. (USAF)

The crew of a B-52F (52-170) after arriving safely back at Andersen AFB. (USAF)

location minimised drag rise at high Mach numbers and served to alleviate load. The wing was designed with a twin-spar torsion box and at first was designed with flaperons but these were replaced on the XB-52 – the YB-52 flying first – by three sections of slotted spoiler ahead of each outer flap.

The YB-52 had six spoiler sections in addition to the outboard flaperons but the XB-52 received small ailerons between the inner and outer flaps. In the final iteration, each wing had seven spoiler sections individually driven by a hydraulic jack and given a deeply serrated trailing edge. The 14 sections could be opened simultaneously to act as air brakes. Most of the rolling energy came from the ailerons but for excessive manoeuvres the spoilers added supplementary management.

The all-flying delta-shaped horizontal tail was responsible for longitudinal control and pivoted around a point at 65% of chord by a screw-jack. Small micro-elevators were attached to the trailing edge with tabs. The all-flying tail was unique on an aircraft of this size and it could move through 13 degrees, the small elevators representing only 10% of the chord. Trim was important on the B-52 and one aircraft was lost because of an incorrect trim setting. The enormous, 48ft tall tail fin contained hinges that allowed it to fold to the right for hangar door clearance and on the G and H series variants fin height was reduced to 40.6ft.

Through several variants Boeing retained the functional layout and operational purpose of the various flight control elements until the ailerons were removed on the G and H variants, leaving the spoilers to provide lateral control. The space between the flaps housed the Lundy ALE-27 chaff dispenser which had five channels through which tape was dispensed after being cut to lengths required for the perceived threat frequency. Readdressing the overall rationales for flight control, the reduced fin height was accompanied by the fitting of hydraulically powered rudder and elevators. The large moving stabiliser and the faster moving, and very much smaller, elevator on this variant required awareness on the part of the pilot that no amount of elevator would help raise the nose on landing.

Two electrically driven hydraulic systems were employed to move the flight controls, with pumps on all engines except Nos 2 and 8. Each pump served a specific group of services and there was no way for the crew to interconnect working services with those failed by a faulty pump. Because of this, one side of the main gear, fore or aft, could fail together with its brakes and without an opportunity for a manual reset and compensating crossfeed. This has been criticised by pilots of this and other aircraft when briefed on the vicissitudes

volume was increased, ultimately making space for fuel. This design also lent itself to a commercial derivative and that triggered the first Boeing jet airliner, the 707, which made use of the thicker wing root mounted in a low position on the fuselage, an ideal position to locate the main landing gear.

There was a fight to convince the Air Force that the thick wing root was the answer but the elegance of the design was self-evident: low empty weight, reduced drag, large wing area providing high lift-over-drag and a spacious fuselage. It fell to Boeing aerodynamicist Vaughan Blumenthal to push for the thick wing approach. His calculations were supported by German aerodynamicist Dr Goethert, one of the many who had careers in the US after the end of the war. Nevertheless, the entire aircraft was designed for low stress levels, with the aircraft limit set at 2g and reduced further on later variants.

As designed, with a span of 185ft at the centreline in the fuselage it had a thickness ratio of 16.2%, reducing to 15% at the massive bridge frame, to 10.3% at 25% span, 9.4% at 57% span and 8% at the tip. With 8 degrees of washout, the root was at a greater incidence than the tip with the highest part of the chord at the top of the fuselage. Essentially it was an NACA-64 series aerofoil section, modified and adapted with a 66-series profile at the tip. With extreme flexibility, the maximum deflection was an astounding 22ft up and 10ft down. Due to lessons learned from the B-47, the B-52 wing was given a surface area of 4,000sq ft – nearly three times that of its predecessor – and range was aided by its 8.55:1 aspect ratio.

The integrated approach put the paired engine pod struts at critical locations 34.16ft and 60ft from the fuselage centreline to act as wing fences and tuned to avoid flutter. Their precise

In service until 1997, the B53 nuclear bomb had a yield of 9MT – the most powerful bomb in the American inventory. Up to this point the B-52 was still supporting air-drop gravity weapons for strategic targets. (USAF)

of the B-52 and some proposals have been made for improving that situation, even to having a manual crossover option to take systems into failed synchronism to prevent compound failure.

The decidedly unspectacular fuselage contained a surprisingly cramped pressurised cockpit and a bomb bay 28ft long and 6ft wide with fuel tanks located from immediately aft of the cockpit to aft of the rear main landing gear. Clearly,

options existed for using the spacious bomb bay for pressurised compartments supporting two additional crewmembers able to operate cameras and other electronic systems when equipped for reconnaissance missions. The forward pressurised compartment had a pilot and co-pilot facing forward with the ECM officer behind the co-pilot facing aft. The bombardier-navigator and radar navigator were side-by side facing forward

in the lower section of the forward compartment. A tail gunner was seated in his own pressurised compartment forward of the gun turret. On B-52G and H variants the gunner was moved forward and seated adjacent to the rear-facing electronics officer.

Early in the operational career of the B-52, considerable crew discomfort was attributed to the poor standard of flying gear and an inability to heat all areas of the pressurised compartment to a common temperature. While considerable progress had been made in aeronautical design and engineering, the standard MC-1 pressure suits were uncomfortable and added to the discomfort from the range of required equipment, including parachutes and survival gear. Worn over winter underwear, heavy underclothing and with thick boots, the general unpleasantness of the condition did nothing to offset fatigue. Little it seemed, had changed since the Second World War.

While the pilots and the ECM crewmember were relatively warm, the two lower crewmembers had their feet against the lower fuselage and outside temperatures would typically be far below freezing. But if that section was heated to the correct level, the upper three crewmembers were left sweltering in high temperatures. Only over time would these anomalies be sorted out.

The design of the aircraft made it necessary to place the landing gear in the same tandem configuration as for the B-47, with two main twin-wheel trucks at

The Douglas Skybolt nuclear stand-off missile was developed in the late 1950s as a potential solution to the increasing vulnerability of bombers over their targets. Each B-52 was to carry four, as seen here on the eighth B-52H (60-008). (USAF)

The AGM-86 ALCM in flight. (USAF)

Uploading AGM-86 ALCMs on a B-52H at Minot AFB, North Dakota. (USAF)

a track of 11.33ft between oleo legs and a wheelbase of 49.75ft. For additional stability, as with the B-47, two outriggers were provided, these being small, single-wheel units which extend a maximum 6ft to the ground and retract inwards. With an outrigger track of 148ft – the widest landing gear track of any aircraft ever built – moving the aircraft around requires special care to avoid the outriggers 'walking' off the tarmac.

The main gear adopted a unique retraction geometry by rotating up and in opposing directions, the right gear aft and the left gear forward so that they all lie along the centreline but in separate bays closed out by triangular doors.

Perhaps surprisingly, the arrangement of the landing gear was one of the most closely guarded secrets when the aircraft was launched, the light structure and astonishingly tight turning radius an ingenious design which had the front wheels steerable and a crabbing ability for +/-20-degrees of turn, keeping the wheels pointing down the runway while the aircraft was aligned with the wind. In other aspects the wheels were remarkably close in design to those on the B-47, with multi-disc, anti-skid brakes and similar tyres. Front and rear paired legs could turn in opposite directions for manoeuvring on the ground or in the same direction for take-off and

landing. It took some familiarisation for the pilot to feel comfortable taking off in a strong crosswind looking out of the side window.

The configuration of the B-52's fuel tankage varied throughout its life, the B-52B having five self-sealing tanks in each wing, a large tank within the bridge across the top of the fuselage, one tank forward and a further five tanks aft across the top of the bomb bay for a total of 37,550 US gallons. The B-52D had capacity for 42,110 US gallons while the B-52H with its wet wing and a rearrangement of wing storage has capacity for 47,975 US gallons.

Structural changes to the B-52G were the most significant in the type's history and provided the biggest wet wing yet seen. The spars remained largely the same but the upper and lower skins were redesigned and supplied as large machined panels without joints. Eight layers of primers and sealants were applied to the main torsion box and each half-wing, 115ft in length, was coated with large quantities of sealer. A 15-man scuba-diving team entered the wing to check on consistency and to trim any dried excess. The additional fuel carried this way allowed replacement of the large 3,000 US gallon jettisonable underwing tanks with standard USAF 700 US gallon fixed tanks. A further structural modification was to strengthen flap skins and the internal structure from excessive vibration from the engines.

Progressively more powerful engines were fitted to successive variants as identified above but for a large part of this aircraft's life it was underpowered and lacking in the performance promised when the aircraft was initially accepted. Serious consequences of a fully loaded B-52 suffering an engine problem on take-off led to calls for a RATO system, as with the B-47. A development programme was begun but cancelled in April 1954, at which point Pratt & Whitney developed the water injection system for the J57-P-29WA.

Despite several modifications to that outlined in the variants subsection, the B-52G incorporated a massive 10,000lb water tank between the forward fuselage fuel tank and the crew compartment. Fed by four pumps in a front truck bay, it provided for 110sec supply of water for the engines. Armed before reaching the runway for take-off, it provided feed directed to the engines

as they reached 86% thrust but there was always the risk of failure to an adjacent engine should its paired twin fail to get a sufficient supply.

BOMBS AND MISSILES

Compared to the gun-bristling B-36, the new all-jet Boeing bombers put a stake in the ground for shifting defence from hot metal to electrons. Boeing, in agreement with the Air Force, designed the B-52 with only a nod to convention by locating a rear gunner armed with four 0.50-calibre machine guns strapped to a turret in the fuselage tail. It was an unforgiving spot, the gunner sitting behind the jettisonable gun pod in a position from which, in an emergency, he had to bail out and take to the silk.

The G and H series variants did away with that position and put the gunner in the forward pressurised compartment. The H-series had a six-barrel M61 20mm Gatling gun installed – but this was removed from all aircraft in 1991 and never replaced.

The rated bomb capacity of the B-52B and D was 43,000lb while that for the B-52F was 50,000lb after structural modifications driven by a proposal for them to carry the GAM-63 RASCAL air-to-surface missile, an option never adopted. Upgrades and added capabilities to significantly increase the B-52D bomb load were begun in December 1965 with the so-called Big Belly modifications. The Air Force worked intensively with Boeing to significantly strengthen the variant for a higher bomb load – up to almost 60,000lb. Other opportunities arising from Big Belly mods allowed the B-52D to carry out mine-laying duties at sea, although modifications completed in late 1971 were only utilised in that mission after President Nixon ordered the mining of North Vietnamese harbours and river inlets on 8 May 1972.

While treated with modifications and upgrades common to all variants, 28 B-52Fs were subject to the South Bay project between June and October 1964. This strengthened the aircraft to carry 24 x 750lb bombs externally. In June 1965, 46 more B-52Fs were so modified under Sun Bath, specifically requested by Robert McNamara to accommodate needs driven by an escalation in operations in the Vietnam War. Prime coordinator for this activity, Air Force Logistics Command's Oklahoma Air Materiel Area had to scavenge war reserve stocks from several units of Tactical Air Command to complete the work on time.

The G and H variants were equipped to carry the AGM-28 Hound Dog stand-off weapon and the GAM-72 Quail decoy, the latter equipped with electronics and a radar cross-section which rendered it virtually indistinguishable from that of a B-52. Built by McDonnell and powered by a J85 turbojet engine, the first Quail entered service on 13 September 1960 and within three years SAC had almost 500 on hand. By the early 1970s, improvements to radar technology rendered them virtually useless, US training exercises successfully discriminating the real B-52 from the decoy in 21 out of 23 attempts.

Predating the imperative to fly low, in March 1956 SAC evaluated options for launching stand-off missiles from less vulnerable airspace. This followed the British decision of September 1954 seeking what eventually became the Blue Steel ASM, designed and built by Avro for the RAF's V-force and deployed operationally with Bomber Command from February 1963.

The B-52G had many improvements and interior changes including 'wet' wings and a completely modified tail gun layout – with the gunner now operating it remotely from the forward pressurised crew compartment. (USAF)

B-52Gs carried the Quail decoy between 1960 and 1976. One is pictured here alongside a B-52D (56-0695). (USAF)

Bigger and with a range of 785 miles at Mach 2, compared to Blue Steel's 575 miles at Mach 3, Hound Dog (named after the Elvis Presley song) carried a thermonuclear warhead with optional yield of 1MT or 4MT. Powered by a 7,500lb thrust J52 turbojet, Hound Dog could actually be used to help the B-52 get off the ground if fired up during take-off. The missile entered service in July 1960 with 29 SAC Wings operational with it by June 1962. After a production run of just 53 examples, Blue Steel was retired in 1970 when the UK's nuclear deterrent went to the Royal Navy and its Polaris SLBM. But Hound Dog production surged, with almost 600 in SAC service by 1963, taken off alert in June 1975 and retired from the inventory at the 42nd BW at Loring AFB in June 1978.

One weapon system earmarked for the B-52G/H variants never made it into operational service but the concept is worth noting for the impact it had, after its cancellation, on development of the air-launched cruise missile of the early 1970s. As early as the mid-1950s, with development of the Atlas and Titan ICBMs as a national priority, the Air Force wanted to take the advances in guidance platforms essential for those weapons and apply them to air-launched missiles of which Hound Dog was a precursor, but as a stand-off weapon rather than an air-launched ballistic missile (ALBM).

Suspicious of the vulnerability of land-based ICBMs, then projected to become operational around 1960, the 'bomber mafia' sought to enhance strike capability and survivability by giving SAC the equipment to launch ALBMs up to 1,500 miles from their target. That was equal to the distance between the east coast of the UK and Moscow or more than the distance from New York to Houston.

With experience of managing Hound Dog for the B-52G/H, the Air Force sought a cooperative programme with the UK for such a weapon under WS-138A, from 1960 designated GAM-87 and named Skybolt.

Largely understated in its cooperation with the RAF, the programme was part of an information exchange involving shared technical knowledge of the rocket motors for Atlas which were the basis of the Rolls-Royce RZ.2 for the Blue Streak Intermediate Range Ballistic Missile (IRBM). The British cancelled Blue Streak in April 1960 in favour of Skybolt.

The Americans wanted the UK involved from the outset to broaden political support and to share costs in the procurement phase. The Air Force was pushing hard for Skybolt, despite efforts at the Pentagon to kill it off, because it wanted to outdo the Navy with its Polaris SLBM, then entering final stages of development. Sucking the British into this inter-service rivalry could only bring trouble – which it did.

A B-52G of the 60th BS, at Andersen AFB, Guam, dropping Mk 82 500lb bombs. (USAF)

The initial design of Skybolt was capable of just about half the performance of the final version anticipated but the first test shots were failures until, on 19 December 1962, the sixth test was successful. B-52Gs and Hs would each have been able to carry four Skybolts, but three days after its performance was successfully demonstrated at last it was cancelled by President Kennedy on the advice of Defense Secretary Robert McNamara – who thought that ICBMs and SLBMs were adequate.

Having given basing rights to the US for its Polaris submarines at Faslane, Scotland, in exchange for procurement of Skybolt, the British government was furious and in a conciliatory response Kennedy agreed to a UK purchase of

Polaris missiles for its submarines. The last Skybolt development round had been fired by a B-52G down the Atlantic Missile Range on 23 December 1962, a day after its formal cancellation.

But survivability of the B-52 against enemy air defences and the potential to add flexibility to nuclear warfighting had been the sole logical purpose of stand-off missiles and ALBMs. The Air Force justified Skybolt on its ability for use as a countervalue weapon against the population and civilian leadership after an exchange of ICBMs and SLBMs against opposing military targets. This was an empowering factor in maintaining a strong capability with the manned bomber and was hailed as a second-strike option and assured destruction.

The bomb bay of a B-52H at Barksdale ASFB. Over the last 70 years B-52 internal payloads have included nuclear and conventional gravity bombs, cruise missiles, decoys and photographic and electronic intelligence gathering equipment. (USAF)

With many strategists believing that true deterrence resided in countervalue, it was not hard for the Air Force to retain that policy against those in the McNamara camp who favoured push-button warfare. While this was an enduring attempt to find the ultimate solution, survivability of the bomber force became the dominant aspect when the B-52G and H variants were introduced.

STAND-OFF WEAPONS

One of the biggest changes to the B-52 programme came with the advent in October 1971 of the Boeing AGM-69A Short Range Attack Missile (SRAM). The first aircraft modified to carry it was delivered to the 42nd BW at Loring AFB in March 1972. As eventually deployed, each B-52G and H could carry 20 SRAMs, eight inside the aft section of the bomb bay, the remainder on the exterior pylons. From this emerged the AGM-86 Air Launched Cruise Missile (ALCM) powered by a Williams F107 turbofan engine more commonly found in crop-dusters.

Although entering service with the B-52H in August 1981, it was to achieve its greatest publicity when seven B-52Gs from Barksdale AFB launched 35 ALCMs at military targets during the opening rounds of Operation Desert Storm in January 1991. Successive evolution of the ALCM resulted in the development of both conventional and nuclear-armed missiles, giving the B-52 a longer lease of life.

With a GPS-assisted Litton inertial navigation system, the conventional AGM-86C/D variants were also carried by the B-52H and whether the nuclear AGM-86B or the conventional ALCM, six can be carried on each underwing pylon in addition to 12 in the bomb bay. With a range of at least 1,500 miles, the nuclear AGM-86B has a Terrain Contour Matching (TERCOM) guidance system enabling it to fly a pre-selected and sometimes highly circuitous flight path to its target using radar against pre-set maps, weaving around air defence sites at different altitudes and making route prediction almost impossible to compute.

By the early 1980s the Air Force had been studying a new ALCM with low RCS for exclusively low-altitude penetration and incorporating forward-swept wings with stealthy shaping and materials technology. Developed by General Dynamics, the AGM-129A carried the same nuclear warhead as the AGM-86B and propulsion was also by Williams turbofan engine but the weapon had a range of up to 2,300 miles at subsonic speed and was capable of maintaining flight for up to five hours. This was an exclusively strategic nuclear weapon and although plans originally anticipated it for the B-1B too, only the B-52H was ever equipped with the AGM-129A. Delivered between June 1990 and August 1993, the missile entered service in 1991 with 461 being produced in total. Strategic arms talks resulted in its retirement in April 2012.

Based on the longevity and ageing of the current generation of AGM-86B, the nuclear bomber force of B-52, B-1 and B-2/B-21 will be equipped with the Long Range Stand-Off (LRSO) missile now being developed by Raytheon. With a range of about 1,800 miles the missile will be married up to the new W80-4 nuclear warhead with a dialled-in yield option of 5KT or 150KT. A conventional warhead variant was cancelled. The LRSO is expected to be in service by 2026 at the latest and to completely replace the existing ALCM force. It is the latest in a long line of stand-off weapons going back 70 years – but the weapons themselves were only part of the story.

Coincident with the decision in 1950 to give the B-52 a low-level capability, and to equip it with Hound Dog and Quail, SAC wanted the AN/ALQ-27 ECM package available for every B-52. It had high hopes for this system as a counter to SAM and AAM threats and to provide early-warning of airborne and ground-control radar and fire control systems. But when the price tag for retrofitting 572 B-52s with it was calculated at more than $1bn, it was abruptly cancelled by the Air Staff. Instead a cocktail of mixed ECM and quick-reaction capability systems would be installed in the B-52H on the production line and retrofitted to other variants still in the inventory.

However, problems with the electronic support programmes were added to with the 'Big Four' modifications for beefing up the aircraft to support low-level operations. Many

Only the B-52H variant remains in service today. With a projected life into the 2050s, according to current inventory planning, it will eventually serve alongside the B-21 Raider. (USAF)

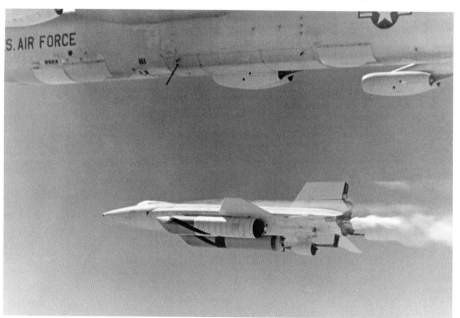

A NASA NB-52B launches the X-15A-2 rocket powered research aircraft, one of 199 flights made by the three manned X-15s. (NASA)

NASA's NB-52B carries the unmanned X-43A hypersonic research vehicle attached to a Pegasus rocket, one of which achieved a record speed of almost Mach 10. (NASA)

of those problems can be viewed in retrospect as symptomatic of a simplistic approach to requirements.

SAC believed that it was only necessary to install an improved bombing and navigation system, a modified Doppler radar, a terrain-avoidance radar, low altitude altimeters and associated missiles to get the job done. In reality, airframes had to be modified and that differed according to the variant and the production model, impacting workload and cost. The C and D aircraft would prove the most expensive to convert.

Bringing the aircraft down from 30,000ft to 800ft increased the gust frequency 200 times and there was little knowledge about the stresses that could be expected. Some data was available from the B-47 programme but the bigger size and much greater wing span and area of the B-52 made it necessary to conduct real tests and a B-52F was singled out for this purpose. This testing programme, perhaps unsurprisingly, revealed that the necessarily modifications would be significant and that the costs would be substantial.

Mandatory modifications in the H-Stress Program consisted of two phases. Firstly, nine fixes would be required when the aircraft reached

2,000 flying hours. The second phase, at 2,500hrs, required modification of the panel splice on the inner section of the upper wing and reinforcement of the lower wing panel which supported both inboard and outboard engine pods. It also required reinforcement of the upper wing fuel probe doors and strengthening of the bottom portion of the fuselage bulkhead. Completed by 1962, this was secondary to the 'Big Four' modifications but then a third phase was added – requiring wing inspections and repair of cracks as necessary in the early variants.

From the outset fuel leaks were a persistent problem, caused principally by broken heavy duty band (Marman) clamps. Under the 1957 Blue Band programme solution, all aircraft were equipped with new aluminium clamps but these proved just as troublesome and under the Hard Shell retrofit programme a new and more durable stainless steel strap clamp, specially designed by Boeing, was fitted. But when these too began to split because of poor latch pins, in 1958 the Quickclip replacement put a safety strap around the improved clamps. Several broken strap clamps were reported but they held in place due to the strapping. It quickly became a permanent feature, preventing the loss of fuel and

large quantities sloshing around outside the tank bags.

Just a couple of months before the October 1962 Cuban Missile Crisis, two B-52Hs at Homestead AFB, Florida, were found to have cracks at the wing-fuselage joint. Attention focused on the taper-lock fasteners as these were known to be subject to corrosion when the aircraft was under stress or in adverse climatic conditions. Consequently, Project Straight Pin was set up to modify wing terminal fasteners on the entire fleet and to clean up cracked fitting holes by oversize reaming. There were also issues with landing gear cylinders but the solution was to use a different alloy to make them less susceptible to stress corrosion.

From the beginning, the development of the B-52 followed a concurrent evolution of airframe and engine in the belief that it would eventually produce the desired performance. But the push to get as many B-52s into operational service as possible early in the programme was a delicate balance between resources spent on turning out new aircraft and those spent on improving it. In the end, evolution of airframe, engine, systems and operational procedures went hand-in-hand – this long and successful process underpinning the B-52's continued survival.

FLATTOP FOLLIES

A Navy Douglas EA-3B Skywarrior (146452) from VQ-1 off the carrier USS *Constellation* (CVA-63) in 1974, the basis for the Air Force B-66. (USN)

Following its tremendous successes in the air war over the Pacific against Japan, the US Navy emerged from the Second World War feeling that it was the United States' most effective global strike force. As such, it was natural to assume that Navy bombers would carry the nuclear deterrent to its targets around the world should that become necessary.

But the independence of the US Air Force in 1947 created a powerful rival for this role and ignited a long and enduring struggle for funds and priority. The Navy's plan to break the Air Force monopoly on nuclear bombers initially centred on the CVA-58 *United States* series of super-carriers planned shortly after the war. Each would have a deck length of 1,000ft to support long-range nuclear strike aircraft on a par in capability with land-based strategic bombers.

The search for a suitable aircraft began in January 1948 with a requirement for a maximum gross weight of 100,000lb, a design range of 2,300 miles and power provided by two turbojet engines in the 10,000lb class. Eight manufacturers were in the running but few could envisage achieving those requirements for the weight required.

DOUGLAS A-3 SKYWARRIOR AND B-66 DESTROYER

The brainchild of the already legendary Ed Heinemann, the Douglas A3D proposal was designed to a maximum take-off weight of 68,000lb for operation from standard *Midway*-class carriers, in the (not unreasonable as it turned out) belief that the super-carriers would never be built. At the end of April 1949, a month after its keel was laid, the *United States*

was indeed cancelled and three months later Douglas got the contract to build the A3D Skywarrior.

Its basic layout was conventional and conservative while also possessing innovation and foresight, much reliance being placed on electronics, avionics and mission flexibility. The high-mounted wing had a 36-degree sweep angle with a 6.75:1 aspect ratio, a super-efficient thickness ratio of 10% at the root tapering to 8.5% at the tip and an incidence of two degrees. The inboard trailing edge had high-lift slotted flaps and the wings folded from a deployed span of 72.5ft to 45.41ft for carrier storage. Power was to have been provided by the Westinghouse YJ40 engine but this was replaced by the Pratt & Whitney J57 for production aircraft.

Douglas was not provided with precise dimensions for the A-bombs

that the Skywarrior would be carrying and as such its fuselage ended up fatter than necessary. Nevertheless, while undramatic in outline the aircraft was aerodynamically refined and a remarkably close match to the original size, weight and performance requirement. Appropriately, it got the blessing of the Navy Bureau of Aeronautics (BuAer) with their acceptance of weight tests to 84,000lb, the heaviest for any carrier-based aircraft.

The Navy bought 282 and it served for a remarkably long time – from 1956 to 1991 – becoming the A-3 in 1962, seeing combat during the Vietnam War and being adapted for a variety of roles. Even before the type's first flight on 28 October 1952 however, the Air Force had been impressed. With a payload and combat-radius equivalent to the B-47, it seemed

A rocket boosted take-off for an A3D-1 from NAS Jacksonville, Florida. (USN)

like a type that the Air Force should operate. And so began the tortuous and not altogether satisfactory adaptation of a naval aircraft for landlubbers.

A great deal of controversy surrounds the next steps taken in getting hold of the A3D and adapting it to Air Force requirements. A mere de-navalisation was originally intended but a train of changes was set in motion which would bring unique and perhaps unnecessary problems.

At first the Air Force wanted a straightforward transfer to a land-based bomber and provided the designation B-66 Destroyer when it placed a contract with Douglas for RB-66A reconnaissance and B-66B bomber variants, production preference going to the bomber. But the Air Force then insisted on changes which included not only a different engine but also revisions to aspects of the design and engineering, largely because of the wide range of roles anticipated.

The A-3 had been designed for high-altitude nuclear strike from carriers but the Air Force wanted it as a low-altitude bomber and, secondarily, as a reconnaissance platform. As a result, the B-66's wing's were given a longer root chord and changes were made to the flaps and ailerons. The fuselage was almost a complete redesign; structural strengthening for the arrestor hook and catapult linkages was removed and three ejection seats were installed for the pressurised crew compartment. This had a very different forward window and nose section which was now longer, more pointed and with a different profile which also included a flight refuelling probe.

A different engine was selected too – the 10,200lb thrust Allison J71. This offered more power, granted, but it also meant a large number of engine-related systems had to be redesigned along with the hydraulics.

The RB-66A made its first flight on 28 June 1954 followed by the B-66B six months later and the first of 294 aircraft entered service with the Air Force in March 1956, the type eventually being phased out in 1974. The reconnaissance variant played an important role in gathering information during the Cuban Missile Crisis and again in Vietnam. Several were operated out of RAF Chalveston and one was shot down over East Germany. Unlike the Navy, the Air Force never employed the aircraft as a bomber but it had the capacity to support a wide range of covert, overt and disruptive tactical roles.

NORTH AMERICAN A-5 VIGILANTE

With the subsonic Skywarrior and the Destroyer less than a year away from entering service with the Navy and the Air Force, in July 1955 North American Aviation (NAA) was placed under contract for detailed design of

Developed into a land-based light bomber, the B-66 was a complete rework of the Navy Skywarrior and caused considerable trouble due to the Air Force insisting on a range of changes and modifications. (USAF)

The RB-66C was developed in 1953 to incorporate a four-man crew of observers working electronic countermeasures from a pressurised capsule in the bomb bay. (USAF)

The Navy was determined to possess a supersonic nuclear bomber by the mid-1950s and in response North American developed the A3J Vigilante, one of the more elegant bombers of the decade. This reconnaissance RA-5C was operated by RVAH-7 in 1979. (USN)

what the Navy clumsily referred to as the North American General Purpose Attack Weapon – or NAGPAW. Unlike the Douglas types, this was to be a Mach 2, low-altitude conventional attack aircraft powered by two 10,000lb thrust General Electric J79 turbojets, 17,000lb with afterburner. Having started out as an unsolicited design from NAA, designationed NA-233, it found favour and the Navy placed a contract for two prototypes in September 1956.

The initial concept had been worked up by NAA's Frank G. Compton, chief designer at the Columbus, Ohio, facility with requirements shaped by experience in the Korean War but the Navy changed that when it saw the drawings, earmarking it as a replacement for the Skywarrior. With an insatiable appetite for high-performance attack and nuclear strike aircraft, the Navy liked the idea of having a bomber with performance close to that of Convair's B-58 Hustler, then

Flattop Follies

Vigilante squadrons saw service in the Vietnam War where, despite technical problems resulting from its sophisticated defensive and offensive avionics systems, the aircraft performed well as a reconnaissance platform. (USN)

As a bomber, the Vigilante could carry nuclear or conventional weapons in the internal bomb bay or on two external hard points. (USN)

Much of the technology applied to aircraft in the late 1960s was developed on systems tried out in the Vigilante, here represented by an aircraft of RVAH-3. (USN)

nearing completion for the Air Force. But to get the nuclear weapon in what was a very slim fuselage required a unique and ingenious configuration.

The basic design philosophy behind NA-233 was a clean, aerodynamically shaped fuselage with a high wing possessing significant sweepback and powered by two J79 turbojet engines. Its Mach 2 design target created difficulties for low-speed handling since the optimised wing required large flaps for deck landings and the clean fuselage left little room for a conventional bomb bay. What Compton did is unique in the history of flown combat aircraft and, perhaps fortunately, was never used in aggression. A tunnel structure was designed between the engines with a void 30ft in length, accessed via a 14ft long door at the front of the long bay. The concept envisaged two 275 US gallon fuel containers centre and aft and a nuclear weapon at the front, all three attached to each other after being loaded separately. The first tank being uplifted and rolled back down the tunnel, followed by the second tank, pushed back and joined to the first, followed by the weapon uplifted directly at the front. The operating procedure would be to deplete the centre and aft bay tanks before reaching the target, then to release all three elements.

On command from the cockpit, the tail cone would be jettisoned and the train

of empty tanks and warload ejected out the back from between the afterburners. It appeared practical in theory but real problems were encountered when testing got under way. It was found that after separation the entire triple-pack floated around in the disrupted airflow behind the aircraft – upsetting any pre-deployment precision achieved by the AN/ASB-12 bombing computer, which compared radar images with target pictures on tape managed by the VERDAN (Versatile Digital Analyzer) computer.

The Vigilante was certainly elegant in appearance, with a 701sq ft wing area and a leading edge sweepback of 37.5 degrees. Thickness/chord ratio was 4.9% at the root and 3.5% at the tip, and the outer 65in of wing folded for carrier deck operations. The entire leading edge was fitted to hinges operated by ball screw-jacks and deployed at various settings for take-off and landing. The inboard trailing edge supported large flaps, blown at a depression angle greater than 7 degrees, providing twice the available lift at 50 degrees. Dispensing with ailerons, lateral control was achieved by a set of spoilers on both upper and lower surfaces and unique in aircraft design.

In triple sets each side of the wing, inner and centre spoilers were hinged on the upper surface at the front and on lower surfaces at the back with the reverse attachments on the outer spoilers. All control surfaces were driven

by the standard 3,000lb per square inch hydraulic system common to all US aircraft driving mechanical actuators. Fly-by-wire was incorporated as a back-up.

The fuselage contained separate cockpits for pilot and bomber-navigator in tandem with their own ejection seats produced by North American. NAA designed the second place cockpit without windows, believing this would help the occupant see the illuminated displays, but negative feedback forced a change and small side windows were added. With an eye to long range missions, a retractable aerial refuelling probe was installed on the left side of the nose. The crew were to have the latest electronics and avionics, although some of those took time to filter through to deployment and would only be retrospectively installed after delivery.

Identified as the A3J before the 1962 redesignations, the first A-5 Vigilante made its first flight on 31 August 1958 and was followed by the second aircraft three months later. Carrier trials began in July 1960, the Navy anxious to show it off to garner support for carrier operations. At the time it was seeking Congressional support for a fleet defence fighter, which eventually became entangled with the TFX programme and the resulting F-111. Operational units began to receive the Vigilante in 1962 but there were serious issues with maintenance and the unreliability of its electronics.

Long forgotten and anti-climactic, an idea that ran out of time, Martin's P6M Seamaster – the only flying boat designed as a nuclear bomber. (USN)

By this time the Navy was beginning to lose interest in an airborne nuclear delivery system, having already placed the Polaris SLBM in full-scale deployment, and the Vigilante found its true niche as a reconnaissance platform, the RA-5C, the first example of which flew on 30 June 1962 and entered service in 1964. It excelled on operations in the Vietnam War but in total only 167 were built. It remained in service until 1979 with all but 30 built or adapted for the reconnaissance role.

Sadly, the Vigilante has never really gained the recognition it deserves and its somewhat less glamorous role as an intelligence-gathering and reconnaissance asset condemned it to relative obscurity. Nevertheless, it achieved the astonishing altitude of 91,446ft while carrying a 2,000lb load and snatched some records which, for whatever reason, are still classified. Although never a bomber in the truest sense of the description, it was designed for that role and demonstrates the outstanding and innovative practices of aircraft designers and their teams in an age where individuals still had an important job to do in guiding companies and providing solutions by their own creative talents.

MARTIN P6M SEAMASTER

Immediately after the demise of the super-carrier USS *United States* in April 1949, the Navy set up plans for a flying boat attack force capable of delivering a nuclear punch and operating from closer to enemy targets than it believed the Air Force could. If it was unable to have a carrier big enough for strategic bombers, it would put the bomber in the water and operate from there!

A performance requirement was agreed in April 1951 and on 30 July the Bureau of Aeronautics issued a request for proposals from 12 manufacturers for a seaplane with a 30,000lb bomb load and 1,500 mile range. Martin and Convair were the only respondents. The Navy wanted a subsonic conventional and nuclear bomber operating off floating support tenders and capable of minelaying. Winning bidder

Martin took some technical design details from its XB-51 and incorporated them into what was named SeaMaster.

Designed initially for a Curtiss-Wright ramjet engine, development troubles forced a switch to the Allison J71 carried above the wing, which had a 40-degree sweepback and tip tanks which doubled as floats. The highly secret programme got an equally covert rollout on 21 December 1954, followed by a first flight on 14 July 1955. Trials exposed a need to cant the engines outboard slightly due to thermal plume impingement on the fuselage. The second prototype followed but the first was lost on 7 December 1955 when it crashed into Chesapeake Bay killing all four crewmembers. The second crashed on 9 November 1956 during the test of a redesigned tail but both crew ejected to safety.

The production P6M-2 was heavier but exceptionally well built, with a stiff and robust construction that gave it a low-level speed of Mach 0.9, compared to Mach 0.55 for the B-52. The Navy was enthusiastic and started a build programme for support vessels but the writing was on the wall – strategic seaplanes were past their usefulness; long-range, land-based bombers would do the job and, in any event, the Navy now had strategic missiles. In 1959 after the two XMP6M-1s, six YP6M-1s and three production P6M-2s had been built, the programme was scrapped.

It was the end of an era. Martin had tried several years earlier to interest the government in a nuclear-powered flying boat but the size and weight any suitable reactor would require made that an impossible dream. In any event, an aircraft big enough to carry such a device would be better suited to land-based operations. Martin wanted to take the SeaMaster design and produce an eight-engine airliner which it named SeaMistress but that too was a redundant concept.

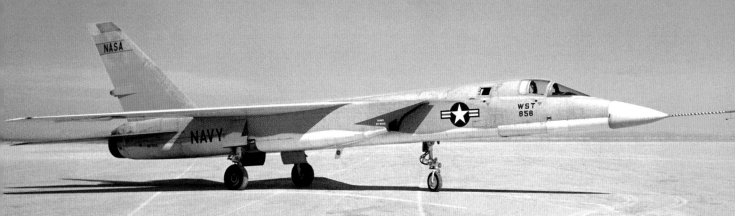

An A-5A bomber without the modified upper fuselage deck characteristics of the reconnaissance versions was operated by NASA from the early 1960s. (NASA)

SEARCHING FOR A SUCCESSOR

Converted from a B-36H, the Convair NB-36 (51-5712) supported the Nuclear Test Aircraft programme for flight tests with a reactor, flown as such during the 1950s but not activated. Here accompanied by a B-50 chase plane. (USAF)

As soon as the B-52 entered service in 1955 the Air Force began looking for a replacement. Possibilities ranged from a nuclear-powered aircraft to a Mach 3, high-altitude type, both concepts depending on new and untried technology.

The nuclear bomber emerged from the Aircraft Nuclear Propulsion (ANP) programme of the late 1940s in which energy from an on-board nuclear reactor would power adapted turbojets, allowing for sustained, long duration flight limited only by the endurance of the crew, food and water on board. It was a step or two ahead of any enabling technology but the idea had been toyed with since the emergence of nuclear power after the first test reactor had been activated in the United States during 1942. Initially, that research was channelled into an atomic bomb but in the early post-war years the possibilities for power and propulsion seemed endless.

The challenges for an atom-powered aircraft were daunting but several manufacturers received development contracts nevertheless. They included Convair and Lockheed for airframes and General Electric and Pratt &Whitney for the reactor. Convair even flew an experimental reactor in a converted B-36, the NB-36H; 47 flights taking place between September 1955 and March 1957. Although the aircraft carried a 1MW air-cooled reactor in the bomb bay, it was never used for propulsion. It did, however, carry out useful scientific research before the nuclear bomber concept was abandoned.

Experience during the Korean War of 1950-1953 had exposed the vulnerability of US bombers to attack by jet fighters and it had quickly become apparent that threats to the manned bomber would only become increasingly difficult to counter. A B-52 successor would still need the range to reach its targets but it would also need new technology to defeat advanced surface-to-air missiles and jet interceptors.

To this end, in April 1955, six contractors were invited to participate in a design competition defined by General Operational Requirement-96 (GOR-96).

NORTH AMERICAN XB-70A VALKYRIE

To begin the process, the Air Force specified a day or night, all-weather bomber with a minimum unrefuelled combat radius of 4,600 miles, but citing a desirable combat radius of 6,329 miles, a minimum over-the-target altitude of 60,000ft and a cruise at Mach 0.9 for most of the mission, with a Mach 2 dash in and out of the combat zone. Boeing and North American Aviation were the only two manufacturers expressing interest and on 8 November 1955 each received a concept development contract

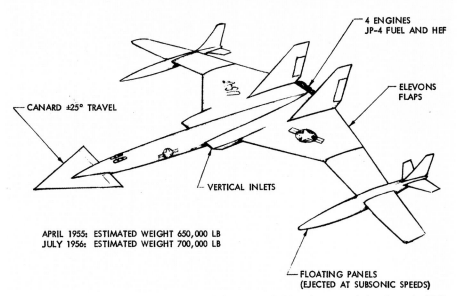

SAC BOMBER ~ AT THE ONSET
CONVENTIONAL CONSTRUCTION, MATERIALS, TECHNOLOGY

4 ENGINES
JP-4 FUEL AND HEF

ELEVONS
FLAPS

CANARD ±25° TRAVEL

VERTICAL INLETS

APRIL 1955: ESTIMATED WEIGHT 650,000 LB
JULY 1956: ESTIMATED WEIGHT 700,000 LB

FLOATING PANELS
(EJECTED AT SUBSONIC SPEEDS)

The Air Force conducted studies on a supersonic long-range B-52 replacement during the early 1950s. Several concepts involved fuel contained in 'floating' outer wing sections. (USAF)

Designed to take maximum advantage of the compression-lift concept with a drooped wing leading edge, the XB-70A was the prototype for what was originally envisaged as a force of 65 Valkyrie bombers. (USAF)

for WS-110A, a weapon system package designed to achieve those targets.

Under the WS concept, a single prime contractor would be responsible for appointing associate contractors and subcontractors for individual systems and subsystems. Where previously individual contracts would be let for airframe or engine, with systems provided by separate government contracts to other companies, under the weapon system process one company would manage it all for the Air Force.

This was intended to speed up procurement with concurrency replacing several competing prototypes. Instead of selecting from several contenders,

procurement contracts would be based on paper studies only, with pre-production test aircraft from the winning bidder flying trials and evaluation flights simultaneously, concurrently with production. This became known as the 'cut and try' approach.

When the designs emerged from each contender in April 1956, they both had floating outer wing tanks with huge fuel pods. Floating, in that they were so wide the outer sections with fuel pods were hinged to provide separate, but connected, lifting components in their own right. The aircraft would use fuel from the outer wing tanks to carry it at Mach 0.9, dropping the tanks and the

With a variable geometry engine inlet and a compression-lift afterbody, the underside of the XB-70 was critical for the enormous performance gains required. (USAF)

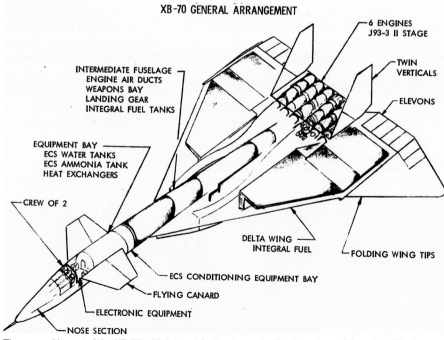

XB-70 GENERAL ARRANGEMENT

INTERMEDIATE FUSELAGE
ENGINE AIR DUCTS
WEAPONS BAY
LANDING GEAR
INTEGRAL FUEL TANKS

6 ENGINES
J93-3 II STAGE

TWIN
VERTICALS

ELEVONS

EQUIPMENT BAY
ECS WATER TANKS
ECS AMMONIA TANK
HEAT EXCHANGERS

CREW OF 2

DELTA WING
INTEGRAL FUEL

FOLDING WING TIPS

ECS CONDITIONING EQUIPMENT BAY

FLYING CANARD

ELECTRONIC EQUIPMENT

NOSE SECTION

The general layout of the XB-70 with integral fuel tanks on the fixed sections of the wing. (North American Aviation)

outer wing sections for a cleaned-up, Mach 2 dash through enemy airspace to the target and back. But to get the range required, each tank was the size of a B-47 and required a wing of its own, all of which were expendable.

Boeing's Model 724-15 had a maximum weight of 710,000lb with each of the two floating wingtips and tanks weighing 180,000lb. The North American proposal was even larger, with a gross weight of 750,000lb. Each contender was 40-50% bigger than a B-52 and required unusually wide runways, reconfigured bases from which to operate and a completely revised operational support infrastructure. Each had one thing in common: they were both totally unacceptable and the floating-wing concept was cancelled on 18 October 1956 just as the solution appeared in research work carried out by scientists at the NACA.

Known as compression-lift, this proposed solution followed the principle of a speedboat surfing on its own bow wave. Developed by Alfred Eggers and Clarence Syvertson, the theory had it that the shock waves created at supersonic speed are angled acutely and proportional to the Mach number. If the waves could be focused on the underside of a large airframe, the whole aircraft could surf on its shock. An aircraft designed to focus those shock waves on its underbody could ride on those waves with greater efficiency than if it cruised subsonic and only engaged in a high speed dash to and from the target. Counterintuitively, such an aircraft could achieve an optimised lift/drag ratio and get a 30% reduction in induced drag by flying at Mach 3 continuously throughout its entire mission.

On 23 December 1957, North American Aviation got a contract to develop its NA-278 proposal for the WS-110A concept and on 6 February 1958 it was designated B-70 and named Valkyrie. It was to be powered by six 19,800lb thrust General Electric YJ93 engines producing 27,200lb with afterburner using JP-6 fuel possessing a lower freezing point and improved thermal oxidative stability.

The very essence of the design addressed construction and performance challenges never encountered before and that story is quite outside the scope of this narrative. Its importance in the story of jet bombers, however, is to acknowledge a landmark in high-speed/high-altitude aircraft engineering with techniques developed specifically for this aircraft. Some of the engineering applications came from missile technologies, particularly those with which North American had prior experience, and a considerable series of advanced manufacturing techniques were applied which would bleed off into other programmes.

With a wing span of 105ft, a wing area of 6,297sq ft, a length of 185ft and a height of 30ft, the XB-70 had a maximum take-off weight of 550,000lb. The wing itself was shaped as a delta planform with a leading edge sweep of 59.8 degrees at 25% chord and outer sections which could pivot downwards by 65 degrees on the action of six hydraulic rams on each side.

This was the secret of the XB-70. With outer wing sections drooping, the massive delta wing would focus supersonic shock waves on the underside and give the aircraft its unique performance: a maximum speed of 2,057mph, or Mach 3.1, a cruise speed of 2,000mph and a range of 5,357 miles with a 10,000lb payload delivered on a thrust/weight ratio of 0.314 and a lift/drag ratio of 6:1. Maximum rated altitude was 79,950ft. The mission profile envisaged acceleration to Mach 1.37 at 25,000ft followed by a short cruise before accelerating to Mach 3 achieved at 65,000ft – gradually increasing to the maximum altitude of 71,900ft before descending.

More than two-thirds of the structure by weight was fabricated from a special

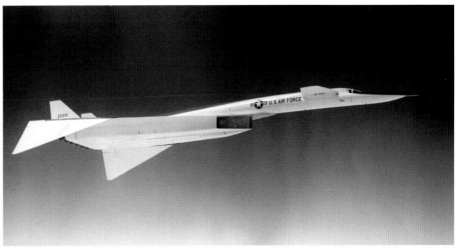

Mach 3 cruise was highly efficient with drooped outer wing sections, as verified through flight tests between 1964 and 1966 – even though the B-70 bomber programme had been cancelled in 1961. (USAF)

One of only two XB-70s was destroyed in a crash on 8 June 1966. It was caused by the collision of an F-104 piloted by Joe Walker, seen here with the red tail shortly before it got sucked into the XB-70s starboard vertical tail, shearing it off. (USAF)

The English Electric Canberra B.2 formed the basis for the Martin B-57A, of which only eight were built. It first flew in July 1953 prior to a few changes. (USAF)

Externally identical to the B-57B, which had tandem-seat crew positions, the B-57C shown here (53-3831) with the Nevada Air National Guard also had dual controls for training purposes but with all the systems required to operate them as bombers. (USAF)

With cameras installed aft of the bomb bay, the RB-57A was the most prolific of this initial variant, 38 being delivered during 1954. (USAF)

Thirty-two RB-57A reconnaissance aircraft were converted to EB-57As for electronic countermeasures work during the mid-1960s and were still in service for training purposes with the Air National Guard into the 1980s when they were replaced with EF-111 Raven aircraft from the regular Air Force. (USAF)

stainless steel (PH-15-7-Mo) which was shaped by the hot-creep process in a furnace or by deep-freeze at -100°F (-73°C) with unprecedented tolerance to avoid excess weight. The wing incorporated 54 spars with skin sheets joined by TIG (tungsten inert gas) welding and by brazing methods incorporating sterling silver. The entire structure comprised a wet wing which, with fuselage tanks, held 47,708 US gallons of fuel.

The XB-70A was never put into production and only two prototypes were built, the first being rolled out on 11 May 1964, long after it had been abandoned by the government and relegated to experimental tests. The first flight was on 21 September 1964 followed by a test phase which revealed some discrepancies and faults, most of which were sorted out by the time the second aircraft flew on 17 July 1965. Flight tests with both took place simultaneously but the second aircraft (62-0207) crashed after a mid-air collision on 8 June 1966 during a photo-shoot in formation with several other Air Force aircraft.

The sole survivor (62-0001) continued to fly on tests providing information for a planned Supersonic Transport (SST) project which never got off the ground, completing 83 flights before it was delivered to the USAF Museum on 4 February 1969.

As with many examples throughout the history of aviation, the XB-70 was a great success as a design and aero-engineering programme but as a bomber it was outdated long before it reached the metal-cutting stage. The Russians never quite believed that and the prospect of it getting an operational role with SAC inspired the MiG-25, and eventually the MiG-31, designed with the performance to intercept it and shoot it down.

MARTIN B-57

Had it not been for the invasion of South Korea by communist forces from the North on 25 June 1950, the British aircraft industry may never have sold the English Electric Canberra to the United States. Frustrated over its inability to field a successor to the B-26 light tactical bomber, the outbreak of hostilities across a peninsular on the opposite side of the world convinced Air Materiel Command to buy the British bomber.

As it turned out though, the American Canberra, the B-57, would not fly until one week before an armistice and the end of hostilities. But at no point was the selection of this outstanding aircraft in contention and its long-lived history with the USAF, later with NASA and right up to the present day, is legendary. It was used with great effect in South East Asia and elsewhere for several decades of outstanding military service.

The Canberra B.2, which formed the basis for the B-57A, was powered

Two B-57Es, the one in the foreground fulfilling its primary role of target-tow. USAF)

An RB-57D (53-3977 foreground) reconnaissance aircraft with larger wing span and a B-57A displaying mission adaptability. (USAF)

A WB-57F (63-13503) assigned to weather duties and with two TF33-P-11A turbofan engines. NASA operates three for atmospheric and environmental data collection. (USAF)

by the Rolls-Royce AJ.65 engine with a thrust of 6,500lb – but the American variant would instead have a licence-built version of the Armstrong Siddeley Sapphire, the Wright YJ65-W-1, delivering a thrust of 7,500lb; the higher thrust level was required to compensate for additional weight incurred in 'Americanising' the Canberra. From June 1951 a joint US/UK team including engineers and technicians from Martin and English Electric started work to adapt the British bomber to the requirements demanded for the B-57A.

The first flight of the first B-57A (52-1418) took place on 20 July 1953, a 46-minute flight with company test pilots O. E. (Pat) Tibbs and George (Rod) Rodney, who declared it to be totally satisfactory. Under the guidance of B-57A project manager Albert J. Perry, numerous subtle changes had been made to the original Canberra. The most advantageous was the additional power from the J65 engines which, despite teething trouble, did provide a boost in aircraft performance.

The B-57A's wing would remain the same as that designed for the Canberra, with a relatively low aspect ratio of 4.27:1 and a thickness ratio of 12% at the root and 9% at the tip. While it might have been expected from this that the maximum lift/drag ratio would be low, the large wing area of 960sq ft provided a low, zero-drag coefficient of 0.0119 and a maximum lift/drag ratio of 15:1, with conventional control surfaces and high-lift flaps in the trailing edge. The crew layout was completely different to that of the Canberra though. The third crewmember (radio operator-navigator) position was removed and that space occupied by additional equipment.

On 20 August 1953, exactly a month after it made its first flight, the USAF accepted this aircraft at the Martin airfield at Middle Rover, Maryland. But this was only the start to a major development programme which would result in the substantial redesign of the basic aircraft acquired from Britain.

Early in the flight development stage, the decision was made to retire the B-57A and develop the B-57B. Before that, during the previous year, the RB-57A reconnaissance variant had been tagged as a replacement for the piston-engine RB-26, the reconnaissance variant of the B-26 Marauder. Sixty-seven B-57Bs were ordered on 11 August 1952, the first rolled out on 20 July 1953 with a first flight three months later. The B-57B had a completely new cockpit, with the navigator-bombardier in tandem behind the pilot beneath a large bubble canopy of the type fitted to the B-47 and the T-33 trainer. The pilot's seat was aligned with the centreline of the fuselage but the second crewmember was offset to the left to provide space to install the SHORAN receiver-indicator. This also

Searching For A Successor

Convair got the contract to build the XB-58 (55-660) supersonic bomber prototype in 1952. The production variant's sole task would be to deliver a thermonuclear bomb but in a detachable pod which also carried fuel for a range which never did match expectations. (USAF)

allowed installation of the Swedish M-1 toss-bomb computer unit.

The programme was cut from 293 to 202 aircraft in 1954 and the first flight of a production B-57B took place on 18 June 1954; the type entered service with the 345th Bomb Group (Tactical), Langley AFB, later that year.

Twenty of a new high-flying RB-57D reconnaissance version were ordered on 3 January 1955. The most visually prominent feature of the D-series was the bigger wing, increased in span from 64ft to 106ft, or 107.5ft with additional fuel tanks under the wing tips. This increased wing area by 56.25%, from 960sq ft to 1,500sq ft. All the fuel tanks in the fuselage were removed and replaced by 'wet' wing fuel cells. There was no defensive armament and the bomb bay was replaced with avionics equipment. The horizontal stabiliser was changed to a variable incidence, all-flying tail with spoilers added to the outboard wings for assistance with roll control.

Optional nose and tail radomes and electronic equipment would extend fuselage length by up to 28in. The

installation of two J57-P-9 turbojets, with a thrust of 10,000lb each, increased total thrust by 38.8% over the J65-W-5 engines of the RB-57B. The P-9 engines also had anti-icing equipment for use above 70,000ft, a considerable increase on the 48,000ft considered as the operational ceiling for the RB-57B. Later, 10,500lb thrust J57P-37A engines replaced the P-9 engines for a further 5% increase. The first RB-57D made its initial flight on 3 November 1955.

The requirement for a new and more capable aircraft next resulted in the RB-57F, which was to be a conversion programme from the RB-57D. The most radical changes were an even larger wing, bigger tail and the replacement of the J65 turbojets with two P&W TF33-P-11 turbofans, each with a thrust of 16,000lb plus provision for two optional P&W J60-P-9 turbojet engines of 3,300lb each attached to pods suspended outboard of the turbofans. The optional turbojets were only used at high altitude and had to be air-started. The ceiling was classified but the aircraft was cleared to 82,000ft.

A completely new and much larger wing gave the RB-57F a span of 122.4ft and a broader chord. With three main spars, it was fabricated with aluminium honeycomb wing panels and bonded skins of aluminium and fibreglass. The design arrangement had been pioneered by work on the Convair B-58 Hustler, which itself had benefitted from work first done by Martin on the RB-57B. As with the earlier B-series wing, tight seals were applied to reduce drag and inhibit buffeting. The wing flaps were deleted but the spoilers were retained from the D-series. In addition, the tail was modified, the height of the vertical fin increased to 19ft as measured from the ground which, with an increase in width, doubled the surface area. This assisted yaw control at 80,000ft.

At the end of 1963 the first two aircraft were sent to the 7907th Combat Support Wing at Rhein-Main AB, Germany, for patrolling the East European border with massive, long-range oblique HIAC-1 cameras. These had a focal length of 66in and could only be carried by the RB-57F. Four aircraft operated on spy missions and one was shot down on 14 December 1965 during a flight over the Black Sea close to Odessa. Wreckage was recovered but not the crew. In 1968 the same aircraft became WB-57Fs, their primary role to monitor atomic tests conducted by China and India.

During the Vietnam War, the B-57 did exactly what it was sought for during the Korean War 15 years earlier. Statistically, it made a major contribution, conducting 6,518 combat sorties in 1967, 2,626 in 1968 and 1,479 in 1969. But the balance between bombing and reconnaissance sorties shifted significantly over that period, 15% of all combat sorties in 1967

Devoid of a bomb bay, the B-58 had a slender fuselage with four under-wing J75-P-17 turbojet engines and provision for three crewmembers in tandem cockpits. (USAF)

Test pilot Fitzhugh 'Fitz' Fulton poses in the forward cockpit in the XB-58. (USAF)

being reconnaissance missions, with 39% in 1968 and more than 71% in 1969.

Overall, throughout its period of operation in the South-East Asia theatre from 1964 to 1969, as a bomber the B-57 flew 31,802 sorties with loss rates varying between 9.7 per 100,000 sorties in South Vietnam, to 16.2 in North Vietnam and 9.7 in Laos. As a reconnaissance platform, RB-57s flew a total of 5,752 sorties, with losses per thousand at 3.6, zero and 3.5 in those three respective sectors.

In total, of the 403 B-57s built, 36 were lost in combat, a further 15 in ground explosions and 137 crashed for various, non-combat reasons, 60 without fatalities.

Also during the Vietnam War, 16 B-57Bs were modified as B-57G night attack aircraft for stopping nocturnal deliveries through Laos. The conversion included laser targeting equipment which allowed very accurate bombing at night – approximately 75% of all bombs dropped by B-57Gs got to within 15ft of their target. But the G had a very short operational life, all 11 surviving aircraft being returned to the US in April 1972.

The type survives today as a research tool for NASA.

CONVAIR B-58A HUSTLER
The origin of this aircraft dates to studies conducted under an Army Air Force contract awarded to Convair in October 1946 for a Generalized Bomber Study (GEBO I) for the investigation of low aspect ratio wings and delta-wings insofar as they applied to a supersonic bomber. Convair examined a staggering 10,000 concepts and configurations, examining the effects of wing area, aspect ratio, thickness ratio and sweep. Also factored in were the effects of different turbojet and turboprop engines and their impact on speed. With a track record in delta-wing studies powered by jet engines, Convair was a natural choice.

GEBO II, a nine-month study to define a high-speed B-47 successor, was launched on 15 June 1949. In April 1950 a combat radius of up to 4,500 miles at speeds of Mach 1.5 was set, penetrating up to 2,000 miles behind enemy borders. At this point the underpinning concept in mind was a parasitic strike weapon carried aloft and to its drop point by a B-36. By early 1951 a new supersonic bomber concept had been produced which, it was believed, could achieve the requirement of the previous April.

However, on 1 February 1952, General Operational Requirement (GOR) SAB-51 defined a Supersonic Aircraft Bomber with a combat radius of 4,600 miles on a single outbound refuelling plus supersonic dash at 50,000ft, with all-weather operation. It had to be simple to maintain, easy to fly and ready within five years. The aircraft had to be small too, since a RAND report indicated that a low radar cross-section was easier to achieve

by reducing the overall size. But later that year, in a revision to the GOR, a previous requirement for high-speed, low altitude capability was eliminated, on the basis that this would be technologically difficult to achieve and could significantly reduce the chances of getting a successful design by 1957.

The Air Force wanted two aircraft and Boeing's MX-1712 was now competing directly with Convair's MX-1626. Then the Air Force decided to open up the requirement to other contractors – namely Douglas, Lockheed, Martin and North American. When their work failed to impress, the Air Force toyed with the notion of opening it all up to the entire aviation industry.

Then the Weapon System concept was introduced, as previously explained. Instead of competitive fly-offs, as had been the case with the B-47 and the B-52, the B-58 would be a single-source contract, the winner chosen on the basis of paper studies after theoretical analysis and evaluation.

Convair was declared the winner on 18 September 1952. The company's original proposal consisted of a delta-wing design powered by three General Electric J53 turbojet engines, one under each wing and the third in the tail. This 17,000lb thrust engine, 23,700lb with reheat, had been specifically designed for Mach 2 performance but it was not the optimum unit. The arrangement was revised on 11 December 1951, deleting the tail engine and replacing the J53 with the J79, the brainchild of the German-American designer Gerhard Neumann.

Fortunately, a flaw in the delta-configured designs coming out of Convair was resolved in December 1952 when NACA's Richard T. Whitcomb

A YB-58 fitted out for flights with a test J93 engine under the fuselage, the powerplant for the XB-70. (USAF)

Ground tests with a mockup of the B-58 ejectable crew pod – designed to replace ejection seats for escape during supersonic flight. (USAF)

Selectable pod configurations were designed for the B-58 – though the system did not enter service. (USAF)

The 116 B-58 Hustlers only served during the 1960s and were never more than a flawed attempt at giving the penetrating bomber survivability. (USAF)

demonstrated that aerodynamic interference drag inherent with this wing form could be circumvented by distributing the entire cross-sectional area of the aircraft along the direction of flight.

By indenting the fuselage over the wing and creating a 'coke-bottle' effect, the area-rule principle was established and would become a common feature of transonic and supersonic aircraft going forward – reflected in the redesigned YF-102A Delta Dagger which first flew on 20 December 1954. This was a big step forward in aerodynamic solutions and was applied to the B-58. But the changes would take two years to complete, integrating the new aerodynamic effects modelling into the already complex wing and fuselage design. The final configuration was selected by the Air Force on 20 March 1953.

Convair test pilot Beryl A. Erickson was at the controls when the first XB-58 took to the air on 11 November 1956, with systems specialist John D. McEachern and test engineer Charles P. Harrison on the third tandem seat. The first aircraft exceeded Mach 1 on 30 December and was joined by the second XB-58 (55-0661) on 16 February 1957.

The first production B-58A (59-2428, misreported in numerous places as 58-1023) flew in September 1959 and went to the 6592nd Test Squadron at Carswell AFB before assignment to the 43rd BW, Carswell. The B-58 was declared operational on 1 August 1960 and from that date on took an impressive number of awards, prevailing in almost every competition it entered. It secured the Bleriot trophy, the Thompson trophy, the MacKay trophy, the Bendix trophy and the Harmon trophy. The only other unit to operate the bomber was the 305th BW at Bunker AFB, Indiana, later renamed Grissom AFB, from late 1961.

Within a year of its first flight the aircraft had managed Mach 2.11 at over 50,000ft, conducted two successful mission pod drops from 42,000ft at Mach 2, demonstrated a straight-line run for 1.5hrs at more than Mach 1.15, and zoomed without pod from 50,000ft at Mach 2 to 68,000ft at Mach 1.13.

As impressive as all this was, from an operational point of view the aircraft had serious drawbacks. On a single refuelling, the aircraft had a combat radius of 4,373 miles but without refuelling a mere 2,700 miles. A single refuelling required a whole tanker's worth of fuel, whereas two tankers could fill three B-52s, and the delivery cost was far greater per bomb than for the B-52. It came down to what else the B-58 could do and apart from speed to evade interception there was very little to no advantage.

Critics seized upon an accurate press report that, at a cost of $3bn for 118 aircraft ($25m each), the B-58 was worth more than its weight in gold.

Another stopgap attempt at providing fast, low-level strike was the General Dynamics FB-111, procured to replace the B-58 Hustler. The type was a variant of the F-111A fighter-bomber which had been developed as a replacement for the F-105 Thunderchief. (USAF)

The Electronically Agile Radar specifically developed for the low flying FB-111, from which the B-1B Lancer's AN/APQ-164 was developed. (Wikicommons, Daderot)

Projected costs over the full production run of 116 airframes ran to each being priced at $14m. The established cost for a B-52 was $6-7m and the B-47 a mere $2m. The operating costs were much greater due to the unique nature of the aircraft's requirements during servicing and maintenance. Plans for a longer-range B-58B with a redesigned interior, greater internal fuel capacity and several other refinements were abandoned. But it did have a negative consequence in another sense.

Previously, only fighters had broken the sound barrier and then only rarely and in limited areas. With the advent of the Mach 2 bomber the effect was raised as a potential annoyance to the civilian population – which in turn could be politically counter-productive. In July 1959 the Air Force took 55-0660 for tests

over the Wallops Island, Virginia, test range to measure the effect.

The results found that there was indeed a socially undesirable acoustic impact. In short order, supersonic flights of all types over land were prohibited – with a few exceptions for very remote and largely unpopulated areas. Individual states passed their own laws, forming the framework in the early 1970s which would deny the Anglo-French Concorde Mach 2 airliner access to supersonic overflight corridors across the United States.

Every aspect of the B-58's design and engineering was new and pioneering. Designed for sustained Mach 2 flight, the temperature and structural stress levels were defining boundaries, with a materials temperature of 260°F (127°C) and a load factor of 2g at maximum take-off weight of 163,000lb, or 3g at a predicted combat weight of 100,000lb. Based on these factors, total airframe life was calculated to be 7,000hrs.

Most of its structural material was aluminium, or steel in areas exposed to exceptionally high temperatures. Long before detailed design had been completed, in addition to aluminium alloys, engineers selected a range of fibreglass honeycomb sandwich core structures, adhesives and composites as well as new lubricants, sealants and coolant fluids for use on the B-58.

The delta-wing had a leading edge sweep of 60 degrees and a trailing edge sweep of -10 degrees with a 3-degree incidence angle. The wing had a thickness ratio of 4.08%, an aspect ratio of 2.096 and a total area of 1,364sq ft across a span of 56.75ft, minus elevons. With a total length of 96.75ft the fuselage supported the wing mid-fuselage, the wing itself being a full cantilever with

cambered leading edges and outboard tips. Leading edges were of sandwich construction without any form of internal bracing and the wing itself was of multi-spar construction with panel coverings secured by titanium screws.

The inboard bulkheads adjacent to the wheel well were flanged away to allow retraction space for the main landing gear. The individual spars were contoured conformal with the aerofoil itself and the sweepback in spars close to areas around the wingtip section provided added rigidity, a key design goal in the wing fitments. The corrugated aluminium spars were spaced 11-15in apart with no chordwise ribs, only special members for securing the elevons, engine nacelles and the main landing gear. The cross section of the wing at the main landing gear station was increased so as to obtain the void necessary for full enclosure.

The underslung mission pod extended below the nose to the midway point of the forward landing gear well. To facilitate retraction, the twin-wheel bogie was attached to a dual-leg trapeze which lifted it up and forward before raising it further and back into the well. In this way the gear avoided colliding with the nose of the pod.

Key to range was fuel and a wet wing was inevitable given the small size of the aircraft; total fuel load was 100,070lb across both wings and fuselage tanks. Sealed on the outside during construction and assembly, due to the shallow depth of the wing the seams were heavily insulated from leaks and this afforded minimum weight for maximum sealing.

The four engine nacelles were designed for minimum frontal area, faired into a conformal structure specifically sized for the J79 engine, with semi-monocoque construction. Each nacelle was equipped with a central spike, variable in position to control the airflow and maintain an efficient volume passing to the engine and proportional to the speed of the aircraft. Designed to move fore and aft, the spike remained in the retracted position up to Mach 1.42, after which activation introduced power to an actuator which moved it forward at a rate proportional to the speed. The J79-GE-5 engine produced 15,600lb thrust at 7,460rpm with reheat or 9,700lb dry. This axial-flow engine had a 17-stage compressor, 10 annular combustion chambers, a three-stage turbine, afterburner and variable exhaust nozzle.

The B-58 was one of the first aircraft to provide the pilot with an audible warning of a crucial parameter or of a potentially hazardous situation. Known as 'Bitching Betty', the taped recording was stored on a device developed by Northrop – a female voice being chosen by ballot as clearer, and getting faster attention. It was also used to inform the crew that an emergency procedure had been selected by the electronic sensors into which it was wired. This concept,

Searching For A Successor

F-111E/FB-111A THREE-VIEW

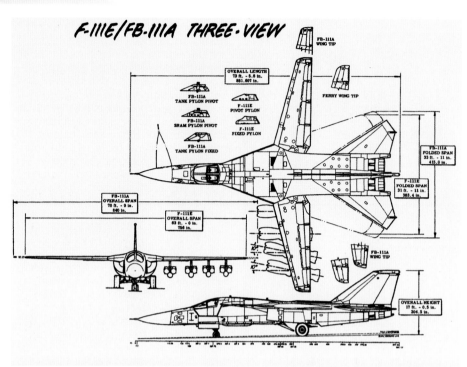

The general arrangement of the FB-111 compared to the F-111E, displaying the longer wingspan inherited from the Navy's aborted F-111B and the location of underwing pylons. (General Dynamics)

Configured for night flying, the F-111's cockpit layout and operational flight routines benefit from side-by-side seating. (USAF)

used to avoid crew-overload in strike aircraft during the Vietnam War, became the inspiration for the 'voice' of the HAL computer in 2001: A Space Odyssey and moved into automobiles during the 1970s and 1980s. It is common today in car GPS systems.

The B-58 was the only jet bomber not to have an internal bomb bay, the carriage of nuclear weapons under the inboard wing pylons being a later addition to the aircraft's lethality. Instead, the aircraft's underslung mission pod could contain fuel, nuclear weapons or other equipment in a bewildering variety of configurations.

One early pod configuration, the 27,108lb MC-1, was envisaged as a rocket-propelled bomb container with a stand-off range of 160 miles. During a

flight time of 65sec, a 15,000lb thrust Bell LR81-BA-1 motor would power the pod through a pre-programmed flight path from a wide range of optional deployment speeds and altitudes.

The MB-1C pod initially became the standard for the B-58. Weighing 36,087lb when fully fuelled and carrying an atomic weapon, it had a length of 57ft and a maximum diameter of 5ft. This pod included fore and aft fuel tanks, a forward equipment bay and a tail section with fins. It was attached to the underside of the fuselage by three hooks, pneumatically retracted for release. During a mission it would supply fuel to the aircraft until, over the target, it would be released in its entirety – the atomic weapon and the empty tanks falling together.

However, in practice there were serious and largely insoluble problems with fuel leakage from the pod tanks and this prevented its further employment after initial production lots.

The definitive pod consisted of two components, each of which could be detached separately. There were two fuel tanks in the lower component, which had a length of 54ft, a diameter of 5ft and a weight of 26,000lb. The upper component also had two tanks but with the nuclear device positioned between them. It had a length of 35ft, a diameter of 3.5ft and a loaded weight of 11,970lb.

In December 1965, Secretary of Defense Robert McNamara announced the decision to remove the B-58 from the inventory by 1970, retire 345 older B-52s and buy 210 FB-111 bombers, a variant of the F-111 tactical fighter-bomber. It was a convoluted saga that would run for almost 20 years before resolution. Peak inventory was reported by SAC in 1964 with 94 Hustlers on strength, followed by progressive decline, with the last recorded in 1969, the year the FB-111, now also considerably reduced in expected numbers, entered service. The B-58 was struck from the register on 31 January 1970, following an announcement three months earlier that many bases would be closed.

GENERAL DYNAMICS FB-111

During the late 1950s the Air Force's Tactical Air Command began looking for a successor to its F-100 and F-105 fighter-bombers, while the Navy needed a new fleet air defence fighter. Both had begun issuing requirements when Robert McNamara was appointed Secretary of Defense in 1961.

McNamara noted a marked similarity in those requirements – the ability to carry heavy loads of fuel and weapons, high supersonic performance, two engines, two crew, variable geometry wings – and determined that all requirements could conceivably be met by a single aircraft, albeit with adaptations particular to the needs of the service using it. This would theoretically ensure massive savings not only in development but also in parts and spares going forward.

The Air Force and the Navy protested vehemently that their requirements were different and that separate programmes were necessary – but McNamara nevertheless gave the go-ahead for a single programme – Tactical Fighter Experimental (TFX). The TFX requirements were largely based on what the Air Force wanted, much to the Navy's chagrin, and proposals came in from Boeing, General Dynamics (formerly Convair), Lockheed, McDonnell, North American and Republic.

General Dynamics' pitch was chosen in November 1962 because it offered greater commonality between the Air Force and Navy versions. The result was the F-111A, the first example of which flew on 21 December 1964, and the proposed Navy version, the F-111B, which first flew on 18 May 1965. The F-111A was accepted by the Air Force but the Navy variant was cancelled and it eventually bought the Grumman F-14 instead – once McNamara was out of the picture.

The Air Force F-111A, powered by two Pratt & Whitney TF30 engines delivering 18,500lb thrust with afterburner, entered an extended test phase between December 1964 and March 1972, an additional 11 aircraft being added to the original development and test programme. Considerable problems with weight increases and engine troubles ensued but the first flight of the initial production version took place on 12 February 1967 with added trials endorsing the general characteristics of the aircraft and encouraging accelerated plans to send it to the war in Vietnam for combat evaluation.

It was distinctively different from the norm for Air Force fighters/fighter-bombers of the period, in that the cockpit had side-by-side seating and of course it famously pioneered the use in service of variable geometry wings. GD gave it a single pivot point for each wing located in a glove box outboard of the fuselage and faired to the latter by an extended fillet blending to the airframe just aft of the cockpit.

The wing could sweep between 16 degrees (fully forward) to 72.5 degrees and possessed aspect ratios of 6.75 and 1.57, respectively. The two sweep screw jacks were interconnected with both wings controlled by either one. Pitch and roll control were provided by horizontal stabilisers moving together or differentially. As designed, wing sweep was locked at 26 degrees with store pylons, or 55 degrees for some oversize loads on inboard stations.

Full-span flaps and slats permitted optimum low-speed lift and spoilers were added for roll augmentation forward of 45 degrees. Overall performance requirements pushed the design in several respects including the soft-field operation which dictated protection from air intake debris ingestion with slots in the lower fuselage to blow material away. The landing gear too was large and mounted on a crossbeam with a centre shock-absorber. The retraction system used a parallelogram mechanism to keep the wheels adjacent to each other before folding forward between the intake ducts.

The engine itself was a development programme only marginally ahead of the airframe in engineering design and test and its performance relied heavily on intake geometry which was both functional and elegant in design. Adopting a variable inlet spike-and-cone concept, flight trials disclosed a sensitivity of the TF30 engine to sudden thrust changes or altitude regimes where it would experience compressor stalls and surges, all of which was traced to the inlet.

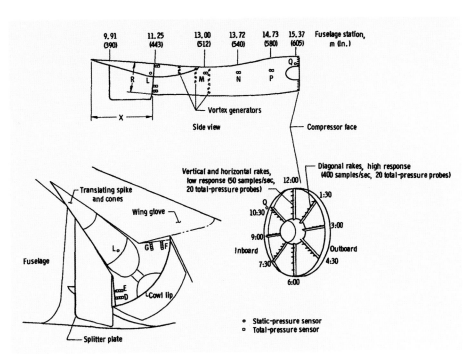

The much modified inlet and intake geometry which evolved through the manufacturer's Triple Plow programme. (General Dynamics)

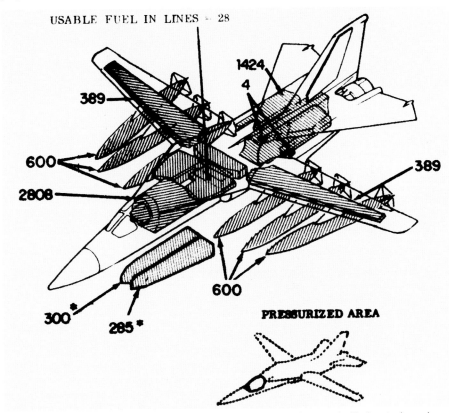

Refined for range, the internal fuel capacity of the FB-111 was supplemented with drop tanks and additional tank capacity in the forward bomb bay. (USAF)

The location of the inlet was beneath the forward part of the wing/fuselage root fairing right where the disturbed air from the wing impinged on the fuselage. This sent stagnant air into the engine and the total problem involving both the sensitivity of the engine and the design of the inlet duct became a major programme for GD and P&W.

The TF30-P-1 was fitted to start with, then improvements were made to a P-3

variant whereby afterburner thrust was modulated by way of five separate burner injectors, increasing thrust in equal increments from 20% to 100%. This increased stability and also improved fuel efficiency. But it came at a price, dropping commonality from 85% to 70% due to major changes to the aft section of the fuselage.

The inlet issue was addressed through the Triple Plow programme, the first

FB-IIIA PRODUCTION BREAKDOWN
B-I 3-on PRODUCTION

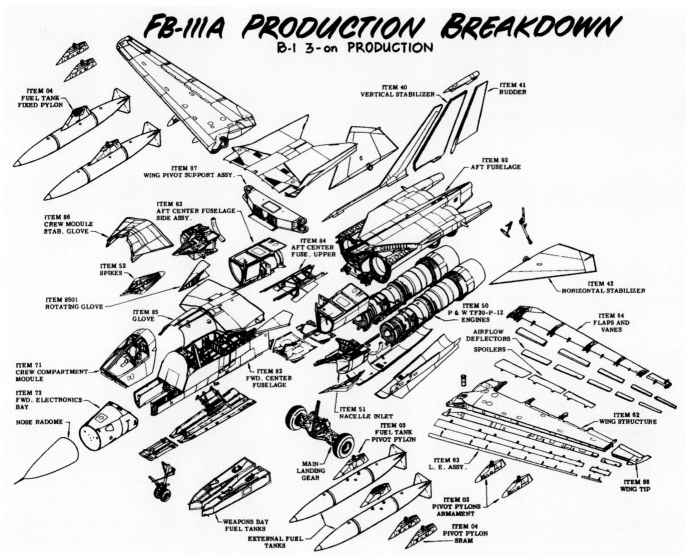

ITEM 04
FUEL TANK
FIXED PYLON

ITEM 40
VERTICAL STABILIZER

ITEM 41
RUDDER

ITEM 92
AFT FUSELAGE

ITEM 87
WING PIVOT SUPPORT ASSY.

ITEM 83
AFT CENTER FUSELAGE
SIDE ASSY.

ITEM 86
CREW MODULE
STAB. GLOVE

ITEM 84
AFT CENTER
FUSE. UPPER

ITEM 42
HORIZONTAL STABILIZER

ITEM 52
SPIKES

ITEM 8501
ROTATING GLOVE

ITEM 85
GLOVE

ITEM 50
P & W TF30-P-12
ENGINES

AIRFLOW
DEFLECTORS

SPOILERS

ITEM 64
FLAPS AND
VANES

ITEM 71
CREW COMPARTMENT
MODULE

ITEM 82
FWD. CENTER
FUSELAGE

ITEM 73
FWD. ELECTRONICS
BAY

NOSE RADOME

ITEM 51
NACELLE INLET

ITEM 03
FUEL TANK
PIVOT PYLON

ITEM 62
WING STRUCTURE

MAIN
LANDING
GEAR

ITEM 63
L. E. ASSY.

ITEM 66
WING TIP

ITEM 03
PIVOT PYLONS
ARMAMENT

WEAPONS BAY
FUEL TANKS

ITEM 04
PIVOT PYLON
SRAM

EXTERNAL FUEL
TANKS

A detailed overview of systems and equipment distribution in the FB-111. Note the internal fuel tanks optional for the forward bomb bay and the underwing drop tanks for greater range. (General Dynamics)

phase of which moved the splitter plate further out from the fuselage and retained the inlet cone with a third plough added to the existing two to suck in boundary air beneath the underside of the wing.

Flow was further improved by adding 20 vortex generators in each inlet. This was first flown on the 31st production aircraft on 24 September 1967. The Triple Plow II upgrade appeared two years later and removed the splitter plate completely, with the cone lengthened by 18in and placed a little farther away from the fuselage. Collectively these improvements raised top speed from Mach 2.2 to Mach 2.5.

As part of the evaluation phase, the Air Force sent six F-111As to Vietnam. The first combat mission was on the night of 28 March 1968 when a single aircraft (66-0018) conducted a single-pass strike against a coastal military storage post, getting in and out without trouble. By 22 April some 55 'Combat Lancer' missions had been flown with mixed results and three losses – 50% of the aircraft sent.

The F-111A received heavy criticism in the media as a result but it later transpired

that all three aircraft had been lost due to horizontal stabiliser malfunctions, rather than to enemy action.

By February 1972, the F-111 had completed 150,000hrs of testing and records show that it had a 40% better safety record than the next safest combat aircraft, the Convair F-106. Next a series of improvements, modifications and upgrades were combined under the Harvest Reaper programme, delayed slightly while a review of lessons from Combat Lancer was conducted.

The last of 158 F-111As, including test and evaluation aircraft, was delivered on 30 August 1969, 10 days after the first flight of the F-111E which had been developed to incorporate Triple Plow II improvements on the production line. This offered better stores management and attack radar, a total of 94 of this type being procured with the last delivered on 28 May 1971.

Out of alphabetical sequence due to its protracted development, the F-111D had been approved back in January 1966 and the first of 96 took to the air on 15 May 1970. It became the most technologically

advanced of the type, incorporating Autonetics' complex and outrageously expensive Mark II avionics suite.

The final variant of this tactical fighter-bomber, the F-111F made its first flight on 13 October 1971, the last of 106 incorporating improved TF30-P-100 engines, better and less costly avionics and minor upgrades. Additional upgrades were applied to this variant during the 1980s but it represented the definitive F-111 for the role originally envisaged.

But there were others, including the F-111K, identified as the RAF variant but cancelled by the British government in 1965, and the F-111C which was the export version for Australia which was essentially an F-111A but with the longer wings of the F-111B and the strengthened undercarriage of the FB-111. A final variation emerged from the basic F-111A, 42 of which were converted into the EF-111A Raven electronic warfare aircraft which served with the Air Force from 1983 to 1998.

Back in 1965, Secretary McNamara had cancelled the B-58 Hustler and was preparing to retire all B-52s by 1971.

Proposed as a successor to the FB-111 with longer range, advanced electronics, better performance and cost reductions, the FB-111H was a non-starter. It appears here in period concept art. (General Dynamics)

Strategic Air Command urgently needed a new aircraft and McNamara had little hesitation in ordering a strategic bomber version of the F-111 to fill the gap. SAC had been attempting to acquire a new long-range supersonic bomber under the Advanced Manned Strategic Aircraft (AMSA) programme, which would eventually deliver the B-1A, but McNamara's strategy was to leave long-range strike to ICBMs. All long-range and strategic bombers were to be eliminated and the SAC would have to use the same aircraft as everyone else – the SAC variant being designated FB-111A.

The possibility of developing the F-111 into an SAC bomber had been proposed by GD in late 1963 with two options. Under McNamara's plan of 10 December 1965, the Air Force would get 263 FB-111As to replace 345 B-52s and 80 B-58s. SAC pressed for FB-111A availability by mid-1968 but McNamara stalled so that the FB-111A procurement decision was not made until 7 February 1966, with the FB-111A attached to a production order for the F-111A under WS-129A.

The first FB-111A – a converted F-111A – made its first flight on 31 July 1967. SAC got to fly a production example on 13 July 1968 while the first seven aircraft entered a lengthy test phase which was not completed until mid-1972. Production was then cut to 126 in November 1968 and then back to 76 in March 1969. This was due to technical uncertainties about the aircraft's performance, delays to development of the advanced avionics and general programme costs.

The final cut was made by the incoming Nixon Administration's Secretary of Defense Melvin Laird in conjunction with a decision to formally progress the AMSA programme and thereby the B-1A.

Creating the FB-111A from the F-111A required a simple set of changes originally, but the necessary alterations became more and more extensive over time, transforming the aircraft

in specification and performance. Structural changes included the longer wings of the cancelled Navy F-111B, a maximum internal fuel load of 5,623 US gallons including that in two optional aft weapons bay tanks, plus the option of six underwing jettisonable 600 US gallon tanks. Overall the range of the FB-111A was 3,170 miles compared with 2,660 miles for the fighter-bomber.

Mass grew to a maximum take-off weight of 119,243lb, a mid-air refuelled weight of 122,900lb and a maximum landing weight of 109,000lb. The heavier aircraft required a stiffer and more robust landing gear, stressed to a sink rate of 8ft per second. Redesigned brakes were needed too.

A key element in the FB-111A was the Autonetics Mark II avionics suite initially planned for the F-111D, soaring costs for which had already slashed production of that variant. A scaled-back Mark IIB in development for the F-111F was thus imported to the FB-111A. Some differences were required so as to adapt it to the SAC mission, including automatic stores release, and it had satellite communication and star-tracker navigation for updates to the inertial navigation system. Integrated with the evolution of the Autonetics avionics was the Short Range Attack Missile (SRAM), developed as a replacement for the AGM-28 Hound Dog stand-off weapon.

SRAM was an integral part of the AMSA bid but it was also directed to the B-52 and the FB-111A with the specific function of taking out radars and SAM clusters with a conventional or W69, 200KT nuclear warhead. The FB-111A could carry four SRAMs but the missile did not enter service until April 1972. Other weapons carried by the FB-111A included a range of conventional bombs or optional B-43, B-57 and B-61 nuclear weapons. Total weapons load for most missions was 10,000lb, although the aircraft was capable of carrying more than that for very short strikes.

The FB-111A entered service with the 4007th Combat Crew Training squadron of the 340th BG on 8 October 1969. The last was handed over to SAC on 30 June 1971, serving with the 380th BW and the 509th BW, the year in which the FB-111A become combat operational. Over the next two years, the Air Force put the aircraft through a series of upgrade programmes, with improved ECM and other modifications. With much reduced range compared to the B-52, the FB-111A had limited capacity for both deployment options and targets within the Soviet Union and the Warsaw Pact countries and their dedicated assignments remain classified to this day.

It took a long time to get the Mark II and the SRAM missile integrated and it was not declared operational until 1974. Following the cancellation of the B-1A in 1977, General Dynamics tried unsuccessfully to sell an improved variant, the proposed FB-111B in which 155 FB-111As would have been modified with a longer, 88ft fuselage incorporating extra fuel for greater range and additional volume for advanced avionics. Two years later GD presented equally unsuccessful design plans for an FB-111H, with F101 engines replacing the TF30s and considerable changes which would have produced a completely different aircraft.

In 1988, the type's role now redundant, 35 FB-111As began conversion back to the tactical fighter-bomber role under the designation F-111G and the remaining FB-111As were retired from 1990 to 1991.

The FB-111A had served SAC well and progressed the operational envelope through the use of advanced avionics and radar systems. As an interim between the B-58A and the B-1A, it provided an operational stop-gap which outperformed the expectations of many, especially critics who opined their views without experiencing the aircraft first-hand. It served SAC as a Mach 2 bomber for 22 years, bridging the gap between tactical and strategic roles, a capability which would remain intact for the B-1B and B-2.

ROCKWELL B-1A AND B-1B LANCER

First Flight: 23 December 1974

The search for a successor to the B-52 resumed with the cancellation of the B-70 in September 1961 when RAND examined far-out options for a future bomber force: a hypersonic, Mach 5-8 boost-glide bomber; a supersonic, high-altitude bomber with a performance similar to the B-70; or a low-altitude transonic/supersonic bomber. The latter was seen as the most promising and relevant to the unfolding threats anticipated for the 1970s/80s. RAND favoured a high-subsonic, low-altitude penetration speed with extended range.

With hindsight it could be concluded that the search for a B-52 replacement was orientated in the wrong direction. Major strides in the evolution of air defence systems had already made the concept of a high-speed/high-altitude penetrating bomber redundant. There had already been several false starts and uncertain paths, leading to the B-58 and the FB-111A, although the latter did give SAC a world-leading low-level, supersonic, all-weather strategic bomber.

A wide range of Air Force bomber studies had been under way since the mid-1950s, adhering to the logical principle that the start of flight tests for a new aircraft should trigger studies for its successor. In some respects it was this logic which kept the bomber-mafia fuelled with enthusiasm for big aircraft dropping lots of munitions on distant targets. The initial rush of Air Force studies known as SLAB (Subsonic Low Altitude Bomber) began in 1961 and was completed by June 1962. The result was a call for something with a 12,000lb bomb load and a range of 12,660 miles, of which 4,949 miles had to be at low level.

Quickly thereafter came ERSA (Extended Range Strike Aircraft) postulating a 10,000lb bomb load and a range of 10,070 miles, of which 2,877 miles would be flown at a height of 500ft or less. The Air Force specified a take-off weight of no more than 600,000lb and the use of variable-geometry wings to support low-level and high-speed dash.

Both were superseded in August 1963 by LAMP (Low Altitude Manned Penetrator), considerably downsizing the gross weight to 350,000lb with a bomb load of 20,000lb and with a range of 7,135 miles, of which 2,300 miles would be at low altitude. Implicit in all three was a realisation that some form of low-altitude capability was essential. In addition, the calculations showed that a less costly approach to delivering gravity bombs or stand-off weapons would be by way of less reliance on speed and more on bomb load and range.

By mid-1963 a Manned Aircraft Studies Steering Group (MASSG) had been set up to appraise all these disparate studies and requirements. Led by Lt Gen James Ferguson a wider range of possibilities were examined, embracing supersonic reconnaissance aircraft, long-endurance types and also the LAMP concept which the group decided was the most promising. Noted missile czar Gen Bernard A. Schriever, commanding the Air Force Systems Command (AFSC), met with the Project Forecast team – looking into long-range requirements for the Air Force – and the MASSG in October 1963 to sum up the various thoughts and rationales for specific requirements and technical configurations. Their conclusion was yet another in the long line of increasingly tortured acronyms – Advanced Manned Precision Strike System (AMPSS).

A B-1B performs a fly-by during a firepower demonstration, displaying the sleek lines and efficient aerodynamic qualities of this semi-stealthy bomber. (USAF)

Boeing, General Dynamics and North American Aviation were asked to conduct low-level studies of AMPSS a few weeks later. This proved fruitless since all three utilised unrealistic costing and schedule data while approaching the requirement in very disparate ways. As previously indicated, Secretary McNamara was now in charge and was barely lukewarm over the whole bomber issue. He kept an unhelpfully tight rein on the money and the resources available to the industry analysts.

By mid-1964 the confused tangle of requirements and possible solutions had reached an impasse and AMPSS was superseded by the Advanced Manned Strategic Aircraft (AMSA) study, defined in July that year as a supersonic bomber with a gross weight of 375,000lb and a range of 7,250 miles, of which 2,300 miles had to be flown at low level. Maximum speed would be Mach 2.2 rather than the Mach 3 specified for the B-70, unusual conservatism for an Air Force never shy of demanding unachievable capabilities!

The search for a cost-effective solution impelled McNamara to continue low-level funding of AMSA and associated activity to allow new technologies to grow and feed both unmanned missile and manned aircraft programmes. He was unable to accept the need for a B-52 successor, yet when the three contracted companies issued their reports at the end of 1964 there was hope that some decision was pending, optimism encouraged several months later when General Electric and Pratt & Whitney were funded to build demonstrator AMSA candidate engines.

But the decision that came was the one on 10 December 1965 in which McNamara announced retirement of B-58s and B-52C and F variants by mid-1971 and procurement of the FB-111A, as described in the preceding section. His logic was based on pricing estimates that AMSA would cost $9-11bn compared with $1.9bn for a fleet of FB-111As. The Pentagon refused to fund AMSA as a development programme, although a contract for advanced avionics went to Autonetics (a division of what was now North American Rockwell) and IBM for work on systems which could be of use on AMSA, if it ever got approved. This also embraced 10 subcontractors on work to develop specific hardware sets, including forward-looking radar, Doppler radar and infrared surveillance equipment, and this did much to advance the state of the art when approval finally came.

And that was where it rested for the next three years until, with McNamara gone, on 6 November 1968 an AMSA Development Concept Paper was circulated through the Pentagon which stipulated that the new bomber would be required to fly at Mach 0.85-0.95 and have a dash capability of Mach 1.2 flying

Rollout of the first B-1A on 26 October 1974 in anti-flash white with a modest workforce in attendance. (Rockwell International)

Only the first three B-1A prototypes were finished in white, the fourth emerging in a trial camouflage scheme of sand, brown and green effect. (Rockwell International)

200ft above rolling terrain. At high altitude it was required to achieve Mach 2.2. This became the single most important evaluation of the AMSA programme and would have repercussions across to the B-1A. Shared with the highest officials in the Pentagon, the paper proposed four optional ways to proceed.

OPTIONS AND CHOICES

The first option was for a three-year design competition but no prototypes, during which trade-off studies of different configurations, wind tunnel tests, detailed design and production options would be completed. A production decision would be made based on this activity and only

Rockwell B-1A and B-1B Lancer

then would a decision be made as to the value of the programme to SAC. This approach would provide an unassailable mountain of verified data enabling informed decisions and provide authentic cost and contractual requirements. The disadvantage was that there would be no prototype and no flight testing.

Option two supported a 15-month definition phase following which a contractor would be selected, the design frozen and development production

contracts negotiated. This option would eliminate the need to fund contractors for three years and could get the aircraft into service earlier because it would move more rapidly into production. It was the epitome of concurrency but had high risk and because the design would be frozen at the end of the contract definition phase the specification would be set eight years before the aircraft achieved operational status. There was even lower confidence that the Air Force could

anticipate technological developments, and engineering as well as manufacturing capabilities that far in advance.

The third option would delay a systems development decision for a year, a period during which it would continue on the same path it had been on for several years. It would be the minimum cost option in the short term but lack the effort required to solve the concept's basic technological challenges, such as that most basic of all – meeting the specification. It lacked any momentum, reiterated the slow pace of the McNamara years and would do nothing to advance the programme to production or service entry. The fourth option was the same as the first but require the contractors to examine subsonic designs as an analogue against which the more ambitious primary requirement could be assessed both on effort, timescale and cost.

The general consensus supported the first option although some voices were raised for option four, if only to keep open options on alternative concepts and implementation strategies. In the end it was agreed to go with that and to conduct trade-off studies on subsonic systems and periodically review the subsonic/supersonic issue at a programme level, on which in 1968 there was no consensus.

For eight years from January 1961, the Kennedy and Johnson era had seen a surge in conflict across South-East Asia, a massive growth in the defence budget and a near decimation in the manned aircraft programmes, especially bombers. When Nixon became President in January 1969 everything changed. Pledged to end the war in Vietnam, Nixon was not shy when it came to taking force to the enemy, sanctioning an expansion of the bombing campaign in a successful effort to drive the communists to the conference table and to the Paris Peace Talks.

Two key players were brought in: Melvin R. Laird as Secretary of Defense and Robert C. Seamans, Jr, (formerly of NASA) as Secretary of the Air Force. Both liked bombers and each supported the manned penetrator as an instrument of foreign policy, applicable to a flexible conventional or nuclear war. And both men were determined to provide the Air Force with a successor to the B-52 – not merely a replacement.

As a sign of their committed intention, in April 1969 Seamans applied the designation B-1A to what had during the previous five years been known as the AMSA. By the end of that year there had been some balancing between desirable performance and cost and the Mach 1.2 low-altitude speed requirement had been reduced to Mach 0.95 and the bombload capacity reduced from 32 to 24 SRAM attack missiles. Once again, four development options were

The underside of the fourth prototype (76-014) showing the mottle-line between the low level camouflage and the white undersurface, together with reduced size for the USAF wing insignia. (USAF)

CREW MODULE ESCAPE SYSTEM

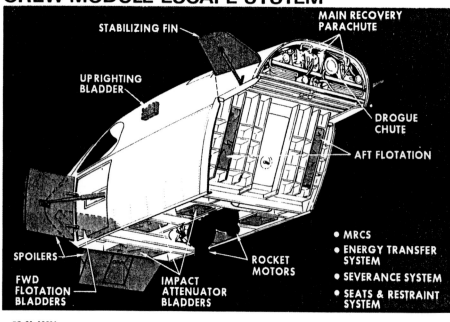

STABILIZING FIN

MAIN RECOVERY PARACHUTE

UPRIGHTING BLADDER

DROGUE CHUTE

AFT FLOTATION

SPOILERS

ROCKET MOTORS

FWD FLOTATION BLADDERS

IMPACT ATTENUATOR BLADDERS

- MRCS
- ENERGY TRANSFER SYSTEM
- SEVERANCE SYSTEM
- SEATS & RESTRAINT SYSTEM

DS-81-10591

(002A)

The B-1A was designed with a complex crew escape pod but this was replaced with the Aces II ejection seat. (Rockwell International)

Set up for a press photo-shoot, a B-1A prototype with the proposed crew escape pod beyond its tail. (Rockwell International)

set out to replace those laid down by the Development Concept Paper of 1968.

The first postulated a six-month design competition followed by a source selection decision to accelerate the programme and get into full-scale development during 1969, reducing costs by up to 13%. Although it would eliminate a lot of initial paper studies, which were increasingly suspect as a sensible way to decide the future of the US bomber force, it was high risk because the configuration would be decided prior to flight test.

The second option was to spend three months soliciting proposals from industry from which two contenders would be selected for a six-month detailed definition phase, after which a single contractor would be chosen. While providing more base data upon which to decide on a specific design it would add 3% to the cost.

A third option would extend the competition into hardware development so that judgements could be made through prototyping. That approach had been proven historically to carry the best end result but it could cost more and delay decisions over procurement. The fourth option was to postpone the design competition and re-examine requirements, although this smacked of McNamara rules and nobody wanted those. After much voting at the Pentagon, the first option was selected.

Paradoxically, a new request for proposals was delayed until 3 November

1969 in an effort to speed up acquisition by putting the requirement through a more thorough, Pentagon-wide review process – clearing the way for pre-determined agreement on specifications and mission profiles. Thus, engineering development really began in March 1969

and prepared the way for industry further down the decision track.

By now a fundamental decision had been reached about the speed of the aircraft and since 1968 a Mach 2.2 capability had been written in. This would dictate aspects of the airframe,

The first B-1A prototype (74-0158) with the F101-100 engine specially developed for this aircraft as far back as the requirement posed by the Advanced Manned Strategic Aircraft (AMSA) programme. (Rockwell International)

Rockwell B-1A and B-1B Lancer

MAJOR AREAS OF REDESIGN
- **New B-1B drawings** = 4827
- **Revised B-1 drawings for B-1B** = 1015 } 17,132 drawings
- **Existing B-1 drawings** = 11,290

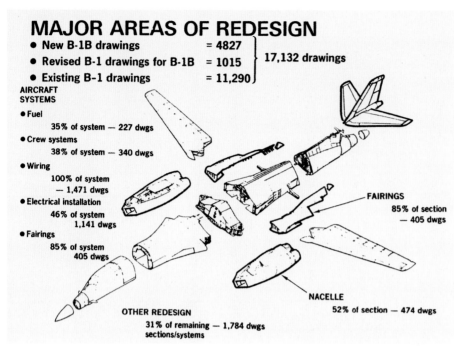

AIRCRAFT SYSTEMS
- Fuel
  35% of system — 227 dwgs
- Crew systems
  38% of system — 340 dwgs
- Wiring
  100% of system — 1,471 dwgs
- Electrical installation
  46% of system 1,141 dwgs
- Fairings
  85% of system 405 dwgs

FAIRINGS
85% of section — 405 dwgs

NACELLE
52% of section — 474 dwgs

OTHER REDESIGN
31% of remaining — 1,784 dwgs sections/systems

When the B-1 programme was reinstated in October 1981 the B-1B emerged as a low-level bomber and cruise missile carrier after several years' work to adapt the original design to the needs of the 1980s and beyond. (Rockwell International)

B-1B STRUCTURAL MODE CONTROL SYSTEM

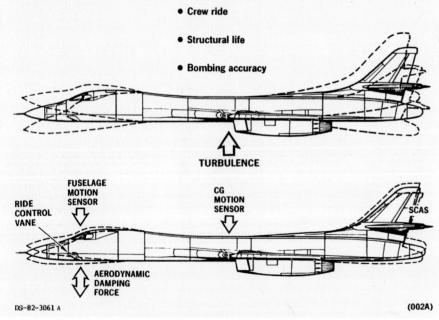

- Crew ride
- Structural life
- Bombing accuracy

TURBULENCE

RIDE CONTROL VANE

FUSELAGE MOTION SENSOR

CG MOTION SENSOR

SCAS

AERODYNAMIC DAMPING FORCE

DS-82-3061 A   (002A)

From the crew training manual for the B-1B, aspects of the Structural Mode Control System (SMCS), an integration of control logic and software for selective damping and motions sensors in aircraft attitude and in the centre of gravity. (Rockwell International)

particularly the engine inlet geometry, and require that crew escape be made by means of a capsule. In fact, many of the features of the B-1A requirement blended the range and lift capacity of the B-52 with the speed and low-altitude capability of the FB-111A.

The Air Force Source Evaluation Board and its 600 representatives met on 8 December 1969 and began a lengthy examination of design options as presented by the four bidding contenders, Lockheed having joined the three original

companies. On 19 December further avionics development contracts went to Autonetics and IBM but prospective defence budgets for 1970 and 1971 were reduced and that required readjustment of cost appraisals. The scrutiny was intense and the detail extensive, with several months spent examining multiple options.

The Pentagon announced on 5 June 1970 that North American Rockwell had been selected to build the B-1A (most references from this date deleting the 'A' applied initially), with five flying test aircraft

and two test articles. General Electric would supply the engines under an initial contract for 40 units. Gone was the concurrency concept and a new 'fly-before-you-buy' programme was introduced under the new systems concept.

The Air Force could only estimate the number of aircraft it might get – that would be up to Congress – but it planned on 244, a figure considered by most analysts to be wildly optimistic. Some 200hrs of flight tests would precede a production decision, following 18,000hrs of wind tunnel tests and 12,000hrs on the engines. Overall, 1,060 flight hours were to be completed, with Phase I contractor and Phase II Air Force testing.

As always in these decisions, the selection of North American Rockwell had been based on political, economic, partisan, technical and cost bases. Politicians wanted an actuarial spread of work across the United States so that at least some of it would be spent in their local constituencies; in fact 3,000 suppliers in 47 States had contracts on the B-1A programme. Economic grounds were fired by competition and governments like a lot of thriving contenders to drive down prices; Rockwell's work on the Apollo programme was winding down, production of the F-100 Super Sabre was drawing to a close, the commercial Sabreliner was going nowhere and the F-15 contract had gone to McDonnell Douglas.

Boeing had the massive Minuteman ICBM contract and General Dynamics would get the equally lucrative Trident SLBM work. Ironically, within three years North American Rockwell would get the Shuttle Orbiter contract. Partisan satisfaction was met by a general consensus on both sides of Congress. Technical and performance marks were strongest too for the winner, as was the cost evaluation.

With aforementioned defence budget cuts kicking in, on 18 January 1971 the number of flight test aircraft was cut back to three, the number of engines to 27 and specific materials, such as titanium, reduced for cost savings. The impact would set back the first flight from March to April 1974 with a production decision in April 1975 preceding initial operational capability by December 1979 on acceptance of the 65th aircraft – a two year delay on the initial schedule. It was at this point that some of the avionics development programmes were reduced and greater reliance placed on the exotic equipment being developed for the F-111D and the FB-111A.

On 29 September the Air Force decided to split the avionics into offensive and defensive systems and requests for the former work went out to 27 companies. Five responded, with Boeing eventually getting the contract on 13 April 1972. The defensive avionics was submitted to 23 companies of which

An early plan to give the B-1B less sweep was abandoned in favour of strengthened structures for the turbulent air close to the ground. The maximum 67.5-degree sweepback angle was retained, as shown here by the fourth B-1A prototype which did much of the avionics development work for the B-1B. (USAF)

two responded but the complexity of the requirement shifted the Air Force to split that into two. Revised requests went out on 17 May but it came to nothing, the Air Force deciding that due to complexity it would use one of its existing subsystems.

The mock-up was inspected in late October 1971 and 297 changes were requested – not an excessive number given the complexity of the aircraft. The sheer performance of the type was evident in its overall design: a blended wing-body interface for the dual pivot boxes supporting the two variable geometry wings.

With four F101 engines in paired boxes beneath the fixed inboard wing sections close to the centre of gravity, the stability of the aircraft would be enhanced in low-level flying. With a high thrust/weight ratio it could achieve high getaway and fly-out speeds while using short runways and reduced response rates due to automated checkout. Equipped with terrain-following radar the B-1A was expected to have a low radar cross-section (RCS), which was already being researched in several design facilities across the US and would very soon see the emergence of the F-117A and the Advanced Technology Bomber – the B-2.

During 1972 two clear technology problem areas appeared: the capsule escape system for the bomber's four-man crew and the F101 engines. An intense effort was mounted to solve issues with turbine blade failures and unacceptable oil consumption in the F101 and by early 1972 these issues were receding. Encouraging too was a programme review in April 1972 which appeared to endorse expectations of

The second prototype B-1A (74-0159) – built as an avionics test vehicle – displays the integration of the wedge-shaped engine intake box and the configuration of the landing gear. (Rockwell International)

a first flight in April 1974. By mid-1973 an overall slowdown in work on the B-1A cast doubts on that confidence and with further delays anticipated to the second and third aircraft, test pilots would not get in the 200hrs required for a production decision with that date now moving out to May 1976.

Seamans' successor, Air Force Secretary John L. McLucas, reported to Congress in July 1973 that the first aircraft was falling behind schedule and that production of the second had

also been delayed due to an inability on the part of the government to pay for overtime at the contractor plant, pushing the first flight further into mid-1974.

Congress held a special investigative hearing on 27 July 1973, during which severe criticism was levelled at both the contractor and the Air Force by partisan politicians with a history of attacking the defence industry in general and the aerospace industry in particular – notably Senator William Proxmire, noted for his opposition to the US Supersonic

Rockwell B-1A and B-1B Lancer

With wings swept forward to a maximum 15-degree of sweep, this overhead shot shows the inboard trailing edge glove slot immediately above the paired engine nacelles. (USAF)

Transport (SST) programme and to the Anglo-French Concorde gaining operating rights in the US.

Several technical changes had already been made, with decisions effecting both the performance of the B-1A and the costs. The engine inlets were changed from mixed compression type to a simpler, external compression design which cut weight by 1,400lb and saved $46m at the acceptable cost of shaving Mach 0.1 off the maximum speed of the aircraft. Some problems were experienced with the wing carry-through box for the variable-sweep wings and with subcontractors falling behind on their deliveries. In July 1973 it was decided to delay the assembly of the second and third airframes to reallocate the workforce on catching up and to defer the production decision to May 1976.

DESIGN AND REDESIGN

Two major reviews of the programme took place between July 1973 and September 1974 which impacted technical issues. Consideration was now given to dispensing with moveable engine inlets altogether

Frontal view showing the B-1B's engine intake boxes. (Wikicommons Dsdugan)

– cutting weight by 1,200lb and saving $230m – but this would reduce top speed from Mach 2.1 to Mach 1.6. That brought criticism from some savvy congressmen who questioned why Mach 2.2 had been so fervently guarded when Mach 1.6 was suddenly acceptable. Continued problems with the complex ejection capsule resulted in the decision to replace it with four individual Weber Aces II ejection seats, the technology of which was by this date considerably more advanced than when the capsule had been planned.

Political and Pentagon pressure to cut costs even brought suggestions to adopt a fixed wing, since at least 15% of the development cost, some claiming up to 40%, was attributable to engineering work on the variable-geometry concept. The Air Force did seriously consider making this switch but decided that the disruption to the overall programme and the rewriting of the requirement and justification for it would have proved more costly and time consuming in the end. But there were consequences for the weight and cost growth.

Maximum weight had now grown by almost 10%, from 360,000lb to

395,000lb, reducing range by 8% and increasing the take-off run from 6,500ft to 7,500ft. Nevertheless, the aircraft was still judged successful on projected performance. There were still serious concerns about finance in Congress however, opponents claiming costs had increased from an estimated $11.2bn in 1970 to $22.9bn in 1976. From this, the estimated unit cost per aircraft had increased over the same period from $46m to $100m. But these remained estimates. In the final accounting sheet, with inflation factored in, the procurement programme cost had actually increased by approximately 12%. Also, from 1971, a fourth prototype had been factored in to the development and flight test inventory.

North American Rockwell, just Rockwell International from 1973, had set up a North American Aircraft Operations structure with the B-1 Division at Inglewood, California, with assembly at Air Force Plant 42 at Palmdale, California. It was from there that the first prototype (74-0158) was rolled out on 26 October 1974. Piloted by Charles Bock, it made its first flight on 23 December and landed at Edwards Air Force Base 1hr 25min later. Also on board were Col Emil Sturmthal, commander of the B-1 Joint Test Force at Edwards as co-pilot and Richard Abrams, the manager of flight test planning and control for Rockwell. The fourth crew position was filled with test instrumentation.

The second prototype (74-0159) was at this date undergoing static testing at Lockheed's Palmdale facility and would not get airborne before 1976, the third (74-0160) would be the second aircraft to join the flight test programme in 1975. The fourth prototype (76-0174) would commence flight testing on 14 February 1979, equipped with the most advanced defensive and offensive electronics placed in any combat aircraft to that date.

Powered by four 16,150lb thrust General Electric F101-GE-100 afterburning turbofan engines delivering 29,850lb thrust with reheat, the B-1A had a span of 136.75ft fully forward at the 15-degree position and 78.2ft in the fully swept 67.5deg position. The wing had an area of 1,946sq ft, less than half that of the B-52, an aspect ratio of 9.6 and was fitted with single-slot flaps, leading edge slats and external compression inlet and spoilers. It was 150.2ft long and 33.6ft high and would carry a crew of pilot, co-pilot and offensive and defensive systems operators. Empty weight was 173,000lb and maximum take-off weight was 389,000lb. With a top speed of 1,390mph and a cruise speed of 647mph, it had a range of 6,100 miles and a service ceiling of 60,000ft.

With a maximum internal bomb load of 75,000lb and an external load of up to 40,000lb, it could carry 24 SRAM on a rotary missile launcher in the bomb bay and eight SRAM on underwing stores pylons. Maximum internal fuel

capacity was 30,786 US gallons with an additional 3,318 US gallons in a separate and optional weapons bay tank. The fourth prototype had an internal fuel load of 30,107 US gallons and 6,614 US gallons in two optional weapon bay tanks. Maximum combat radius was 3,265 miles with a 50,000lb bomb load at an over-the-target speed of Mach 0.85. With a 25,000lb warload, combat radius was 2,650 miles at a target speed of Mach 2.1.

A quick reaction, low altitude penetration capability was provided by the offensive avionics system, forward-looking AN/APQ-144 radar, the Doppler AN/APN-200, a terrain-following AN/APQ-146 and an AN/APN-194 altitude radar with dual-inertial AN/AJN-17 units adapted to operate with real-time digital controls. The defensive avionics were restricted to known threats to low-altitude penetration runs and consisted of RF surveillance and ECM equipment adapted to the digital flight control system.

The first three aircraft were finished in a gloss all white paint with black nose radome but the fourth prototype had a curious camouflage mix of green, brown and tan to signify its low-level role and the changing nature of the aircraft's primary job. This had become both necessary and opportune with the known development of look-down/shoot-down radar on selected Soviet aircraft threatening any low-flying intruders and the development of the long-range, Air Launched Cruise Missile (ALCM) described earlier in association with the B-52. Awareness of Soviet capability was verified when Russian pilot Victor Belenko defected with his MiG-25, along with its instruction manual, in September 1976 and spent many hours briefing US officials.

The US had a lead on the development of airborne radar which could discriminate targets from ground clutter when it developed the AN/ASG-18 fire-control system in the early 1960s, intended carriers being the B-58 and the YF-12. The Russians applied their equivalent Saphir-23P to the MiG-23 interceptor from the late 1970s. As we will see in the next section, the development of low-observables technology for evading radar detection was already well under way by the time the B-1A began flight tests. There were several programmes either in development or under contract which concentrated on the size of the radar cross-section achieved either by shape, thermal or acoustic constraints or by the use of special materials.

Just as the bomber's role had shifted from flying fast and high to flying fast and low, the march of technology shifted the emphasis once again – from penetration to standoff release of cruise missiles. The concept wasn't new but now the technology was available to make such systems effective and the 1970s saw the emergence of the long-range cruise weapon.

B-1B PROPULSION SYSTEM

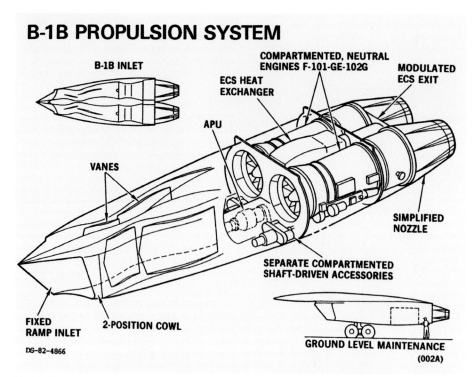

The B-1B was powered by four General Electric F101-102 series afterburning turbofan engines fed by air ducted through a two-position cowl and four side vanes. (Rockwell International)

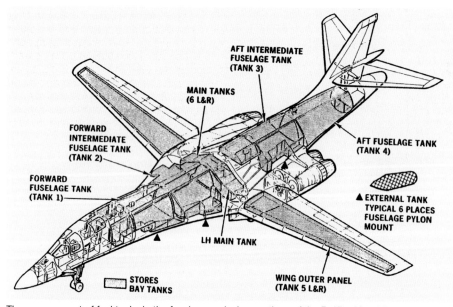

The arrangement of fuel tanks in the fuselage and wing sections of the B-1B with additional tanks on optional, underwing stores points. (Rockwell International)

The maturing application of terrain-contour-matching (TERCOM) capabilities improved accuracy and provided more flight route options, while advanced navigation capabilities were supported by the Navstar global positioning system. The rapid maturation of all these factors led to the decision by President Carter, announced on 30 June 1977 to cancel the B-1A. Unknown to all but a few, he did this as stealth technologies were about to be tested in the air on a single-seat attack aircraft (misdirected as a 'fighter', the F-117A) and an aircraft already under contract, the Advanced Technology Bomber (eventually the B-2).

The stated reason was the stand-off role now available to the existing B-52, which was soon to be equipped with cruise missiles. Carter said this obviated the need for the B-1A. Between the resignation of President Nixon on 9 August 1974 and the inauguration of Jimmy Carter on 20 January 1977, the unelected interim President Gerald Ford, formerly Nixon's Vice President, prioritised national stability and forbad radical policy changes. Ford had authorised production for the new bomber but it was not an irrevocable decision. Nevertheless, Congress allowed flight testing on the B-1A to continue so as not to undo a decade of rigorous work

and considerable government-funded technology development. The second prototype reached Mach 2.25 on 5 October 1978.

ENTER THE B-1B
After the decision to cancel the B-1A, the Air Force pressed for an increase in flight activity with procurement of two additional prototypes. Work had already begun on the fifth and sixth aircraft, Congress had allocated the necessary funds, and it was also pointed out that cancelling them would cost as much as building them but Carter still went ahead with the cancellation in February 1978.

While blocking any further development of the B-1A, Carter enthused over the ALCM's potential. This was limited by the B-52's carrying capacity however, so he sought a review of existing large commercial aircraft for the role of LRCA – essentially a bulk ALCM-carrier launching its missile from outside hostile airspace. Behind the scenes, Carter remained supportive of the F-117A and B-2 bomber programmes but could not say so publicly due to their highly classified nature.

As industry and the defence establishment began to discuss the LRCA, unsolicited proposals appeared suggesting the Boeing 747, McDonnell Douglas DC-10 and Lockheed C-5 Galaxy as candidates. Rockwell International and the Air Force added the B-1A to the list. The Carter Administration rebuffed all approaches to apply an existing commercial aircraft to the role, or to rethink its decision on the B-1A. But events were unfolding which would bring about the downfall of Carter and the resurrection of the B-1.

With the invasion of Afghanistan by Russia in 1979 and the escalation of Soviet strategic and theatre weapons throughout Warsaw Pact countries, universal concern over the consequences of the failed Strategic Arms Limitation Talks under the Nixon Administration raised issues about national security and the apparent decline in US military power. Carter withdrew the SALT II treaty from debate in Congress and took steps to consolidate US firepower. But it was too little too late and by 1980 there was wide debate in Washington DC about the need for a new strategic bomber.

Much of the discussion focused on the vulnerability of subsonic cruise missiles to attack and being shot down long before reaching their targets. There were also concerns about the durability of complex, electronically controlled weapons kept in storage for many years prior to use, and about the inability of ALCMs to find moving targets such as road-mobile ballistic missiles.

On 4 November 1980 the American public voted Ronald Reagan as the next President. Entering office on 20 January 1981, Reagan had pledged to undo what he perceived as a decade of neglect for

Engine inlet geometry of the B-1B is displayed by this aircraft of the 9th BS at Dyess AFB, Texas – the oldest active bomb squadron in the US Air Force. (David Baker)

the armed services and faced multiple choices and three clear options regarding the bomber issue. Congress had already decided that a new bomber was needed and that it had to be in service by 1987. On the table were the B-1A, the FB-111H, the ATB and – a distant outsider – commercial cruise missile launchers.

The first option was to let things ride and take their course. The second option was to bypass both an improved version of the B-1A, known as the B-1B, and the ATB and buy the FB-111H in large numbers. But as good as the new F-111 derivative was it would not have cruise missile carrying capacity nor would it have the range. For various reasons the commercial carrier was rejected as a non-starter.

The third option was to build just the B-1B.

Reviewing all these factors, the Air Force was determined to get the stealthy ATB and Congress liked the idea of its promised technology, awareness of the fighter and bomber programmes now being a matter of public discussion, albeit without any knowledge of shape, size or specifications for those exotic projects.

The Air Force had never really liked the FB-111A due to its limited bomb load and range, seeing the ATB as the best option in the long run. However, it was prepared to accept the FB-111H or the B-1B as an interim until the stealth bomber arrived on the ramp. There were serious concerns, though, that the B-1B could sap support for the ATB and leave the Air Force without a true penetrating bomber.

A B-1B takes off from Ellsworth AFB, South Dakota. The trailing edge spoilers and the wing sweep glove slot above the engines are visible. (USAF)

Rockwell B-1A and B-1B Lancer

COMPARTMENT LOCATIONS

TAIL WARNING
RADAR BAY

INTERMEDIATE
WEAPONS BAY

WING CARRY-THRU
AND MAIN FUEL TANKS

EQUIPMENT TUNNEL

AFT AVIONICS BAY

AFT FUEL TANK

AFT WEAPONS BAY AND AFT
INTERMEDIATE FUSELAGE
FUEL TANK

MAIN GEAR WELL AND
AVIONICS BAY

FORWARD INTERMEDIATE
FUSELAGE FUEL TANK

ENGINE COMPARTMENT

APU COMPARTMENT

FORWARD FUSELAGE
FUEL TANK

ADG COMPARTMENT

CREW ENTRY
WAY

WING FUEL TANK
(L AND R)

CREW
COMPARTMENT

AERIAL REFUEL
RECEPTACLE

FORWARD
WEAPONS
BAY

FORWARD
AVIONICS
BAY

WING GLOVE
AVIONICS BAY
(L AND R)

NACELLE INLET

ECS BAY
(L AND R)

CENTRAL
AVIONICS BAY

NOSE GEAR
WHEEL WELL

CHEEK COMPARTMENTS (L AND R)

DS-82-3051

(002A)

Map of the B-1B systems and subsystems accessible through external panels and doors. In the stand-down between the B-1A and B-1B, design teams worked on improving accessibility as a vital part of the aircraft's acceptance. (Rockwell International)

The antenna for the AN/APQ-140 Ku-band radar developed for the B-1A in the late 1960s, seen here at the National Electronics Museum. (Wikicommons Daderot)

A sizeable majority of staffers at Air Force headquarters favoured rushing the improved B-1B into service and proceeding on pace with the ATB, seeing the former as a better low-altitude bomber than the B-52 and a better strategic system than the FB-111H. It would have greater penetration potential due to a smattering of stealth features for reduced RCS, 10% lower than the B-1A and only 1% that of the B-52.

Changes included shaped engine inlets, radar-absorbent material (RAM)

on critical areas of the structure and significant improvements including shielded aspects of the wing and fuselage to eliminate sharp points and wing-sweep cavities which would be strong radar reflectors. The B-1B would be quickest into service of all options and that alone offered political capital for the Reagan Administration, showing that it was swiftly meeting its electoral pledges on defence.

After decades of uncertainty, the Air Force wanted the bomber set irreversibly on track to deployment before the 1984 election – in case Reagan was ousted and his successor decided to cancel the B-1B, as Carter had done to its precursor.

In parallel, the B-1A prototypes were winding down their own flight test programme, having achieved almost 1,900hrs in the air. The fourth and last prototype made the type's final flight on 29 April 1981.

Following the inevitable deliberation over options, on 2 October 1981 Reagan announced the decision to build 100 B-1Bs with service introduction in 1986 and final delivery to the Air Force by 1988. In addition, the ATB was to proceed with a requirement for 132 aircraft in service in 1991 or 1992. The B-52Ds would be retired while the G and H variants of the venerable bomber would become cruise missile carriers.

The B-1B would be the sole penetrator from 1986 until the early 1990s. At this point, the B-2 would take on that role and the B-1B would relieve the B-52 as the cruise missile launcher. The agreement to limit B-1B production to 100 aircraft assuaged fears that the type would threaten the ongoing

development of the more expensive stealth bomber.

In January 1982 Rockwell International signed a $2.2bn contract for the initial tranche of work on the B-1B which secured 58,000 jobs in the supply chain of 3,000 companies, 22,000 employees being at Rockwell working toward a first flight in early 1985. By the end of 1982, 16,300 of the aircraft's 18,000 production drawings had been completed, 41,000 of the 68,000 manufacturing orders required had been written, 54,000 of 58,000 tool orders had been released and 16,000 parts had been fabricated for the first two production aircraft.

BUILDING THE LANCER

From the contracted go-ahead, the rapid pace was supported by an equally robust budget, growing from over $2bn in 1982 to $4.6bn in 1984 and by 1985 about 78% of the total procurement cost had been allocated. Rockwell claimed that the degree of commonality with the B-1A was 80-90% - the engines alone having 95% of parts in common. Seemingly a relatively simple upgrade to the B-1A, the B-1B was deceptively ambitious and incorporated a radically different offensive avionics system, a new terrain-following radar and a new flight control system demanded by the heavier airframe.

The fundamental operating difference between the two types was the reduction in maximum speed from Mach 2.2 to Mach 1.25 and this was reflected in several differences between the B-1A and the B-1B. The design weight of the B-1B was significantly greater, with modifications for ALCM carriage adding 7,000lb, a 50,000lb payload and 25,000lb of additional fuel. With a gross weight of 477,000lb, the B-1B was 82,000lb heavier than the B-1A. This meant flight test data acquired from the B-1A was no longer relevant. With an empty weight of 180,500lb, the B-1B had a theoretical internal payload capability of 75,000lb, a maximum external load of 50,000lb and a design flight mass of 395,000lb with a maximum flight weight of 477,000lb.

Dimensionally, the B-1B was close to the B-1A, with a length of 147.2ft and a wingspan of 136.7ft fully forward and 78.2ft fully swept designed to NACA 69-190-2. Power was provided by four GE F101-GE-102 engines delivering a thrust of 17,390lb or 30,750lb with afterburner. The engine had a simplified nozzle with fewer active segments and engine bleed ports in a neutral position, removing the need for a left and right engine build-up and allowing installation of any engine in any position.

Air turbine starters were added to the engine accessory drive gearboxes as well as cross-bleed capability for starting. Accordingly, the APUs were of revised design to reflect the new start capability. Throughout, speed and ease of maintenance was a key factor in

Leading edge slats stand proud of the B-1B's wing leading edges in this plan view. (USAF)

improving reaction times and combat availability. Each engine had just 12 disconnect points, making a complete engine change possible within half an hour. Unlike the B-1A, the engine inlet nacelle had a serpentine path to the compressor stage with guide vanes on the interior channelling the air flow, a two-position cowl and fixed ramp inlet.

The four-man crew had the same ACES ejection seats as fitted to the B-1A, with instructor personnel having parachutes and an exit hatch through the underside of the nose section at the crew entry ladder well. With a total volume of 330cu ft, the avionics bays were situated in forward, central and aft fuselage locations, in addition to the two main gear wheel wells. An additional bay was installed in the horizontal stabiliser fairing to contain the tail radar and another in the aft intermediate tank at the weapons bay bulkhead to house missile electronic equipment.

The fuselage, wing carry-through and outer wing panel tanks contained most of the fuel storage in eight integral tanks, six in the fuselage and one in each wing with two supplementary weapons bay tanks optional. In addition, new for the B-1B were two windows, one each for the offensive and defensive system operators and a new relocatable

Beginning in 2012, the Integrated Battle Station upgrade programme brought together the Fully Integrated Air Data Link, the Vertical Situational Display Unit and the Central Integrated Test System, all of which carry forward into the cockpit and onto the displays and controls. (USAF)

Rockwell B-1A and B-1B Lancer

The AN/APG-66 installed in early B-1B aircraft and seen here, has been replaced by the Scalable Agile Beam Radar together with a new attitude indicator. (Wikicommons, Daderot)

Two B-1Bs overflying the rural expanses of Wyoming, indicative of their low-level flying capabilities. (USAF)

With a 'pop-up' presence around the world, Air Combat Command has a more international show of strength than Strategic Air Command ever did, as a B-1B overflies the pyramids of ancient Egypt. (USAF)

bulkhead was added to the forward weapons bay.

Three 15ft long bays were available for internal weapons storage, two forward of the wing carry-through structure and a third aft of the main landing gear wells. The two forward bays had a non-stress-loaded moveable bulkhead to reposition the partitioning of the two forward bays into one 22ft long bay and one 8ft bay. Or, it could be left out for a single 31ft long forward bay. Fuel tanks could be carried in any or all of the three bomb bays with multiple installation options.

External stores could be accommodated on six dual-missile and two single-missile pylons, with the former capable of carrying six optional, jettisonable fuel tanks for added range. The internal and external payload of the B-1B was more than twice that of the B-52D and in area the weapons bay had a total volume of 1,643cu ft versus 1,043cu ft for the B-52.

The aesthetic lines of the B-1B resulted from the area-rule fuselage to prevent boundary layer air separation with the blended wing-body design presenting a very clean frontal area where the wing emerges from the fuselage, reduced drag and additional lift coming from the fuselage portion of the inner wing box. Unlike the B-1A, the B-1B was designed throughout for a fail-operational/fail-operational/fail-safe capability, in which a single systems failure would not imperial the mission and a second single system failure would not prevent the aircraft from returning intact to base. This represented a design goal of 99.99% reliability across the system spectrum and had been derived directly from Rockwell's (North American Aviation) work on the design and development of the NASA Space Shuttle.

Considerable changes were introduced to the material and associated manufacturing processes due to the relaxation of performance criteria. 2024 or 7075 aluminium alloys were used throughout with the four primary fuselage sections, box sections and both paired engine nacelles in aluminium reinforced with steel and titanium structural members. Titanium was also used in the wing carry-through structure and wing root attachment points in addition to the pins, with advanced composite materials including glass-fibre reinforced plastics in the expanded wing flap area. Poly Quartz was employed in the nose and tail cones in addition to the side radar fairings. The hydraulic system employed a 4,000lb per square inch system, rather than the traditional 3,000lb per square inch used in previous US military aircraft, providing a one-third increase in pressure to four separate systems.

While the power increase was not proportional to the pressure it did allow the use of smaller and lighter components. Only the B-70 and the Anglo-French

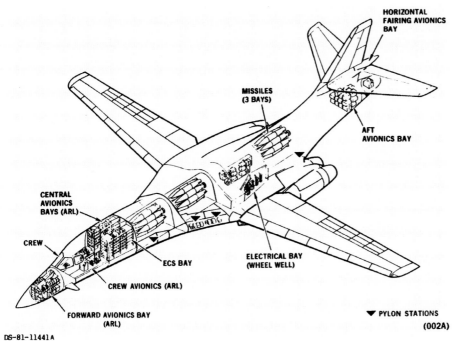

HORIZONTAL
FAIRING AVIONICS
BAY

MISSILES
(3 BAYS)

AFT
AVIONICS BAY

CENTRAL
AVIONICS
BAYS (ARL)

CREW

ELECTRICAL BAY
(WHEEL WELL)

ECS BAY

CREW AVIONICS (ARL)

FORWARD AVIONICS BAY
(ARL)

▼ PYLON STATIONS
(002A)

DS-81-11441A

A general configuration drawing displaying the internal layout of avionics and weapons bays together with access areas for electrical and environmental control systems. (Rockwell International)

Looking up into the bomb bay of an early B-1B. Changes implemented through an upgrade programme have increased capacity to allow installation of the Common Strategic Rotary Launcher (CSRL). (via David Baker)

Concorde had previously used this high-pressure hydraulic system. Motors in place of cylinders were used throughout the airframe where the actuation loads were not so severe, allowing more precise control. Redundant fail-safe supply lines were usually routed on different sides of the aircraft so that damage to one would not necessarily disable the other. The hydraulic pumps were located on different engines to avoid a pressure loss from engine or pump failure.

Redesigned steel landing gear supported the additional weight of the aircraft. As it had evolved, the B-1B was far from a rough-field bomber and the landing gear reflected that. Located inboard of the engine nacelles, the main gear consisted of a four-wheel bogie on each leg which was configured to fold inwards and to the rear, with the wheels stowing in the vertical plane. Produced by Cleveland Pneumatic, the gear had Goodyear wheels with carbon brakes and tyre pressures of 250lb per square inch, restricting operations from all but the most hardened of runways.

No weaponised defensive armament was considered for the B-1B, this being the first US aircraft to enter service specifically designed as a bomber without guns. The primary defensive system was the AN/ALQ-161A built by AIL Systems (now L3Harris), initially consisting of an RF surveillance system with appropriate ECM systems, tail-warning function, ASQ-184 management system and a 108-element chaff-dispensing system located in the upper part of the fuselage. Development problems persisted after the system was taken off breadboard tests in the laboratory and integrated with the aircraft during flights tests. The system was installed initially before a major problem-solving exercise kicked in.

With a weight of 5,000lb and consuming 120kW of power, the AN/ALQ-161A provided 360-degree receive and jamming coverage against a large number of simultaneous threats, detecting incoming missiles from the aft sector. The ECM system filtered threats according to their lethality and automatically reacted against them. In jamming mode it emitted only in a certain direction but discriminated against those targeted and only emitted a brief jamming signal when doing otherwise might reveal the aircraft's presence.

Searching for a solution to the system's problems, the Air Force examined a wide range of alternatives but remained with the original hardware and frequent software updates. One significant early embarrassment was a tendency of the system to illuminate the presence of the aircraft when it was meant to be veiling it.

It also suffered electronic leakage and signals from some active jamming frequencies bled into and jammed passive receivers. And in some cases the defensive

Rockwell B-1A and B-1B Lancer

avionics signals interfered with those from the offensive system which resulted in the practice of not operating the two systems at the same time. Most of these problems had been sorted out by late 1988 with the realisation that, as good as it was, it was never going to live up to its advertising.

Then there were additional problems which only came to light on tests and exercises. Although the defensive system could locate and track some threats, it could not cover the entire spectrum it was designed to, with the tail warning radar especially vulnerable in this regard. The receiver/processor was unable to adequately process the number of threats it was supposed to and could be overwhelmed in a high-threat environment. In all too many instances, the crew had to manually jam enemy radar and missile systems.

The push to iron out the defensive avionics suite's bugs kept growing and eventually would absorb $1bn with only minimal improvements. Half of the additional cost would be spent on the tail warning radar, which was required to operate perfectly to allow the crew to manually control the ECM. Not until 1991 was the flight testing of the core system completed with modifications proceeding through to the mid-1990s. The Air Force only stabilised the offensive and defensive avionics seven years after the B-1B entered service.

The B-1B's offensive avionics included the Westinghouse (now Northrop Grumman) AN/APQ-164 – which consisted of a ten-mode, low-observables, dual-axis (+/-60deg) phased-array antenna.

Coming from the F-16 programme, this was the first development and production installation of an electronically scanned array radar system and had been checked out first on a B-52 in 1977. Operating in X-band, this was essentially two radars in one with the second set of line-replaceable units on reserve standby, the prime elements consisting of a 44in by 22in antenna with 1,526 phase

A CSRL in a B-1B bomb bay. The aircraft has also received an upgrade to accommodate a new suite of hypersonic missiles. (via David Baker)

Seen here being armed at Hahn AB, Germany, the 500lb (227kg) Mk 82 general-purpose munition was a low-drag 'dumb' bomb, up to 84 of which could be dispensed from the B-1B. (USAF)

control modules, video signal processor and target indicator. It provided a high resolution synthetic aperture radar for navigation and weapon targeting, with automatic terrain-following and terrain-avoidance capability. Modified from the AN/APG-66, the radar could be upgraded with a multi-target track software mode for AMRAAM deployment on other platforms.

The B-1B could also carry the Lockheed Martin AN/AAQ-33 Sniper pod located on the underside of the fuselage just aft of the crew access hatch and ladder. Essentially performing the role of the LANTIRN system, but with up to five times better detection range, it incorporated a high definition, mid-wave forward looking infrared radar (FLIR). This contained sensors for advanced image stabilisation, observing and tracking targets through smoke and clouds and in high or no-light conditions. It has been used on a wide variety of combat aircraft including the B-52.

Two B-1A prototypes (the second and fourth aircraft) were modified for tests involving improvements and systems which were to be incorporated in the B-1B, including air load testing and engine inlet development. The No 2 aircraft began flying in support of this activity on 23 March 1983. An incorrect fuel transfer by a crewmember on board during a flight on 29 August 1984 moved the centre of gravity aft of the acceptable flight limit, causing the aircraft to become uncontrollable.

At an altitude of 1,515ft the command pilot Maj Richard V. Reynolds pulled the escape handle and the capsule (this aircraft had the crew escape capsule, rather than ejection seats) separated but the parachute risers failed to deploy properly. The pod hit the ground with a force of 40g, killing the programme chief test pilot Tommie Douglas 'Doug' Benefeld and seriously injuring the other crewmembers including Reynolds and Capt Otto J. Waniczek, Jr. The report found pilot error, in that the transfer switch to move fuel between tanks to adjust the centre of gravity as the wings were swept forward for a low altitude test had not been flicked. The nose pitched up and the aircraft stalled into a spin.

As a consequence of this accident, a new fuel management system from Simmonds was introduced to automatically integrate fuel operations and maintain the centre of gravity. To extend the already credible range of the B-1B, a flight refuelling socket was fitted above the nose to facilitate high-speed top-ups from an aerial tanker.

The primary flight controls consisted of a two-section rudder controlling yaw with four spoiler panels on the upper surface of each wing. Moveable horizontal stabilisers controlled pitch by symmetrical deflection and roll control by asymmetric motion of those surfaces and by deflection of the four-section wing spoilers. Each wing had full-span slats in seven sections and six sections of single-slotted flaps extending to 40 degrees and terminating well inboard of the wing tips, where ailerons would have been. The wings pivoted on 6Al-4V titanium pins in large spherical steel bearings carried at the tips of the wide and deep carry-through box, which was fabricated from a similar titanium alloy.

With much of the B-1B's mission flown close to the ground, the Air Force pushed demand for what the programme called the Low-Altitude Ride Control (LARC), later defined as the Structural Mode Control System (SMCS). With this, the stresses caused by turbulence bending and flexing the aircraft were reduced and the ride for the crew made not unduly disruptive. It quickly became apparent that

Clips of Mk 82 bombs are loaded on board a B-1B of the 28th BS at Dyess AFB, Texas, a unit specialising in training. (USAF)

this could not be controlled by the primary flight control surfaces. Driven largely by its heavier weight, two canards were added with 30 degrees anhedral, driven by signals from the vertical and lateral accelerometers in the forward section of the fuselage. With anhedral, the canard surfaces could respond to oscillations in yaw as well as pitch.

The flight control system produced three inherent problems: two involving stall inhibitor systems (SIS-I and SIS-II) and the third involving a stability enhancement system. SIS-1 was expected to be installed by the time the B-1B entered service in 1986 but it was redesigned three times before being retrofitted to the entire fleet – this work being completed only in April 1988. Both SIS-II and a stability enhancer could not be completed before 1994 and the cost

Armourers with 2,000lb (907kg) GBU-31 JDAMs destined for a B-1B. (USAF)

Rockwell B-1A and B-1B Lancer

Trainees from the 28th BS put on a chaff-dispensing show for photographic chase planes. (USAF)

Strongly considered for integration with the B-1B, and seen here carried by a B-52H in June 2019, the AGM-183A Mach 7 missile with a range of 1,000 miles would provide the ultimate stand-off capability against heavily defended targets. Each B-1B could carry 31 internally and externally. (USAF)

of retrofit, rather than integrating this on the production line, was significant.

In critical assessment of the B-1B, the Air Force was judged to have made a significant error in becoming the programme manager but not having sufficient administrative resources to adequately handle all the many technological problems simultaneously. Even so, a lot of applied technology from other programmes helped the B-1B get into operational service, including the IBM AP-101 main computer which had been developed for the Space Shuttle and would also be retrofitted to the B-52. It was programmed with JOVIAL.

Developed in the 1960s as a language based on ALGOL 58, JOVIAL was designed for integrated and embedded systems and was a prudent choice for knitting together a range of disparate systems and subsystems. Several modifications would accrue through a series of upgrades, including the incorporation of GPS from 1995.

LANCER FLIES

The first production B-1B rolled out of the Palmdale factory on 4 September 1984, only six days after the loss of the second B-1A prototype which had been modified for trials. It made its first flight

on 18 October and became a permanent test aircraft. The second aircraft took to the air on 4 May 1985 and was flown to Dyess AFB, Texas, to join the 337th BS of the 96th BW, this unit receiving the first 15 aircraft. It was with this deployment that the type became operational in September 1986. The next 14 aircraft made up the full complement for the 96th BW with the rest of the production aircraft going to the 28th BW at Ellsworth AFB, South Dakota, 35 going to the 319th BW at Grand Forks AFB, North Dakota, and the 384th BW at McConnell AFB, Kansas, the last delivered in 1988.

The programme had been largely on schedule due to concurrency, the price paid being the protracted retrofit of essential offensive and defensive systems outlined previously. The fleet was grounded in 1990 due to two engine fires in separate aircraft, that problem being a fault with the first stage fan and the B-1 was returned to service a few months later. Increasingly, with the collapse of the USSR and the unification of Germany, relations between Russia and the West warmed. There were a series of international deals and the role of the bomber fleet shifted dramatically.

The Administration of President George H. W. Bush signed off a plan to redefine the role of the B-1B out of the nuclear triad and into that of a conventional-munitions bomber. The adaptations cost $3bn but gave the aircraft a much longer lease of life. When SAC was deactivated in 1992 and replaced by Air Combat Command (ACC), an extensive programme of conversion established the B-1B as the prime-mover of conventional munitions – but with the flexibility to carry just about any of the

The B-1B is an iconic symbol of US air power and force projection but it has a limited life in the future as autonomous reconnaissance, surveillance and strike systems take over. (USAF)

guided and unguided munitions in the US inventory. On the way to this, by 1995 all the ancillary equipment for supporting the nuclear role had been removed from the aircraft and additional verification was applied in accordance with the START agreement signed with Russia, that being completed by 2011 and open to annual inspections by the Russians.

To some degree, the continued availability of the B-52 and B-2 has precluded many upgrades and modifications which could have been applied to the B-1B. In late 2002, the Air Force had had to cancel plans to fit the aircraft with the Defense System Upgrade Program (DSUP) due to cost and schedule slippages. This would have given the B-1B better survivability in a hostile environment but with the descaling of its role in 21st century air warfare, the costs involved were unaffordable.

Overall, for a while missions were applied to a shifting transfer of role from the continuous bomber presence mission formerly carried out by the B-52 but increasingly taken over by the B-1B, as evidenced by the basing of this aircraft at Andersen AFB, Guam since 2006. Now, that continuous bomber presence has been replaced by the 'dynamic force employment' which aims to have bombers pop up at random anywhere around the globe

to demonstrate an enduring ability to project power. But with just 62 B-1Bs now in the inventory, alongside 76 B-52Hs and 20 B-2s, that leaves a lot of work for the fleet in 2022.

Low-level operations and sustained combat operations over the last 20 years have stressed the airframe of the B-1B and some aircraft currently in service now require up to $30m worth of maintenance and life-extension work to keep them going. The Air Force is to retire 17 B-1Bs leaving 45 aircraft in the inventory, with the first having departed on 17 February 2021. Both the B-1B and B-2 fleets will be wound down as the B-21 begins to enter service.

By the end of this decade the bomber force will consist of the B-52 and the B-21 in a force structure very different to that which the Air Force has operated with since it became independent in 1947. Four of the 17 retired B-1Bs will be preserved in a condition where they could rapidly be brought back into service.

But the modifications continue to come. The B-1B's central integrated test system (CITS) is its diagnostic and recording system – providing the crew with several thousand data points in flight and the Joint Range Extension Applications Protocol (JREAP) provides long-distance tactical communications.

Also, the Fully Integrated Data Link (FIDL) incorporated within that system provides the added advantage of Link-16 and merges with JREAP to push that information into the cockpit with new multifunctional display panels replacing analogue instrument and information displays. But there is only so much that can be done with old aircraft and the B-1B has limited advantage compared with the B-52.

The Air Force looked in detail at future bomber requirements for a Global Strike-Global Persistent (GSGP) attack capability in 2004 and sought solutions to an increasing range of problems, not least being the desire to get bombers back to high altitude for a more direct application of smart weapons and real-time targeting. Boeing (having absorbed Rockwell International's North American Aviation operations) proposed a B-1R which would be powered by the Pratt & Whitney F119 engine used on the F-22 Raptor, restoring a top speed of Mach 2.2 for a 20% cut in range and incorporating an AESA radar with more hard-points for additional munitions. The hope was that an aircraft of this type could destroy ground radar sites and allow targeted bombing from higher altitude, letting other aircraft through for a penetration strike. With the B-2 in service however, nothing came of this.

NORTHROP GRUMMAN
B-2 SPIRIT
First Flight: 17 July 1989

Flying across the countryside of Kent, England, B-2 *Spirit of Mississippi* (82-1071) epitomises the Air Force of the 21st century. (USAF)

The availability of new stealth technologies with which materials engineers could reduce the radar cross-section (RCS) of small combat aircraft was demonstrated through remotely piloted vehicles (RPVs) developed for the last stages of the Vietnam War in the early 1970s. Teledyne Ryan produced a stealthy mini-RPV tested at Eglin AFB, Florida, experience in Vietnam having indicated an overriding need to somehow evade or neutralise Russian-made air defence networks.

Simultaneously, the availability of data from the Lockheed YF-12/SR-71 aircraft prompted DARPA (Defense Advanced Research Projects Agency) in 1974 to fund low-level studies into the possibility of building a small combat aircraft with low-observables characteristics. McDonnell Douglas and Northrop were commissioned in early 1975 to conduct research on how ground-based radar could be negated and countermeasures designed into an airframe with low RCS.

Northrop had a small group of experts with experience in this field such as John Cashen, late of Hughes where he had worked on radar and infrared sensors. Meanwhile, a second player entered the field tangentially when Lockheed's Ed Martin became aware of stealth work during discussions at the Pentagon and this news was transmitted back to Ben Rich, president of the company's Skunk Works, and on to Clarence 'Kelly' Johnson.

Lockheed had a rich history in pioneering radar-absorbent materials (RAM) with the high-temperature plastics used on the SR-71. In September 1975, Lockheed and Northrop were each asked to submit designs in the Experimental Survivable Testbed (XST) programme which would produce pole-top models to measure radar reflectivity, pitching low RCS against respective configurations.

Northrop produced a model designed to prioritise head-on radar against reflections from the rear, whereas DARPA was looking to measure reflectivity levels in quadrants covering 360 degrees, the rear 90-degree 'look' measurement

The Have Blue programme was an attempt to radically transform fighter-bomber design criteria to minimise radar cross-section and apply radar-absorbent materials. It began the true 'stealth' era of combat aircraft. (USAF)

Have Blue and other research projects resulted in the Lockheed Martin F-117A, which was more bomber than fighter, seen here dropping a 5,000lb (2,268kg) GBU-28 laser-guided bomb. (USAF)

Northrop Grumman B-2 Spirit

Structurally defined by the requirements of the stealth programme – an F-117A under construction. (Lockheed Martin)

Developed as a technology demonstrator from its inception in 1976 under the Battlefield Surveillance Aircraft Experimental (BSAX) programme, the Northrop Tacit Blue programme produced a stealthy surveillance aircraft which took to the air in February 1982. (Northrop Grumman)

Inside Tacit Blue. Electronic flight control systems were designed to keep the inherently unstable vehicle in the air and this work would inform the design of the B-2. (USAF)

placed centrally on the tail. Lockheed had a swept-wing aircraft and addressed the rear problem with a notched trailing edge.

Northrop had been unaware of Lockheed's RAM expertise and learned of it too late to build it into its own design. The Lockheed submission was revolutionary and featured flat plates across its surface, whereas Northrop employed blended curves with a top-mounted engine inlet and serpentine duct behind a mesh screen. These combinations were successfully employed by Lockheed on the pole tests and resulted in a contract for the Experimental Survivable Testbed (XST), aka Have Blue, in March 1976.

The story of the Have Blue test aircraft, first flown on 1 December 1977, has been well told in numerous places but suffice to say here that without it, and the F-117A which was to follow, passionate devotes of stealth technology would have had a much more difficult time supporting what became the B-2.

Meanwhile, DARPA and the Air Force had turned their attention to a stealthy reconnaissance aircraft under the Pave Mover programme. Known as the Battlefield Surveillance Aircraft Experimental (BSAX), it had a V-shaped tail with a straight tapered wing, an oversize fuselage with an engine inlet on top and two Garrett ATF3-6 turbofan engines.

Pave Mover was a demonstration programme for wide-area surveillance and in April 1978 Northrop received a contract to build a single example, which made its first flight on 5 February 1982 from Area 51 at Groom Lake, Nevada. Arguably the most unstable aircraft developed and flown to this date, the BSAX employed a quadruple redundant digital fly-by-wire flight control system which provided valuable data later would be incorporated into the B-2 programme.

ADVANCED TECHNOLOGY BOMBER

Before BSAX, after winning XST/Have Blue and taking the lead with stealth technology applications, Lockheed put up proposals for two Advanced Tactical Aircraft concepts: ATA-A which was a single-seat fighter with a 450-mile combat radius and a bomb load of 5,000lb, and ATA-B which was proposed as a replacement for the FB-111A medium bombers, possessing a combat radius of 1,150 miles and a bomb load of 10,000lb. ATA-A became the F-117A but Ben Rich went to SAC and proposed a slightly upgraded ATA-B, larger and with even greater stealth properties.

The Air Force was enthusiastic, believing it could form the basis for a B-52 and B-1A successor, while new intelligence information sparked fears that such an aircraft was needed more urgently than previously thought. Reports on Russia's new MiG-31 interceptor, first flown in 1975, raised alarm – particularly when it was discovered that it had the world's first passive electronically scanned array radar. With a top speed of Mach 2.8, it had been developed as a successor to the MiG-25 and was directly aimed at US bombers.

Having lost out on XST/Have Blue, Northrop imported fresh talent to broaden its design capabilities on stealth concepts. Lockheed pinned its hopes on the ATA-B+ concept. At this point President Jimmy Carter was made clearly aware of the potential to create a new generation of stealth bombers and SAC got a prime supporter in the White House. Congressional leaders were also made privy to the highly classified information.

Between 1977 and 1978 the impetus to create a stealthy bomber gathered momentum, with a wide range of design possibilities being considered, and the go-ahead to actually build one was given in 1978. The following year the Pentagon formally labelled the programme Advanced Technology Bomber (ATB). The F-117A had set a benchmark for stealth and SAC was encouraged to believe that this level of RCS was possible for a much bigger aircraft.

Predictably, Northrop and Lockheed put up the most credible proposals as the Air Force refined its requirement, still based on a need to penetrate deep into Soviet airspace and roam around, taking out military targets at will. The formal definition of requirements for the ATB got under way in January 1980 when a funded study named Advanced Strategic Penetrating Aircraft (ASPA) was started with low-observables (LO) given top priority.

Under the ASPA umbrella, SAC began its own studies on the strategic value of a stealth aircraft. Following Carter's cancellation of the B-1A, there was enthusiasm for reaching out to industry for ideas, since it had been from that sector that stealth projects had emerged. Deputy Chief of Staff for Research and Development at the Pentagon Lt. Gen. Thomas P. Stafford approached Northrop in the second quarter of 1979 and asked for a briefing on the company's approach to LO.

With Stafford on board, the programme moved rapidly toward a request for proposals and this was issued on 1 September 1980 to Lockheed and Northrop. Stafford also played a key role in briefing the Presidential transition team after Ronald Reagan was elected in November – to equip the civilian leadership with the appropriate briefings prior to the inauguration on 20 January 1981. This was vital for rapid policy formulation by the new administration and the implementation of Reagan's pledge to build US military power as well as engage directly with the Soviet leadership for arms reduction talks.

As ever, the Air Force placed high requirements on the ATB, stipulating a

HIGH ALTITUDE PENETRATOR

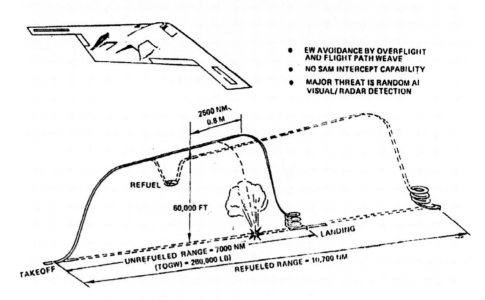

- EW AVOIDANCE BY OVERFLIGHT AND FLIGHT PATH WEAVE
- NO SAM INTERCEPT CAPABILITY
- MAJOR THREAT IS RANDOM AI VISUAL/ RADAR DETECTION

Aero-engineering consultant and think-tank DARPA (Defense Advanced Projects Agency) conducted a detailed study of mission profiles for a high-altitude stealth bomber in 1980, which at the time was considered survivable on the basis of low-observables. (DARPA)

LOW ALTITUDE PENETRATOR

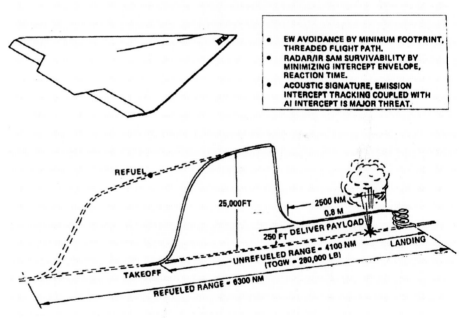

- EW AVOIDANCE BY MINIMUM FOOTPRINT, THREADED FLIGHT PATH.
- RADAR/IR SAM SURVIVABILITY BY MINIMIZING INTERCEPT ENVELOPE, REACTION TIME.
- ACOUSTIC SIGNATURE, EMISSION INTERCEPT TRACKING COUPLED WITH AI INTERCEPT IS MAJOR THREAT.

At the same time as its high-altitude analysis in 1980, DARPA examined the options for a low-altitude penetrator, a mission profile which radically changed the overall design configuration to cope with stress caused by buffeting. Clearly high and low mission profiles required very different geometric flying wing shapes. (DARPA)

range of 6,000 miles with a bomb load of 10,000lb but a maximum possible bomb load close to 40,000lb. The primary objective of the ASPA work was to seek a solution to the long range, high-altitude cruise performance of the Soviet network radar and 14 hypothetical missions were appended to the RFP for calculating range, payload, structural durability and all those elements required to complete the mission regarding weapons, environments and penetration corridors as well as survivability.

Lockheed and Northrop were clear font-runners in the bid to build the ATB but the competition ran for two years before contract selection. Lockheed's design proposal was named Senior Peg, Northrop's Senior Ice. Lockheed's philosophy was to produce a small design which would meet the minimum requirements and offer the Air Force numerical superiority rather than an expensive, highly sophisticated design. The attractiveness of such an approach was precisely what the company had

Northrop Grumman B-2 Spirit

sensed when proposing the ATA-A and ATA-B concepts.

The design Lockheed came up with was minimalist with a strangely extended fuselage at the end of which was a V-shaped tail, borrowing much from the F-117A. It had a flying-wing planform supporting the extended tail with faceted windows and a raked frontal fascia with flat upper fuselage sections and engine inlets covered with mesh. The tail was necessary to ensure stability due to the smaller area of the control surfaces.

In contrast, Northrop opted for a pure flying-wing concept reminiscent of its own XB-35 and YB-49 bomber proposals of the 1940s - aircraft which had been impossible to fly safely without considerable assistance from boosted controls and a great deal of skill. Thirty years later the evolution of fly-by-wire and digital flight control systems allowed such an exotic concept to succeed. The electronics would keep the aircraft in the air and the pilot would direct where it went.

Senior Ice offered performance far greater than the requirement, its shape a continuously changing set of blended curves and sloping contours confounding radar from almost any direction – at least, that was the idea. It had no tail at all and split elevons on the wing trailing edge, which was unlike anything that had flown before. Much larger than Senior Peg, it had greater control surface area and simulation showed a benign and graceful manoeuvrability unlike any other flying wing that had ever flown.

Key to the Northrop design was Irv Waaland, who had come to Northrop from Grumman. It was his drive to define the nature of the radar threat and work back from that which dictated the design – essentially from a technical viewpoint rather than a mission-orientated starting point. Waaland approached the challenge from the basis that he had to come up with a shape which was responsive and capable of maintaining low RCS against multiple bandwidths of radar emissions and not just those that appeared most threatening.

The Northrop design had tremendous climb and ceiling performance too, offering potential for effective operation to at least 70,000ft, although the Air Force would never admit to that. In researching radar frequencies and Russian air defence systems, a uniquely valuable discovery had pointed the Air Force back to a capability it had not sought since the B-70 in the 1950s: high altitude penetration with impunity.

Northrop discovered that over the years Russian radar had become increasingly optimised for detecting low-level intruders, hardly surprising given the attack strategies used by the US Air Force since the introduction of surface-to-air missiles. Air defences were consequently a lot less challenging for

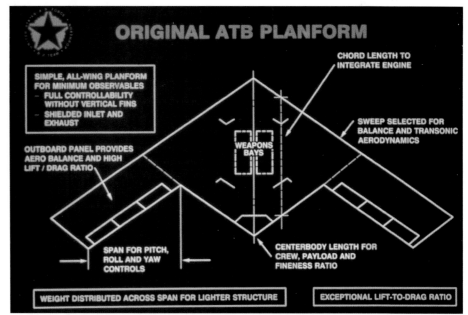

The original Northrop design for the Advanced Technology Bomber programme favoured the prevailing Air Force view that stealth would permit a return to high-altitude penetration. The initial B-2 design was therefore a flying wing based on that mission profile. (Northrop Grumman)

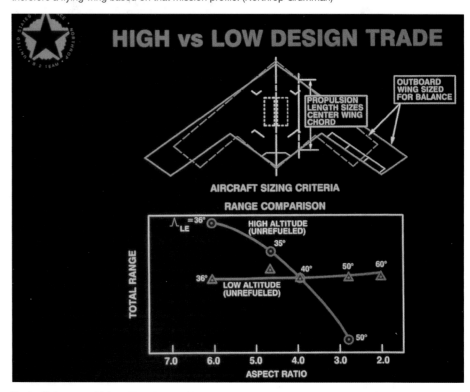

Tradeoffs between high and low flight profiles were defined by changes to the shape of the blended flying wing as indicted by the range and aspect ratio with both cases ignoring in-flight refuelling. (Northrop Grumman)

high-flying aircraft. Therefore, contrary to all received wisdom up to this point, the company's engineers concentrated on creating a high-altitude ATB.

The competition between Lockheed and Northrop became a matter of interpreting the customer's requirement and from the outset Senior Ice appeared to have the edge. In the purest form of stealth, an aircraft would be a flat plate, with no angles to reflect a radiated signal back to its source. But aircraft also need crew, bombs, engines and landing gear.

Each company took a different approach to reconciling these facts.

Without a tail, the length of the centre-body would be determined by the depth needed to accommodate a cockpit, weapon bays and landing gear and it had to be as short as possible to minimise subsonic drag. The ATB would not be supersonic and so could be optimised around those parameters. The chord of the wing was dictated by the slope coming off the centre-body and by the need to carry engines buried in the

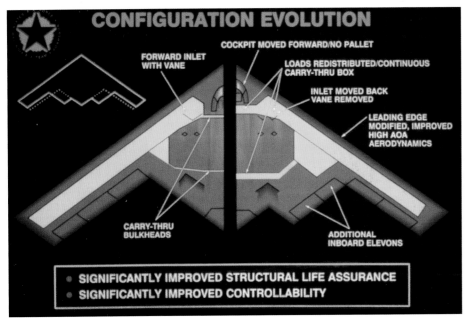

CONFIGURATION EVOLUTION

COCKPIT MOVED FORWARD/NO PALLET

FORWARD INLET WITH VANE

LOADS REDISTRIBUTED/CONTINUOUS CARRY-THRU BOX

INLET MOVED BACK VANE REMOVED

LEADING EDGE MODIFIED, IMPROVED HIGH AOA AERODYNAMICS

CARRY-THRU BULKHEADS

ADDITIONAL INBOARD ELEVONS

- SIGNIFICANTLY IMPROVED STRUCTURAL LIFE ASSURANCE
- SIGNIFICANTLY IMPROVED CONTROLLABILITY

Driven by intelligence information that made it desirable to switch the primary mission to low altitude penetration, the design of the ATB/B-2 switched dramatically, transforming the single W trailing edge of the flying wing into a double-W as shown here on the right hand half of the layout. (Northrop Grumman)

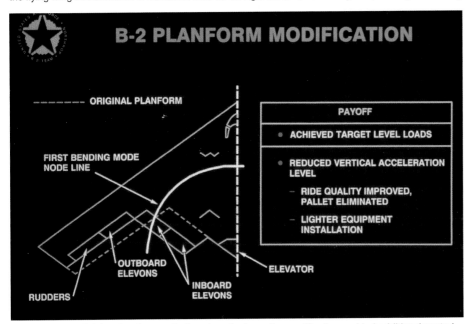

B-2 PLANFORM MODIFICATION

------- ORIGINAL PLANFORM

FIRST BENDING MODE NODE LINE

PAYOFF
● ACHIEVED TARGET LEVEL LOADS
● REDUCED VERTICAL ACCELERATION LEVEL
– RIDE QUALITY IMPROVED, PALLET ELIMINATED
– LIGHTER EQUIPMENT INSTALLATION

OUTBOARD ELEVONS

ELEVATOR

RUDDERS

INBOARD ELEVONS

Specifically highlighting the changes to the wing planform, the modifications added additional control surfaces with a pair of inboard elevons, leaving the drag rudders intact. This alleviated gust problems for the low altitude mission and reduced airframe stress and fatigue. (Northrop Grumman)

aerobody with inlets and serpentine ducts above the blended wing-body form. In this way they would be better shielded from ground radar and difficult to detect from above.

The face-off between Lockheed and Northrop began on 1 December 1980 when the Source Selection Evaluation Board (SSEB) chaired by Col. Joseph T. Glenn gathered to review Senior Ice, with several days spent examining the contents of a 15-volume proposal before moving on to Senior Peg. Having already produced Have Blue and the F-117A, Lockheed was confident that its design would be chosen. But Northrop had excelled during preliminary tests and their full-scale bomber, though more complex

than Lockheed's minimalist contender, had impressed the Air Force.

Northrop's Hal Makarian had come up with a flying wing with only two angles and parallel edges and it was this that attracted the attention of the aerodynamicists for its elegance and simplicity.

As the dual evaluation continued into February 1981, the SSEB provided the Source Selection Advisory Board (SSAB) with continuous briefings about their findings and it was decided that low-altitude capabilities, which had shrewdly also been offered by Northrop, should be prioritised and given greater emphasis in the overall capabilities.

The SSAB issued a Modification Request in April 1981 for an immediate

analysis of what impact switching the primary mission from high to low-altitude penetration would have. A complete resubmission was allowed, since the spectrum of changes was already accepted as being potentially so great that a complete re-examination of the concept might be required.

The return to low-altitude came as a result of new intelligence from Lincoln Laboratory which catalogued and evaluated evolving and perceived Soviet threats. It was decided that the Soviets were already moving to close the gap in their high-altitude defences and that a high-flying ATB might now find itself entering a high-risk area.

Both Lockheed and Northrop were immediately obliged to beef up the structure of their designs, adding 10,000lb of weight. Following these refinements, the SSEB prepared draft contracts anticipating a flight within 48 months of go-ahead but that was considered too risky and extensions were added, first to 60 months, then to 72 months.

ENTER THE NORTHROP B-2

After further pole tests and evaluation of how its design would counter the Soviet air defence threat, Northrop was awarded the B-2 contract on 17 October 1981. This was 15 days after the B-1B had been authorised, with 100 bombers ordered into production. At this date, the Air Force planned to procure 132 B-2s. Key to its success was the division of responsibility: James E. Kinnu was in charge of the B-2 at Northrop with Waaland covering the technical design details and Cashen responsible for the stealth, radar and electronic requirements in both defensive and offensive systems.

Northrop worked a hierarchical structure and demanded a military-style approach to management, with a top-down pattern of work assignments and job functions. Personnel were recruited from the Shuttle programme, including Ed Smith who had been working the Shuttle Orbiter. He became the B-2's chief engineer.

Confidence was high but unanticipated problems were just around the corner. Early in 1983 the aeroelastic analysis of stresses and loads at low-level flying revealed a problem caused by the original positioning of the control surfaces. This was always going to be an issue with any flying-wing configuration and one which had to a certain extent been accepted. As located, these were fine for high-altitude conditions but totally inadequate in extended flight low down. Pitch and roll were handled by trailing edge controls and that exacerbated the effect so the controls had to be moved inboard of the first bending mode back as far as the trailing edge notch.

The underlying problem was in the positioning of the control surfaces which were unable to respond sufficiently to gusts and buffeting due to pressure

Northrop Grumman B-2 Spirit

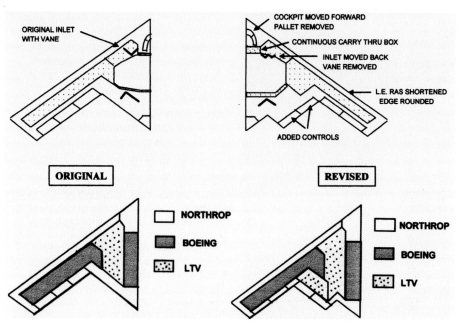

Aeroelastic analysis only available from 1983 showed that the centre of pressure was close to the first wing bending mode line, reducing the effectiveness of the control surfaces and placing 70% of carry-through loads via the weapons bay bulkhead. The double-W configuration was the only way the reconfigured control surfaces could decouple the flight control harmonics from the structural vibration mode. The lower illustration shows changes to work allocation. (DARPA)

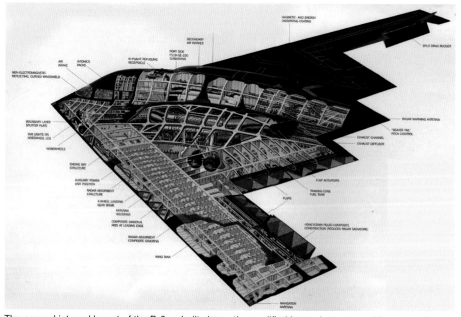

The general internal layout of the B-2 as built shows the modified internal structure with radar-reflective shaping and the application of radar-absorbent materials. (via David Baker)

loads in all the wrong places. Moreover, it was discovered that loads transfer from the outer to the inner wing sections were poor.

Some of the problem was due to demands from the Air Force, which wanted a high subsonic speed at low altitude rather than the optimised Mach 0.55 of the design which had been passed at contract selection and reviewed again at the preliminary design review in October 1982. Initially, this discovery confounded the specialised teams working flight control dynamics but Al Myers was put in charge of the redesign and integrated that activity with the structural dynamics group.

Computer modelling was used to tackle the problem – setting a new standard for this new means of assessing aerodynamic designs in the process. Honeywell and NASA's Langley Research Center also got in on the act, with specialists pulled in from around the country. Thus was born the gust load alleviation system (GLAS).

It appeared that larger flight control surfaces were needed but they also needed to respond faster to command inputs than had previously been the case. Getting large surfaces to respond with the speed required proved challenging. A conventional fighter such as the F-16, similarly unstable and controlled by a

flight control computer, would command movement at 80 degrees per second – but the B-2 needed to achieve 100 degrees per second. In theory it should have been possible to decrease the gust load by around 10% but the faster flight control system cut it back by an unprecedented 40%.

It was soon found that the problem had not all been about the need for faster controls and the positioning of the aero-surfaces however. Within a couple of months it became clear that the entire trailing edge of the wing-body form had to change. Previously, the configuration in planform had been built around a diamond-shaped centrebody with rectangular wing sections added. There were no inboard sections on the aft sides of the diamond on which to place control surfaces. But by adding a further notch cut in the rear outboard centrebody a new surface was created inside the first bending mode, to which new inboard elevons could be attached. And by creating a higher aspect ratio to the rectangular wing sections the overall surface area remained similar.

Another advantage was a stronger centrebody structure and improved shape, with great improvements made to the front of the aircraft and, with the sawtooth trailing edge across the entire aerobody planform, the flight controls were moved well aft of the centre of pressure. In the original configuration, the chord of the centre wing section – essentially the outer section of the diamond body – was determined by the length of the propulsion system, with the outside wing panels sized for balance.

The reconfiguration of the shape with the new double-W trailing edge allowed redistribution of loads via a continuous box and that provided a more elegant arrangement of carry-through bulkheads in the aft section of the body. In that way, the two massive spars could transmit loads and do it more efficiently. It also provided options for modifying the location and shape of the engine inlet face.

The Air Force gave Northrop another challenge – the aircraft might have to land at unfamiliar airfields and in extreme weather environments; at locations with 2,500ft runways and facilities no bigger than those required for a Boeing 737. For take-off from a hot and high location at high angle-of-attack (alpha), with a straight wing leading edge the aircraft in its initial form would not get sufficient airflow across the control surfaces and would stall. At slow take-off speeds and fully loaded, as the alpha angle increases the air flows spanwise, starving the control surfaces along the trailing edge.

The solution was to provide radius on the leading edge only where it was necessary to generate airflow parallel to the line of flight, neither spanwise nor tangentially to the leading edge sweep. This was to change the leading edge

Rollout of the first B-2 (82-1066) took place at Plant 32, Palmdale, California, on 22 November 1988 before a specially invited assembly of politicians, senior Air Force officials and representatives of the prime contractors. (USAF)

dimension of the wing and create a subtle non-linearity to taper the edge radius at critical wing sections, rounder in the middle and thinner at the ends.

All this added $2bn to the overall programme and moved the predicted date of the first flight out to late 1988. But it was creating a new way of designing and building aircraft. Traditionally, an aircraft is assembled on a production line from the inside out but that could not be the case with the B-2. The contours of the external skin had to be exact and the traditionally acceptable irregularities and minute inconsistencies that ended up on the skin wall of an average aircraft would completely unstitch all the hard work done to achieve low RCS. There had to be a carefully composed mathematical model to define the exterior shape, into which would be fitted all the structural and systems/subsystems elements.

CAD, CAM AND NCAD
New tools were being made available through increasingly more powerful computing equipment and 2D design mechanisms during the 1980s. Computer-aided design (CAD) was in its infancy and built on computer-aided manufacturing (CAM), which had preceded it by a decade. CAM evolved from G-code where computers created the patterns required for control machines and placed them on punch cards or tape to increase the flow of accurate copies of a standard, numerical shape.

When computers became sufficiently powerful to handle relatively large volumes of data the CAM replaced punch cards and tape, creating physical items directly from design files. The aviation industry was late to pick this up, development for which had been pioneered in France by the Renault car

company. When CATIA was introduced in the late 1970s, the integration of CAD, CAM and computer-aided engineering made it possible to replace blueprints and physical measuring tools with powerful computerised processing systems.

It was against this background that Northrop's Kinnu made the bold decision to spend money developing a uniquely tailored application of CAD/CAM called NCAD – Northrop Computer Aided Design. The company wrote its own software and patented the process to build on earlier 2D models by matching them to a 3D system called No-Loft. It was this need to design and manufacture from the outside in which convinced Waaland and Cashen that this was the only way it could be achieved.

Northrop's B-2 was the first aviation project to use such an integrated CAD/CAM process and the result was an

aeroplane built straight from a numerical tool. The pioneering part played by Northrop in developing this system was reflected in the majority of aerospace engineers a decade later who said that they first learned these techniques with NCAD. But it involved a lot of companies, as did the entire manufacturing process. Many subcontractors gained measurably from this work and benefited from being involved in the B-2 programme, if only because of that. The B-2's design also stimulated the development of exotic materials, many of which did not exist at the time the ATB was conceived, making it one of the most important programmes in the history of aeronautical engineering.

Developing a production line involved big-name players such as Boeing and Vought. It all came together at a plant in Pico Rivera, east of Los Angeles and north-west of Downey, long ago the headquarters of North American Aviation. Situated only eight miles from Cranford airport, the site had been operated by Ford from 1957 to 1980 during which time it turned out more than 1.4 million automobiles. The 157-acre site was purchased by Northrop and the early design, development and support phases for the B-2 were established there before operations were moved to Plant 42 at Palmdale, California.

During initial briefings given by Northrop to the Air Force in 1979, Waaland had presented the possibility of protecting the aircraft and its crew from the effects of its own nuclear bombs detonating at low level, allowing it to continue with its mission even under these dire circumstances.

None of the materials used in Northrop's previous experience with stealth projects would be transferable to the B-2 – since they would not be able to withstand post-nuclear detonation conditions. Indeed, there were not even any known parameters against which to measure the resilience of radar-

Careful fabrication of internal structural members supported new and revolutionary forms of radar-absorbent material (RAM)

Northrop Grumman B-2 Spirit

Careful examination of the starboard wing leading edge shows accentuation of the differential profile as the underside displays landing gear door, hatches and access panels. (USAF)

absorbent material (RAM) to this extreme environment.

The requirement was then stepped up a notch when SAC demanded that all B-2 avionics equipment be completely hardened against radiation. This included protection from the gamma radiation emitted at detonation, from the following thermal wave which would overtake the departing bomber and from the electromagnetic pulse (EMP) as a consequence of exo-atmospheric gamma rays interacting with the magnetic field.

In seeking appropriate materials, Northrop discovered some very nasty

consequences in the preparation cycle for some that had initially been selected and thought appropriate for the job; the contamination they produced and sometimes the toxic emissions they gave off were unacceptable. The cockpit area got special attention and the windscreen was fitted with a fast-action photochromatic surface. An important aspect of survivability was for the aircraft itself to detect a nuclear flash and shut down its own electronics – preventing them from being fried by the EMP before self-rebooting. Another troubling challenge was to make the aircraft

lightning-proof. That was harder than EMP protection, because the excessive amperage imported when struck could very easily fry wiring.

FLIGHT TIME

The second Preliminary Design Review was held in March and April 1984 to assess and approve configuration and system changes, with the critical design review (CDR) still pencilled in for December 1985. One added complexity was the absence of a mock-up or prototype, the several tens of thousands of 'pages' of engineering drawings

A front view of the bulbous crew compartment and blended intakes with drooping drag brakes. (USAF)

having to comprise the ensemble from which judgement on all aspects of the B-2 would be passed. The CDR involved Northrop, Boeing and Vought and was made with 90% of the structural drawings complete together with 20% of the subsystems.

Delays to the first flight of the B-2 resulted from the change in wing design necessitated by the altered mission profile. During this time the decision to limit production to 132 B-2s was challenged by Northrop, which conducted an evaluation to show (realistically as it happened) that the company could build 24-36 stealth bombers a year, hastening to point out that a longer production run would lower the unit cost over time. But there were real concerns over cost.

The first B-2 airframe, AV-1 (82-1066), would be used to explore the flight envelope and to conduct the early LO capability testing. This was an important step since no amount of pole tests with scale models could effectively characterise the actual radar cross-section of the full-size aircraft. AV-2 (82-1067) would share some of the performance testing and would also be the vehicle to test weapons release. AV-3 (82-1068) was to begin tests of the avionics and to share some for the LO tests as well as demonstrate weapons compatibility. This was the first to carry active defensive and offensive flight systems and would become the primary test aircraft for the low-observables requirements.

AV-4 (82-1069) would also conduct avionics testing and divide the work with AV-3, supporting it in weapons tests. AV-5 (82-1070) would also conduct weapons tests and carry out climatic tests from Eglin AFB, Florida. AV-6 (82-1071) would perform more LO tests and conduct

US Secretary of Defense Mark Esper checks out the B-2 from the pilot's seat, the commander occupying the right-hand position. Note the expansive windows coated with non-reflective finish. (USAF)

evaluation of technical requirements under various flight conditions and carry out type evaluation trials.

Several changes were occurring and one important move was to put Jorge Diaz in charge as chief engineer. It helped that the first six aircraft off the line had assigned roles and their systems and subsystems could be prioritised according to the flight test assignments. It was a delicate balance between managing the overall pace of the programme and true systems management rules when it came to assigning work packages and evaluating supplier-provided equipment, right down to the component level. The prime players – Northrop, Boeing, Vought and engine-builder General Electric – worked together in a unique partnership.

Additional effort was needed on the electronics and avionics development programme and a Boeing C-135A (60-0377) was employed testing navigation and bombing equipment. This included tests with Hughes radar systems in 305 flights during which 1,000hrs were committed to radar and 650hrs to testing navigation systems. Another C-135A (55-3122), was assigned to General Electric's F118 turbofan engine, specially equipped with dedicated test equipment.

Completion of AV-1 was accomplished on production tooling and the rollout ceremony was set for 22 November 1988 with great anticipation. Intense secrecy surrounded the project itself but knowledge of its existence and potential impact on future warfare was rife with drama and hyperbole. Among those who already knew was Jack Northrop. In April 1980, he had received special clearance for a meeting with John Cashen where he was shown a model of the flying-wing ATB, vindication of his lifelong belief in the flying wing form. Visibly moved by the

model he held in his hands, he died 10 months later knowing that his flying wing had bridged the decades and was finally coming home to the Air Force.

The first flight of AV-1 on 17 July 1989 occurred from Runway 04 at Palmdale at the start of a 1hr 52min flight to Edwards ADFB, California. Piloted by Bruce J. Hinds, chief test pilot for the Northrop B-2 division in the left seat and Col Richard S. Crouch, director of the combined test forces, the nose wheel left the runway 22sec after brake release and with the stick eased back at the 3,500ft point, rotating to a planned 7.5-degree pitch but lifting off at 6.5 degrees, at 6.37am local time. Two F-16 chase-planes kept formation on the aircraft, at times moving in to half the B-2's wingspan, but at no point did the aircraft exceed 10,000ft. It was flown for stretches at speeds of 180, 150 and 140kts, the latter being the final approach speed.

Touchdown at Edwards' Runway 22 occurred at 8.29am, 200ft short of the 1,000ft point with a pitch-up of 7.5 degrees, stopping in 4,200ft. There had been no landing gear retraction on this initial flight and the aircraft was in such excellent condition that preparations for the second flight were immediate, rather than an extended post-flight inspection being conducted as originally planned. The crew found the aircraft highly responsive. Crouch found that it "flies like a real airplane" and that it had a "very good roll rate for a big airplane". Hinds added that there was only one overshoot responding to a yaw doublet but that the B-1 was "very well damped, as you would imagine with the big wing".

Easing the aircraft into a concentrated flight test programme, 82-1066 made unsuccessful bids for a second flight on 12 and 15 August before making

Northrop Grumman B-2 Spirit

With a seemingly ungainly appearance when viewed from the side, in the air at slow speed this B-2 (89-0129) shows detail in the landing gear doors. (USAF)

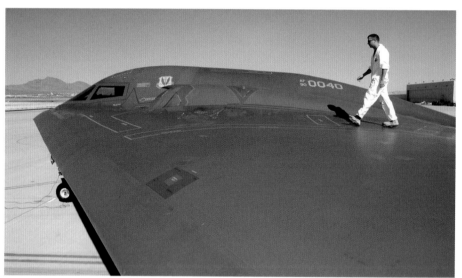

The exterior coating applied to the B-2 has been changed during block upgrades and commercial development of new and improved products increases the low-observables characteristics while reducing maintenance time. (USAF)

A close-up of the forward landing gear leg with detail on B-2 *Spirit of Missouri* (88-0329). (USAF)

it back into the air on the following day when Block 1 testing started evaluation of aerodynamic performance and airworthiness. The flight had to be aborted after testing the landing gear when low oil pressure signalled lubrication issues. The third flight took place on 26 August lasting 4hr 38min, during which a maximum altitude of 25,000ft and a top speed of 300kts (345mph) was achieved.

Aero-manoeuvring tests demonstrated 60-degree bank angles and the aircraft rendezvoused with a KC-10A (79-1951) from March AFB, California, to check procedures for in-flight refuelling. A fourth flight on 21 September was also cut short but as the flight envelope opened up, two days later the fifth flight gave Lt Col John Small the opportunity to fly the aircraft on low-speed tests.

The first in-flight refuelling was successfully accomplished on 8 November during the seventh test flight, when the KC-10A from March AFB transferred

40,000lb of JP-8 to the B-2 about three hours after take-off. JP-8 fuel was just now being adopted throughout the Air Force for its higher flashpoint and being less carcinogenic – but it also has a strong odour, is oily to the touch and is more difficult to wash away. It can also cause headaches and B-2 servicing and maintenance personnel had to take special precautions when using it. As testing accelerated and the flight success rates brought acclaim for the aircraft, all Block 1 work had been completed by June 1990.

The second aircraft (82-1067) made its first flight on 19 October 1990 and flew straight to Edwards AFB. The third B-2 (82-1068) followed on 18 June 1991 and was the first to carry a fully active defensive and offensive avionics suite. It was used to demonstrate full weapons integration and was the basis for the Block 2 low-observables programme. This accounted for 25% of the 3,600hrs of testing. All this activity took place under the auspices of the B-2 Combined Test Force and by 1991 was averaging 30hrs/month of flight time.

In addition to the flight activity, progress was being made by Northrop in reducing manufacturing time, with the second aircraft requiring 1.75 million hours and the seventh around one million hours, compared to 3.5 million hours for AV-1. Targets for the test phase had 80% of the flight envelope explored during the first six months and fully completed within two years, 90% of the propulsion system testing and 70% of the radar signature definition completed by that date.

BUILDING THE B-2

Although the prime contractor had overall responsibility for the B-2 detailed design and manufacture, it employed 131 subcontractors on specialised systems and subsystems. Boeing used 69 subcontractors, General Electric 52 and LTV (Vought) some 32. Overall, at the end of the 1980s during peak development and production, the programme involved 26,000 people of whom 46% were with Northrop.

The entire design and build of the B-2 was different from any previous programme, with the exception of the SR-71 which also had its unique record in the history of exotic aircraft. It was designed to MIL-STD-1760 and brought unique requirements regarding materials, with 80% of the structure comprising composites, some uniquely developed for this aircraft. Most composites consisted of carbon and graphite with glass-fibre woven with cloth or tape and a binder consisting of a polymer.

The usual method was to lay up the cloth or tape in a mould in an orientation according to the strength or structural requirement of the component. To this base the polymer was added and checked for accuracy of mould conformity before being baked in an autoclave at temperatures above 350°F (176°C) and pressures in excess of 100psi.

The composite components weighed one-third less, were considerably stronger and had up to four times the fatigue life of their aluminium equivalents. In further applications, which cut labour manpower by a third, LTV developed an automated process to apply the appropriate amounts of tape or cloth to the contoured tool to produce appropriately shaped structural ribs and stringers. This was marketed to other companies and the entire B-2 composites programme set a trend throughout the aircraft manufacturing world, extending beyond the use of composites to fine-scale cutting and shaping across a wide range of materials including steel, aluminium, titanium and aluminium-lithium.

LTV's computer-controlled superplastic forming cell took CAM to a new level with robotic abrasive water-jet cutters for all kinds of conventional steels and alloys, enabling manufacture of sheets up to 4ft by 12ft in size and up to 0.25in thickness. A five-axis computer-controlled robotic drilling machine could make holes for fasteners and install them while sealing composite or combined composite/ metallic surfaces of up to 18ft by 30ft. This precision prevented a great deal of waste in costly exotic metals and composites.

Load-bearing elements were fabricated from titanium. Driven by the requirements of combat aircraft, titanium came into much greater use during the 1980s because of its high specific properties, good fatigue and tensile strength with some retaining considerable resilience up to 932°F (500°C). Fatigue limits are more predictable with titanium than with aluminium alloys and it has greater resistance to corrosion, although salt in the environment is not good for it. Fabrication with titanium was approximately seven times more costly than with aluminium or steel but the results achieved were deemed worthy of the expense.

The overall layout of the B-2 consists of a deep and roughly diamond-shaped blended centrebody incorporating two side-by-side bomb bays, a cockpit, two main landing gear wells and associated electronics packages. The aerodynamic design was based on computational fluid dynamics (CFD), a tool which was still in development during the emergence of the stealth project. Never imagined as a supersonic aircraft, the CFD for the B-2 was based on a transonic analysis code which discounted the engine flow and incorporated spilling air.

The solutions defined through CFD were tested in wind tunnels to incorporate all manner of conditions including ground-effect and aerial refuelling. The depth of the main aerobody and the thickness/span ratio, the greatest for any bomber fuselage yet built, posed significant challenges.

Stripping off the original coating to apply a new and more effective product during the Block 30 upgrade. (Northrop Grumman)

Aerial refuelling is crucial for many B-2 mission profiles and this nose shot shows the receptacle above and behind the crew compartment. (USAF)

The fully pressurised and air-conditioned cockpit contains two ACES II ejection seats for the crew and blow-out hatches above. The mission commander usually occupies the right seat with the co-pilot to their left. Four very large photochromatically coated windows are displaced far forward of the crew positions and afford a less included-angle visibility than would seem apparent from their size. The crew climb aboard via retractable steps to the rear of the nose leg and can hit an 'instant' switch to start the engines and primary systems, minimising response time. Controls are basically the same as in any other aircraft but throttle quadrants are provided for each pilot, with almost all the controls accessible to both.

As built, the displays conformed to the emerging 'glass cockpit' concept of the late 1980s and cockpit layout made provision for the addition of a third crewmember at some future date, should they be required for workload relief or some unique task independent of flying the aircraft. The Air Force awarded a $109m contract to Northrop Grumman for an aft deck redesign in 2011. The all-colour, nine-tube, electronic flight instrumentation system (EFTIS) displays flight, engine and sensor data with associated avionics and weapons information. With this, the pilot can select take-off, go-to-war, or landing mode via a single three-position switch. In 'go-to-war' mode the aircraft shuts down all inactive systems and arms the weapons in the bomb bays.

Northrop Grumman B-2 Spirit

A B-2 tops up from a KC-135 of the Nebraska Air National Guard, a capability which the Air Force claims extends the range of the bomber beyond 6,900 miles. (USAF)

Four 8in square colour displays handle information from double-redundant control processors. Quadruple-redundant digital flight control computers also manage processing for the passive air-data system and the attitude-motion sensors which are an independent inertial reference system. This allows the flight computer to continue operating even if all air-data is lost. The multi-function displays are backed up on the left side by three electro-mechanical gauges which supply attitude, airspeed and altitude reference data. The automated

fuel control system can also be handled manually in the event of a malfunction.

The weapons bays can accommodate nearly 60,000lb of stores but there is no provision for carrying anything externally. Each of the two bays incorporates a rotary launcher and two bomb rack assemblies and tests have demonstrated successful release of several nuclear bombs, including the B61-11 and B83, and the conventional Mk 82 from the rotary launcher and the CBU-87 conventional weapon from the racks.

The aircraft is also capable of carrying the AGM-129 advanced strategic cruise

missile which has a range of 1,500 miles and as many as 16 JDAMs can be carried. The bomb rack assembly is being upgraded to carry up to 80 JDAMs. It will also be able to carry the joint stand-off weapon (JSOW), the joint air-to-surface stand-off missile (JASSM) and the wind-compensated munition dispenser (WCMD). Another option will be 80 x 254lb Small-Diameter Bombs (SDBs).

In June 2007, Northrop Grumman was contracted to integrate the Boeing Massive Ordnance Penetrator (MOP) weapon, a 30,000lb GPS-guided bomb configured to dig into deeply buried and heavily hardened targets. Since 2013 the B-2 has been able to carry one in each bay. Integrated with the Block 30 upgrade in the late 2000s, a Generic Weapons Interface System (GWIS) was installed to support the B-2 in carrying a range of different weapons on a single mission, allowing the bomber to hit four different target types on one sortie. An added advantage available with the Block 30 upgrades is the aircraft's ability to attack moving targets with PGMs. The work also included upgrades to the displays and to the radar modes.

Countermeasures for the B-2 include a Lockheed Martin radar warning receiver, a defensive aids system from Northrop Grumman and the Lockheed Martin AN/APR-50 defensive armament management system. Operating at the Ku-band, the Raytheon AN/APQ-181 covert strike radar is a multipurpose unit combining terrain following and terrain avoidance modes with a demonstrated capability for hugging the contours at

Deep Strike From Every Angle

If the Army deployed missile batteries with its Long-Range Hypersonic Weapons to Guam, the U.S. territory closest to China, the $40 million missiles could reach the Eastern Coast of China. By contrast, penetrating stealth bombers based in Guam, Australia, Diego Garcia, aided by aerial refuelling, could reach targets across most of China's territory.

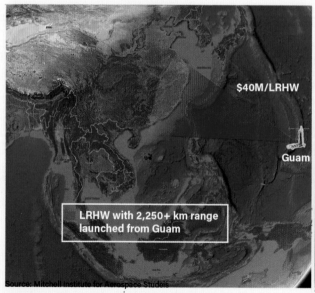

$40M/LRHW

Guam

LRHW with 2,250+ km range launched from Guam

Source: Mitchell Institute for Aerospace Studies

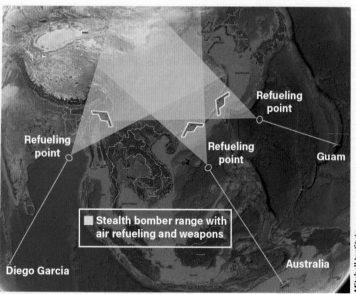

Refueling point

Refueling point

Refueling point

Guam

Stealth bomber range with air refueling and weapons

Diego Garcia

Australia

Mitchell Institute

In the 2020s much debate surrounds the equivalent force-effectiveness of ground-launched ballistic strike systems and the deployment of B-2s from several locations in the region. (Mitchell Institute)

The third B-2 (82-1068) *Spirit of New York* flies up the English Channel off the Kent coast accompanied by two F-35s. (RAF)

less than 200ft. Originally, the radar had a dual-phase antenna, one each on either side of the nose landing gear well. The first aircraft with an active electronically scanned array (AESA) was delivered to the Air Force in April 2009.

This equipment replaces entirely the radar system incorporated when the B-2 was designed during the 1980s but new antennas were not installed until 2012. The navigation suite incorporates a Rockwell Collins TCN-250 TACAN with the VIR-130A instrument landing system. This company also provides the communications equipment and a Milstar military strategic and tactical relay satellite communications system is also fitted. All aircraft now have Link-16 equipment.

The basic wing of the B-2 was taken from a modified NASA laminar profile to incorporate a compound camber with a sharp leading edge. As described in the preceding section on how the B-2 evolved as a design, with a sweep angle of 33 degrees the wing leading edge is critical both to stealth capabilities and aerodynamic performance. It incorporates both sharp and blunt edges, varying in camber from root to tip. For stealth, each straight edge is bent downward, this being most visible at the aircraft's nose with its distinct 'beak-like' appearance.

The inlet for each of the aircraft's engines is integrated into the shape of the wing. The area across the chord of the wing can be divided into two supercritical areas: the region from the leading edge to the inlet over which airflow is accelerated to supersonic speed and then compressed to subsonic speed; and the area from the inlet to the exhaust outlet, where flow is accelerated and recompressed. In cruise flight the air is disrupted all around the inlet and this interaction flows spanwise to the

A B-2 at Andersen AFB, Guam, operating with the Pacific Air Forces in a display of combined operations with US and friendly forces in the region. In recent years the focus of attention has switched from Europe to South East Asia and the region around contested locations in the South China Sea. (USAF)

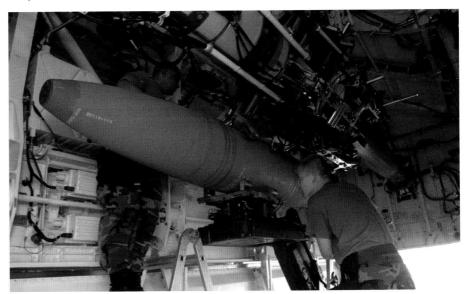

The bomb bay has a wider access uplift capacity for some special weapons identified at the time of the aircraft requirements document but cancelled later. That spaciousness allows current weapons in development to be carried by the B-2. (USAF)

Northrop Grumman B-2 Spirit

Mk 82 bombs being uploaded to a B-2, displaying its conventional role. (USAF)

Capt. Jennifer Wilson (now Lt Col (ret) Jennifer Avery) of the 393rd BS became the first woman to fly as a pilot on the B-2 on 12 February 2002. She is pictured here during Operation Iraqi Freedom in 2003, graduating to the stealth bomber after three years flying the B-1B. (USAF)

The potential of the B-2 to carry almost all conventional air-drop munitions makes it an ideal instrument for supporting fire-fighting or regional conflict. A technicians uploads a JDAM to the spacious bomb bay. (USAF)

tip. This phenomenon made it impossible to precisely predict the upper wing's overall aerodynamic performance short of flight testing.

The leading edge of the wing beginning just outboard of the engine inlets is shaped so as to optimise transonic air flow and to provide shock-resistant compression of that flow at high subsonic speeds. Early in the design phase, a full-scale mock-up of the inlet area showed that flow separation in the curved duct resulted in a loss of power, so retractable auxiliary doors, or scoops, were added above the wing and these give the aircraft a characteristic appearance at all but high cruise speeds and in selected regions of the mission profile.

Most of the aircraft's spars and skin are fabricated from carbon-fibre/epoxy composites which for some sections were the largest fabricated thus far, with spars and some skin sections 70ft long and 1in thick. Because of the need to create a seamless surface assembled from the outside in, skin sections were cured at the same time and this significantly reduced the number of joins. There was concern that the stealthy characteristics designed in to the airframe could be compromised by reflections from the internal structure but RAM was applied to prevent that. A material coating transforms radio energy into thermal energy. As the radar wave encounters the outer layer of, say,

a carbonyl iron particle bed, the bed beneath it transforms the small reflections by a residual reflection which detunes the frequency by half a wavelength. These processes are effective for a wide frequency range and satisfy the need to protect against AAM and SAM sites where most operated between the L-band and the Ku-band.

But wavelengths up to 2m require special attention and for VHF radars in particular a radar-absorbent structure does the job. Particularly on the leading edges, a high-frequency ferromagnetic absorption layer is laid down over a resistive layer which reflects incoming signals to higher frequencies and allows lower frequencies to pass right through. Below these layers, a glass-fibre honeycomb core is treated with an increasingly dense material of high resistivity from front to back covering a wedge-shaped reflective surface. The energy reaching here will be further disrupted and prevented from reflection back to the emitter. Antennas and probes, including pitot tubes, which would usually project from the surface are buried in shaped voids and covered with RAM.

The overall design of the aerobody incorporates access panels covering several grouped sensors to minimise surface breaks. Access to internal systems is via existing apertures such as wheel wells, the crew boarding hatch and the weapons bays and these also provide access to fuelling and inspection electronics. Unusually, there are no drain holes on this aircraft and nothing drips out to the ground. Fluids that do leak are routed by pipes and collected in reservoirs which can be emptied

Along with the F-117A fighter-bomber, the B-2 represents the peak of US jet bomber evolution and the introduction of types specifically designed for low-observables. (USAF)

B-2 *Spirit of Pennsylvania* (93-1087), the 20th and penultimate B-2, in service since August 1997. (USAF)

A close-up view of the engine intake with the slot beneath for sucking in cool air to modify the thermal profile of the engine exhaust. (USAF)

after flight. In all aspects of the design, accessibility was a priority.

As indicated previously, stealth includes thermal signatures where hot exhaust gas emissions can reveal the presence of an aircraft that has not been picked up by radar. Infrared sensors are designed to lock on to those thermal gradients to distinguish them from the surrounding atmosphere. With four engines, the B-2 has a large thermal emission spectrum across a broad band of wavelengths. This is most easily suppressed by reducing the temperature and dispersing thermal gradients.

The engine inlets and exhausts are on the top of the aerobody but the gaseous emissions emerge into free air on top of the main body of the aircraft and well ahead of the trailing edge. The engines have flow-mixers to blend cold bypass air from the secondary inlets with the hot exhaust as it emerges with the exit orifice flat and wide to disperse the gases more broadly and so reduce the temperature per unit volume. The side-angles on the exhaust outlets box in exhaust gas with the air flowing over the aerosurface and that too helps disperse the gases and lower temperatures. To suppress the formation of high-altitude contrails, a chloro-fluorosulphuric acid is injected into the exhaust mixture.

The flight control surfaces are exclusive to the trailing edge of the double-W configuration and make up some 15% of the 5,140sq ft total wing area. There are three elevon surfaces on each side for pitch and roll and a drag-rudder/spoiler at each wing tip for yaw control. The inboard elevons are considered secondary. Each elevon is split into separate surfaces for redundancy and synchronised by the quadruple-redundant flight control system. A 'beaver tail' on the centreline at the extreme rear provides for some pitch control and gust alleviation at low altitude.

The XB-35 and YB-49 control layout formed the basis for control surface design into the wing trailing edge with the concept of drag rudders taken directly from those designs, automatically controlled but with a manual override for selecting a wider opening if required. No high-lift devices are incorporated, partly due to the need to minimise moving sections, gaps or cavities which would otherwise compromise the low RCS. Even with the large main landing gear doors open the aircraft has only very small side forces.

Designed and fabricated by Boeing, the landing gear consists of a conventional tricycle layout with a single Dowty Decoto forward gear strut supporting a twin-wheel assembly with two lights, one above the other on the left side of the nose gear upper main strut. The nose wheel has two doors, one attached to the main gear strut and the other hinged to the right side of the well. The main landing gear retracts forward and up and each has an

Northrop Grumman B-2 Spirit

A B-2 from the 509th BW with an F-35A Lightning II from the Royal Netherlands Air Force during Bomber Task Force Europe 20-2 in March 2020. (USAF)

The 509th Maintenance Squadron at Whiteman AFB has 40 mechanics working to keep the General Electric F118-100 engine for the B-2 maintained and upgraded. (USAF)

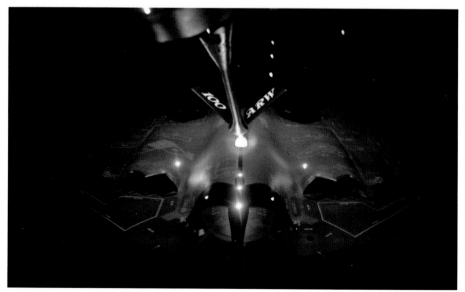

A KC-135 from the 100th ARW refuels a B-2 from the 509th BW late on its way to bomb terrorist camps in Libya on 18 January 2017. (USAF)

articulated, four-wheel bogie with large anti-torque assemblies, the main brakes being carbon disc types.

Each main gear well is covered by a single door hinged on the outer side and powered by a hydraulic ram for opening and closing in synchronism with extension and retraction. All gear doors have serrated edges for minimal radar returns between the doors and the surrounding surface. The landing gear track is 40ft and all tyres are provided by Goodyear Tyre and Rubber Co.

Carrying the designation F118-GE-100 and producing a thrust of 17,300lb, the engine selected for the B-2 was based on the F101-X which was a fighter engine derived from the General Electric F110 used for the B-1B. It was developed from the original in 1983 and has the same fan diameter and configuration in the stator case as the F110 engine for the F-16C/D and F-14D fighters.

The B-2 engine has the smaller low-pressure spool which is scaled up from the F404. Bypass ratio was reduced from 3:1 to 0.87:1. Although a higher bypass ratio would have been better, that would have increased inlet and exhaust dimensions, undesirable for stealth configurations, and would in any case have lost power with altitude. Total fuel tank capacity is about 165,000lb.

A Lockheed Martin integrated processing unit (IPU) was installed in July 2009 as part of a larger upgrade to develop a satellite communications capability and a new computer architecture. In maintenance where time is costly, a new alternate high-frequency material (AHFM) has been developed which is sprayed on to a single vehicle by four robots independently controlled. This greatly reduces maintenance and ensures higher availability rates.

SPIRIT IN THE SKY

The original plan for 132 B-2s did not last long. When the Soviet Union collapsed, so too did the need to counter the Soviet air defence threat. In April 1990, a mere nine months after its first flight, Secretary of Defence Richard Cheney decided to cut B-2 production to just 75 aircraft. Less than two years later, in January 1992, that was reduced to 20 – plus one test aircraft which would not be upgraded. The test aircraft was referred to as the B-2, operational aircraft as the B-2A.

The first delivery to Air Combat Command was on 17 December 1993 when the eighth aircraft (88-0329) named *Spirit of Missouri* arrived at the aircraft's only home base, Whiteman AFB, Missouri, the entire complement eventually to serve with the 13th BS and the 393rd BS of the 509th BW, Eighth Air Force.

Shakedown operations got under way rapidly, with a further four aircraft delivered by the end of 1994. On 12 January 1995, three B-2As were launched in 30 minutes, refuelled and conducted

B-2 *Spirit of Mississippi* (82-1071) in the foreground and *Spirit of New York* (82-1068) accompanied by an F-35 Lightning II along the coast of Kent and East Sussex in the UK. (USAF)

six sorties in a single day. Less than two weeks later they turned up at the Red Flag exercises at Nellis AFB, Nevada, in which they participated for two weeks.

On 11 June 1995, a B-2A flew non-stop to the Paris Air Show and landed for an hour before flying back home with a different crew. Over the next several months, numerous visits were made to foreign locations and in July of 1996 the fleet began to receive the GBU-36/37 GPS-guided bombs with a demonstration in which a single aircraft dropped 16 of these munitions from 40,000ft against 16 targets on a single sortie. A B-2A flew to the RAF Mildenhall air fete in May 1997, thrilling spectators and flying the flag for the USAF. Once the production aircraft had been delivered, the test aircraft were brought to operational standard. The last was handed over to the 509th in January 2000.

Along the way, crews learned a very different way of flying the bomber. The 11 surfaces provided a unique means of thrust-vectoring the engine exhaust and differential throttling of the engines controlling yaw without using the outboard speed brakes. Pilots regard the aircraft as one of the easiest to fly, particularly since the flight control system can fly the B-2 on its own while the crew focus their attention on mission objectives. The designed-in space for a third crewmember proved unnecessary as flight tests and operational exercises demonstrated the effectiveness of a two-person crew.

Variant evolution began with Block 10 and limited capabilities and unable to operate guided weapons, followed by Block 20 which gave the capacity to carry CBU-878/B combined-effects munitions and Mk 84 bombs as well as nuclear gravity bombs. Block 30 gave full JDAM and JSOW capability plus the full defensive avionics suite. Seven of the 21 aircraft delivered were built to Block 30 standard from the outset and the rest were upgraded to it.

The combat effectiveness of the B-2 was ably demonstrated in 1998 during Operation Allied Force against Serbian military infrastructure in Yugoslavia. Some 33% of all selected targets were destroyed in the first two months on missions flown non-stop from Whiteman AFB and back. During Operation Enduring Freedom in 2001, the B-2 made an extended, non-stop flight from Whiteman to Afghanistan and thence to Diego Garcia where it changed crew and returned to Missouri.

Although at first limited to deployment at Whiteman AFB in the US, a transportable hangar was then created which allows the B-2 to operate from forward locations. With a length of 126ft, a width of 250ft and a height of 55ft, the first was located at Diego Garcia in the Indian Ocean. This supported Operation Iraqi Freedom in March and April 2003,

with B-2s flying 22 sorties and releasing a total of 1.5m pounds of munitions.

In March 2005, a squadron of B-2s was deployed to Andersen AFB, Guam, to support USAF Pacific Command. It was there on 23 February 2008 that the only B-2 loss to date occurred – *Spirit of Kansas* crashing on the runway shortly after take-off. An investigation later found that heavy rain had caused moisture to enter skin-flush air data sensors. This condensation caused three pressure transducers to fail, sending inaccurate angle of attack and airspeed data to the flight control computers, which shortly after the wheels lifted from the runway initiated a sudden 30-degree pitch-up manoeuvre.

An unrecoverable stall ensued and the crew ejected as the port wing tip began to dig into the ground beside the runway. The aircraft came down violently, tumbled and burned as its fuel ignited. Both crewmembers survived unharmed. The B-2 fleet was grounded for two months during the investigation but then returned to flight status.

A product of the extraordinary efforts made to reverse the proactive expansion of Soviet military power during the late 1980s, the B-2 remains unparalleled in its capabilities more than 30 years after its first flight. It is the only acknowledged aircraft than can carry large air-to-surface standoff weapons in a stealth configuration.

NORTHROP GRUMMAN B-21

First Flight: 2022

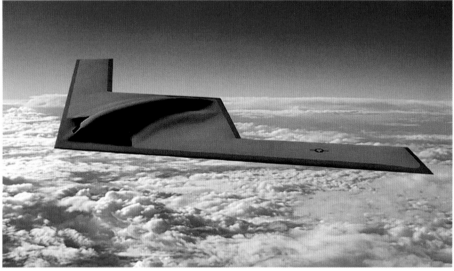

The first officially sanctioned rendition of the B-21 was released on 26 February 2016 when the Air Force revealed the outline of the Long Range Strike Bomber. (USAF)

Released on 6 July 2021, this revised artist's illustration of a B-21 orientates the angle of the aircraft to hide the engine intake geometry, placing the rendition over an image of Edwards AFB, California, where it will conduct flight tests. (USAF)

Toward the end of the last century, fearing that the B-2 programme would fall prey to accelerating capabilities in counter-stealth technology, and seeking to bridge the encroaching gulf in penetration capability, the US Air Force set up the 2037 Bomber study. This examined a range of options from a B-2 replacement to an unmanned UCAV-type system controlled remotely by ground-pilots via satellite.

Next came the Next-Generation Bomber programme in 2001, which aimed to commission a B-2 successor for service entry in 2018, but this was cancelled in 2009. Its successor, the Long Range Strike Bomber study, led to the B-21.

The evolution from B-2 to B-21 was the evolution of the bomber itself from an instrument for dropping munitions, to a combat aircraft with a more diverse role – putting it firmly back in contention as a key player in the contested airspace environment. What emerged from studies carried out between 2010 and 2014 was the need for a survivable battle-management aircraft able to remain on station in hostile areas while managing manned and unmanned assets. It was clear that the B-2 was aging, that it was too expensive and that it would eventually be overwhelmed by new air defence technology.

Experience with counter-insurgency missions over Iraq and Afghanistan demonstrated to the Air Force that a bomber could have intelligence, surveillance and reconnaissance capabilities far beyond those previous conventional bombers had possessed. The B-2 demonstrated that with embedded antennas and a full-stealth treatment it was possible to carry out missions which had previously been deemed too hazardous for such a large and relatively slow platform.

And it was apparent that an aircraft designed from the outset for fusion-warfare, integrating defensive and

Movement of US bomber forces around several overseas locations requires support from ground facilities, as with the portable hangar designed and deployed for receiving the B-21 when required to operate from foreign bases. Evaluated here at the B-21's initial bases at Ellsworth AFB, South Dakota, the Environmental Protection Shelter provides a haven from lengthy exposure to ultraviolet light and protects against snow and adverse weather. (USAF)

offensive avionics into a net-centric platform, would be able to go even further – greatly expanding operational possibilities.

While experience had shown the value of stand-off battle management using aircraft such as the E-3 AWACS or the E-8 JSTARS, it was now thought necessary to put command and control (C&C) capability beyond the forward edge of the battle area (FEBA) and deep into the fray, enabling sensor mapping of enemy airspace to handoff to fighters and strike aircraft.

In addition, rather than having surveillance and reconnaissance aircraft passing back information about targets, it was now possible for the surveillance and reconnaissance aircraft itself to carry smart munitions for threat suppression, attack and strike missions.

To achieve all this, a future bomber would need flexibility and modularity – an 'open architecture' approach to systems integration where new and improved avionics could be easily integrated into an existing airframe without the need for a completely new aircraft.

DECISION GATES

The sheer cost of the B-2 had prevented its procurement in great numbers but the Air Force had a requirement for at least 80-100 aircraft capable of carrying out its mission. Moreover, the extended commitment in cost and manpower to keep the B-2 flying was prohibitive, compromising its use and operational flexibility. Its successor would need to be both cheaper to buy and cheaper to maintain.

The Air Force issued a request for proposals in July 2014 but Northrop

Grumman already had a distinct advantage. It had itself conducted most of the analytical work to show the Air Force what was possible and a select group of politicians were convinced that building on what had been achieved with the existing aircraft was the right move when it came to a successor.

Northrop Grumman's work was vindicated when it was awarded a development contract in October 2015. What they were about to develop was described at this point as a fifth-generation global precision platform.

Under the highest level of security classification until it appears for flight, probably in 2022, the precise layout and physical dimensions of the aircraft were unknown at the time of writing

and only two artist's impressions had been released by the Air Force, the most recent being shown on these pages. Indications are that the B-21, officially designated as such on 26 February 2016, is smaller than the B-2 and although it possesses the same aerobody shaping as its predecessors it has a modified configuration. This is evident in the initial illustration showing a different arrangement of the two engines which it is believed to have, rather than the four which power the B-2, and a lighter gross take-off weight indicated by the less bulky landing gear.

The B-21, given that designation as a signal, it is said, that it is a '21st century bomber', was named Raider at a ceremony on 19 September 2016. This was attended by the last surviving Doolittle 'raider', Lt. Col. Richard E. Cole, who accompanied Gen. James H. Doolittle when he took 16 B-25 Mitchell bombers to attack Tokyo in April 1942. The B-21 passed its critical design review in December 2018 and work progressed on the first five aircraft at Plant 42, Palmdale, California, where the B-2 had been fabricated more than 30 years earlier.

Informed reports appear to indicate outstanding performance from Northrop Grumman, supported by Pratt & Whitney with their F135 engine, BAE Systems, Spirit AeroSystems, Orbital ATK (owned by Northrop Grumman), Rockwell Collins, GKN Industries and Janicki Industries.

Specialised fabrication facilities for the construction work have included a unique coatings plant set up at Plant 42, indicative of the shift toward a more user-friendly RAM with several new technologies providing a less costly, more resilient and more effective product.

Finding a suitable base for maintenance of the B-2 was one of its major drawbacks, so the availability and use of hardier materials has been

With a B-2 standing in for a B-21, which will be recognisably different, an artist's rendering of the Burns & McDonnell Main Operating Base facility which will be constructed for the Raider at Ellsworth AFB. (Burns & McDonnell)

Northrop Grumman B-21

a key element in the decision to build the B-21, as have the potential make it smaller than the B-2 and the ability to integrate it more effectively into a mixed-fleet combat force.

DEPLOYMENT

The test and evaluation phase will be handled by Edwards AFB, California, with Tinker AFB, Oklahoma, responsible for maintenance and 'sustainment'. Active deployment is initially at Ellsworth AFB, South Dakota, followed by Dyess AFB, Texas, and Whiteman AFB, Missouri. The 420th Flight Test Squadron has been reactivated at Edwards and is now the home of the B-21 Combined Test Force.

With a first flight confidently predicted in 2022, timelines and schedules appear to be on plan. It was verified on 8 June 2021 that the first two Raiders had been completed and were entering extended ground tests and engine trials. The Air Force confidently expects the B-21 to be in service by the mid-2020s and beginning the process of replacing the B-1B and the B-2 as it moves toward supporting a bomber force consisting entirely of this aircraft and the B-52.

With increasingly confident assertions that the B-52 will remain in service until the early 2050s, and re-engining plans already well under way for that aircraft, the B-21 is likely to support the B-52 until both retire mid-century. What comes after those may not be a manned aircraft at all and some surprises on that front may yet await initial combat-readiness of the B-21.

The Raider is frequently paired with the top secret Next Generation Air Dominance (NGAD) fighter which some say is already flying from Area 51. If that is so, the B-21 is clearly part of a fully integrated air combat package, leading a new and expanding inventory of manned and unmanned vehicles for command coordination, mission targeting and communication.

In operation, the B-21 is designed to enter hostile airspace and to remain, at altitudes of up to 80,000ft, for long periods of time as it maps electronic threats, launches electronic and active suppression and provides a high level of risk-mitigation for incoming allied aircraft. It is designed to counter air-to-air and surface-to-air threats and give a greater level of air dominance than can be achieved by lower-flying aircraft and conventional strike packages.

More than any other aircraft yet built anywhere, the B-21 restores to a prime role the manned penetrating bomber and vindicates the preservation of that capability across almost 75 years since the end of the Second World War.

Now more than 40 years after it was first planned in factories and think-tanks, the B-2 has set the standard from which legacy programmes have already emerged, the B-21 Raider being an affordable and more sustainable example of that evolution. (USAF)

TYPE SPECIFICATIONS (Listed in order of first flight of type irrespective of variant)

Aircraft	Length	Span	Empty weight	Max weight	Range	Cruise speed	Max speed	Bomb load	First flight
YB-35	53ft	172ft	91,000lb	209,000lb	7,500 miles	240mph	391mph	52,200lb	June 25, 1946
B-36J	162ft	230ft	166,165lb	410,000lb	3,985 miles	230mph	435mph	86,000lb	August 8, 1946
B-45	75.25ft	89ft	45,694lb	91,775lb	1,192 miles	365mph	566mph	22,000lb	March 17, 1947
YB-49	53ft	172ft	88,442lb	193,569lb	9,978 miles	365mph	493mph	16,000lb	October 21, 1947
B-47E	107ft	116ft	80,000lb	221,000lb	2,013 miles	557mph	607mph	25,000lb	December 17, 1947
B-52H	159.25ft	185ft	185,000lb	488,000lb	8,800 miles	509mph	650mph	70,000lb	April 15, 1952
B-57	65.5ft	64ft	27,090lb	53,720lb	950 miles	476mph	598mph	4,500lb	July 20, 1953
B/RB-66	75.2ft	72.5ft	42,549lb	83,000lb	782 miles	528mph	631mph	15,000lb	June 28, 1954
P6M-2	134.25ft	102.5ft	97,439lb	190,000lb	2,083 miles	535mph	686mph	30,450lb	July 14, 1955
B-58	96.8ft	56.75ft	55,560lb	176,890lb	2,000 miles	610mph	1,319mph	19,450lb	November 11, 1956
A-5A	76.5ft	53ft	32,783lb	63,085lb	1,121 miles	590mph	1,322mph	8,000lb	August 31, 1958
XB-70	185ft	105ft	253,600lb	542,000lb	4,287 miles	2,000mph	2,056mph	25,000lb	September 21, 1964
FB-111	75.5ft	70ft/34ft	53,500lb	114,300lb	3,170 miles	650mph	1,650mph	31,500lb	December 21, 1964
B-1B	146ft	137ft/79ft	192,000lb	477,000lb	5,900 miles	595mph	830mph	75,000lb	December 23, 1974
B-2	69ft	172ft	158,000lb	376,000lb	6,900 miles	560mph	630mph	50,000lb	July 17, 1989

Note: Date of first flight is of the type and not the variant given in the specifications.